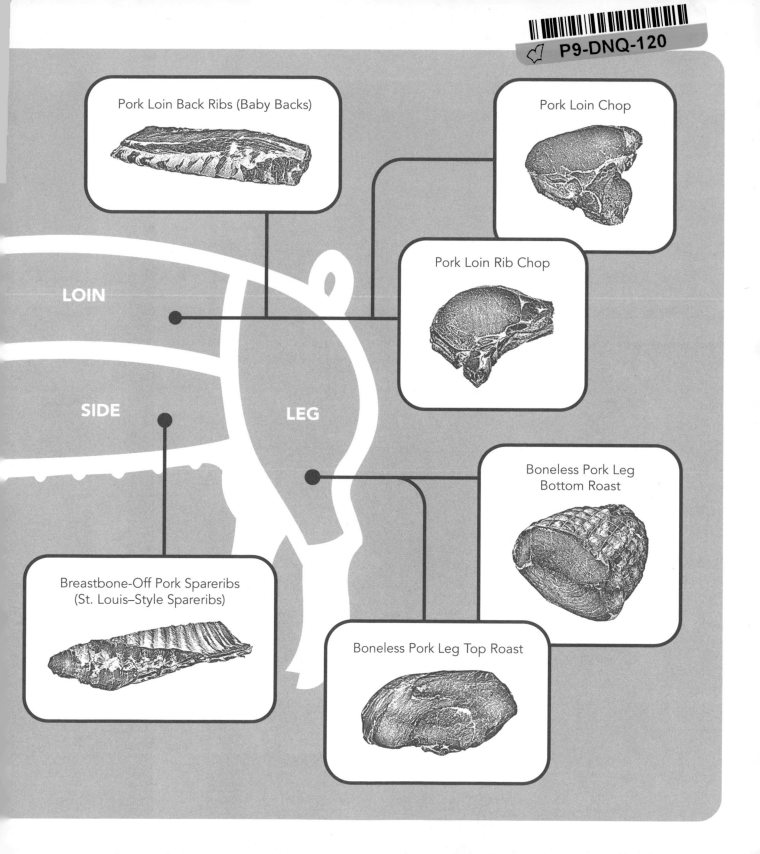

Pork Loin Back Ribs (Baby Backs)

Pork Loin Chop

Pork Loin Rib Chop

LOIN

SIDE

LEG

Boneless Pork Leg Bottom Roast

Breastbone-Off Pork Spareribs (St. Louis–Style Spareribs)

Boneless Pork Leg Top Roast

BRUCE AIDELLS'S
Complete Book *of* Pork

Also by Bruce Aidells

The Complete Meat Cookbook, with Denis Kelly

Bruce Aidells' Complete Sausage Book, with Denis Kelly

Barbecuing, Grilling, and Smoking, with Ron Clark

Real Beer and Good Eats, with Denis Kelly

Flying Sausages, with Denis Kelly

Hot Links and Country Flavors, with Denis Kelly

BRUCE AIDELLS'S
Complete Book *of* Pork

A Guide to Buying, Storing, and Cooking the World's Favorite Meat

BRUCE AIDELLS
WITH LISA WEISS

HarperCollins*Publishers*

HarperCollins books may be purchased for educational, business, or sales promotional use.
For information, please write: Special Markets Department, HarperCollins Publishers Inc.,
10 East 53rd Street, New York, NY 10022.

Some of these recipes were previously published in slightly different form in *Bon Appétit,
Cooking Pleasures, Fine Cooking, Food & Wine, Gourmet,* and the *National Culinary Review.*

FIRST EDITION

Designed by Joel Avirom and Jason Snyder
Design assistant: Meghan Day Healey

Printed on acid-free paper

Library of Congress Cataloging-in-Publication Data

Aidells, Bruce.
    Bruce Aidells's complete book of pork : a guide to buying, storing, and cooking the world's
favorite meat/Bruce Aidells with Lisa Weiss.
        p. cm.
ISBN 0-06-050895-7
1. Cookery (Pork) 2. Pork. 3. Cookery, International. I. Title: Complete book of pork.
II. Weiss, Lisa. III. Title.

TX749.5.P67A33 2004
641.6'64—dc22   2004040896

04 05 06 07 08 ❖/RRD 10 9 8 7 6 5 4 3 2 1

Acknowledgments

FIRST AND FOREMOST I'd like to thank my editor, Susan Friedland, for her commitment to a thorough look at pork cookery and her continued support and guidance in this project. I received excellent legal advice from literary lawyer Susan Grode. Many of the fine recipes included in this book come from fellow chefs and pork enthusiasts, including my wife and contributor, Nancy Oakes, who always has new and creative ways for preparing pork for which I'm appreciative. I'd also like to thank many friends for graciously sharing their recipes: Michelle Aaron, Jeff Bergman, Hugh Carpenter, John Desmond, Franco Dunn, Michael Gassen, Kristin Goldberg, Andrew Hash, Shannon Hayes, Jacob Kenedy, Loni Kuhn, Johnson and May Koo, Christopher Lee, Karen Levin, Pamela Mazzola, Art Meyer, Tom Oden, Alex Padilla, Cindy Pawlcyn, Cindy Peterson, Henry Joe Peterson, Mick Vann, Edy Young, and Ann Yonkers.

Thanks goes to ProPork of Iowa for providing special Berkshire pork, as well as Niman Ranch of California, and DuBreton of Canada for providing all natural pork for our testing. The National Pork Board was especially helpful and generous with advice.

Thanks to the creative team at HarperCollins: designers Joel Avirom and Jason Snyder, and copyeditor Evie Righter.

Contents

Introduction

I'M A RESTLESS COOK AND ADVENTUROUS EATER. What I mean is that once I cook a dish, I'm ready to move on, to explore new culinary horizons. As an adventurous eater, I'm always searching out the next new taste, the next new ethnic cuisine or esoteric dish, and it seems that pretty much wherever I go, wherever my eating adventures take me, pork is featured prominently. But that's not surprising when you consider the long history man has had with the pig. Forty-thousand-year-old cave drawings depict wild boar that our early ancestors hunted in France and Spain and judging from the huge number of boar bones found at ancient camp sites, Mr. Pig was a frequent dinner guest.

In this book I profess no allegiance to any one country, tradition, or cooking style. This book represents my history as a restless cook who has cooked food from scores of cuisines. My first goal is to provide you with recipes for all the cuts of pork, most of which you can find at your local supermarket, as well as less common cuts, such as pork belly and fresh pork shanks, which you will have to search for or buy online. I also confess that in these pages there aren't any recipes for pig's head or chitterlings; even I can't find a reliable source for pig's head, and I don't like chitterlings, and therefore have no interest in cooking them. (I do, however, possess recipes for pig's head, which I'll share with anyone who contacts me.) The recipes I have chosen come from every continent except Antarctica and Australia. In addition to China, Japan, France, Italy, and this land, I've included recipes from Hungary, Poland, Germany, England, Spain, Portugal, North Africa, West Africa, Indonesia, Malaysia, Burma, Vietnam, Goa, India, Latin America, Cuba, the Caribbean, Mexico, Turkey, Greece, and others I've not listed. Some recipes are mine, and some were given to me by friends. They're all culled from my vast collection of my and my friends' favorite pork recipes, and when I reviewed them for inclusion in this book I realized that not only do they reflect my diverse and adventurous cooking inclinations, they are also representative of the world's best pork cookery.

This is a book for all of us who love pork, but because we don't all share the same skill levels, I've written it for the beginning cook as well as the experienced amateur and even the professional chef. I do assume that all of you have at least tried your hand in the kitchen, that you've cooked a pork chop to your satisfaction at some time (or maybe not), made a roast, or braised a stew. For those of you who consider yourself beginners, I've written long sections on basic techniques like grilling, sautéing, and moist-heat cooking. Reading these sections will help you build confidence and knowledge that will enable you to master the techniques. Even experienced cooks, I think, will benefit from a tip or two on seasoning or determining doneness.

A Pig Tale

(Or, A Brief History of the Pig)

IN THE ENTIRE HISTORY OF CIVILIZATION, no animal has provided us more sustenance than the pig. The easily tamed and domesticated ancestors of the Eurasian wild boar, *sus scrofa,* have graced our tables during feasts and famines and have been objects of both repulsion and reverence. In spite of the many cultural taboos against it, more pork is consumed on this planet than any other meat.

Before the domestication of sheep, goats, or dogs, humans had tamed pigs. Actually, some scholars think the pig might even have tamed itself, because those crafty

> *The pig is nothing but an enormous dish which walks while waiting to be served.*
> —CHARLES MONSELET, FRENCH GASTRONOME

wild boars who roamed the earth for 40 million years figured out somewhere around 10,000 B.C. that human beings not only offered them protection from large predators, but also were a source of food (as in garbage). Though scholars disagree about exactly when and where the domestication of the pig first took place, large bone sites have been discovered both in the "fertile crescent" of the Middle East, as well as in China, indicating that domestication must have taken place almost simultaneously (give or take a thousand years). In the "fertile crescent," where it's believed agricultural practices first began, archaeologists uncovered a large collection of boar bones (8,000 B.C.), predating the cultivation of barley and wheat (7,000 B.C.), which indicates that humans were able to catch and tame the boars. The Chinese have written records of pig-keeping that date back to 7,000 B.C., and perhaps the oldest-known written recipe for pork dates to 500 B.C. China: suckling pig, stuffed with dates, wrapped in straw, and pit-roasted.

Several innate traits have made pigs good candidates for domestication. First of all, they're intelligent, ranked only behind humans, whales, dolphins, and primates, which makes them easy to train. (In fact, they can be housebroken and for centuries the Chinese have kept them as pets.) Second, they're affable creatures that like to live and travel in groups; anthropologists believe that boars liked hanging out with humans. No dummies, they enjoyed not only the camaraderie around the campfire, but they could always count on eating any leftovers as well. Third, although boars are known for their ferocity and courage in the wild, their piglets can be easily tamed and bred in captivity.

Our early ancestors must have realized after they first bred pigs that they were on to a good thing. Pigs breed easily and prolifically. The average sow can have a litter every four months with an average of ten piglets per litter. Besides being prolific, pigs can "pork-up" at an astonishing rate. A baby pig weighing 2¼ pounds at birth can put on 130 pounds in just six months. The beauty in the pig's design, however, from a human's point of view, is that it can gain a lot of weight with a minimum of expense or effort on our part. Pigs live to eat. Far from being picky eaters, pigs will devour anything in sight, from seeds, fruits, and nuts on the forest floor, to table scraps, garbage left in city streets, and even human waste (which undoubtedly contributed to their reputation as "unclean" animals). From the beginning of their domestication, pigs have been kept either by pasturing them in forests (pannage), their natural habitat, or by confining them in pens. On the forest floors, pigs could survive on acorns, beechnuts, hazelnuts, wild fruits and berries, worms, tubers, and mushrooms, along with the occasional small bird or rodent. In medieval times, forest taxes were actually calculated on how many pigs could be fed because pigs were more valuable than the wood the trees produced. Though for several millennia pigs derived their main source of food from the forest floor, pannage pigs have all but disappeared from most of rural Europe. They are, however, still found in a few parts of the continent, mainly Spain, famous for its Iberian mountain pigs, which make the sought-after cured ham known as *jamón iberico*.

The Pig in Ancient China, Greece, and Rome

The Chinese were perhaps the first civilized people to truly appreciate the value of the pig and have been keeping and breeding them in great numbers for at least 7,000 years. China is the largest producer (one pig for every three people) and consumer of pork in the world, and the fact that the words "pork" and "meat" are synonymous in the Chinese language is no accident. Somewhere around 4,000 B.C., the emperor decreed that everyone in the realm had to breed and raise pigs. The Chinese love their pigs and have often bestowed places of honor in their households on them, and not just at the dinner table. Pigs are pets, too, although even ones raised in the home were usually not spared from slaughter. The Chinese character for home is comprised of the symbol for "swine" beneath the character for "roof." Statuettes of pigs have graced tombs from the Chou Dynasty (1,100 B.C.) through the Han Dynasty (A.D. 200) and were meant to assure prosperity in the afterlife.

From Asia, the domestication of the pig spread throughout the Middle East and Europe. There are numerous references to pigs throughout ancient literature and mythology. Demeter, the Greek goddess of agriculture, was believed to actually be a pig in human form, or sometimes a human in pig form, and to keep her happy, suckling pigs were sacrificed to her before the planting of corn. To this day, suckling pigs are often a part of Greek celebratory tradition. Homer mentions both domesticated pigs and wild boars in the *Iliad* and *Odyssey* and Circe changed men who courted her into swine (but Odysseus made her change them back). Athenaeus, the second-century B.C. Greek gourmet, declares that baby Zeus was suckled by a sow (and later killed by a boar), and in his treatise on food, *Learned Banquet*, enthused about roasted, pickled, salted, and boiled pig's meat as ingredients for good living.

The Romans, too, loved pigs and it seems huge herds of pigs were roaming all over what now is considered Italy as early as 1,000 B.C. Varro, a first-century scholar on agriculture, laid out detailed instructions for pig breeding, feeding, and keeping, based on traditions that had already been in place for several centuries. And who hasn't heard about those prodigious Roman appetites for food and extravagant banquets? Juvenal, a Roman satirist, called pigs "animals borne for feasting," and rare is the account of one of those famous feasts that fails to mention a pig. Apicius, the first-century Roman culinary expert who wrote one of the oldest-known cookbooks, *De Re Coquinaria,* described a banquet where a pig was boned through the throat, then the intestinal cavity was stuffed with sausages, chicken dumplings, snails, small game birds, dates, and blood puddings. At the same time, a guild of artisans called the

Botulari specialized in the making of fine sausages. But, unfortunately, the sausages they made were also quite deadly—and thus the derivation of the word "botulism" from Botulari. Eventually a Roman emperor noticed that his heralded legions were dying off after a sausage feasting and finally prohibited the production of these dangerous treats. When sausage-making did start up again in the Empire, sausage makers learned the importance of adding enough salt (which probably contained traces of nitrates) to their products, and botulism was inhibited. Along came the first marketing genius, and the name changed from one based on *botulism* to a word derived from the Latin word for salted or salty, *salsus*. *Salsicce,* the Italian word for sausage, has been the word of choice ever since. (The English word "sausage" is also derived from the Latin *salsus*.)

In addition to the rare parts of the pig that were sold at the Roman Forum Suarium, or pork market, shoppers could find all kinds of imported hams and sausages. It also was probably no coincidence that the *Salinae,* or salt market, was located right next door, so that along with fresh meat, salt could be purchased for curing it. Supposedly Julius Caesar (100–44 B.C.) was so crazy about Gaul hams that he had them imported to feed his armies. A recipe from 200 B.C. describes pork covered with salt for seventeen days, steeped in vinegar, hung and dried, then smoked for another two days.

The Pig in Europe

After the fall of Rome, and for many centuries afterward, pigs became the most important source of dietary meat for people all over the continent. The first pigs were fed on mast, nuts from the forest floor, but eventually as forests became fewer and smaller, pigs were kept in pens and fed house scraps or surplus crops. However, during the Middle Ages, when pigs were still herded in forests, it became traditional for them to be slaughtered in the late fall, just before their forest food supplies became scarce, when the animals were at their plumpest and when the weather turned cold enough so that the meat could be "put up" before it spoiled. The annual community pig slaughter became a tradition in many communities and was cause for celebration. There were *Schlachtfests* in Germany, *boucheries* in France, *matanzas* in Spain, and the *festa del porco* in Italy, or the day the pig is killed. One large well-fed pig could keep one large family or sometimes a small village well fed throughout the winter—not on fresh pork roasts but on preserved meats. Before refrigeration, which didn't come about until the late nineteenth and early twentieth centuries, most meat needed to be preserved, usually with salt. After the pig was butchered, usually a little of the meat was set aside to eat fresh and then most of it was turned into hams, sausages, pâtés, and confits, which could be kept through the winter. The fat of the pig was turned into lard, the skin was tanned and used for leather, and the bristles were often stuffed into mattresses. (The fat of the pig was particularly important in the cold climates, which could not support olive trees.) All over the continent and British Isles, techniques for salt-curing and preserving pork were developed that were unique to the various regions and are particularly notable in the salt-curing of the leg-of-pork, or what we commonly refer to as ham.

Curing and Smoking

Curing means preserving, by removing and replacing some of the water in pork with salt. Usually this is accomplished one of two ways: **dry-curing**, which is done by coating the meat in salt; or **brine-curing**, which requires soaking the meat in a solution of salt and water (and often sugar, sodium nitrite, and spices in addition to the water). If enough water is removed, bacteria and other microorganisms can no longer grow. This is why country ham and dry salami does not go bad at room temperature.

Smoking is a process in which meat is exposed to concentrated smoke, which is absorbed and diffused from the surface to the interior. Smoking reduces moisture in meat, concentrating flavors and firming up the texture. If the process is done long enough, and also when combined with adequate salt and air-drying, smoking can completely preserve meats (like country ham), so that they no longer spoil at room temperature.

Factors such as the kind of pig, what it eats, the ingredients in the cure, how it's stored or aged, all play into the differences in hams. Today we're still enjoying hams such as the French *jambon de Bayonne,* Italian *prosciutto,* Spanish *serrano* and *iberico,* British York ham, and German Westphalian, to name a few. In addition to the well-known European cured hams, the Chinese were also curing pork and Yunnan ham is one of the finest hams in the world.

The Pig in North America

Pigs inhabit every continent on earth save Antarctica, and they didn't just get there by swimming (although pigs are good swimmers). Though all the great recipes for pork in this country and in Mexico and Latin America might lead one to think that pigs are native to North America, in fact, the first pigs to arrive in the New World came on ships with the explorers De Soto and Columbus.

Christopher Columbus brought eight pigs with him on his second voyage to the New World in 1493 and the ancestors of those pigs are still roaming the brush throughout the Caribbean and South and Central America. The thirteen sows and two boars that Hernando De Soto brought with him to Florida in 1539 were so prolific that within one year they had multiplied to 300. Three years later, after De Soto's expedition had trekked 3,000 miles of what is today the southern United States in search of gold, they still had 700 pigs (even though they had lost 400 of them along the way). The progeny of those pigs are still living in the woods of Virginia, Georgia, the Carolinas, and Florida and are familiarly known as razorbacks, an important feral food source in the South to this day.

Most expeditions to America carried pigs with them. Today there are descendants of Spanish, British, French, African, and Italian swine stock that thrived in the New World, full of forests with nuts (hickory, pecan, and acorns) and wild fruit, a warm, temperate climate, and plenty of water. The pigs brought to Jamestown in 1607 by British colonists increased in numbers so quickly that they overran the town and had to be confined to their own island, "Hog Island," where they were free to run "hog wild." In the Northern colonies, pigs were introduced by Dutch settlers and salted or barreled pork, long a staple in European households and a provision on ships, quickly became the colonies' biggest export. Settlers discovered that their semi-feral pigs could be easily fattened with surplus crops of Indian corn for little or no expense, slaughtered, salted, packed in barrels, and used for trade. Huge herds of pigs were driven to market to be processed into salt pork for shipment all over the world and eventually the port cities of Boston, New York, and Philadelphia grew up to accommodate the industry. In addition to salt pork, the colonists began curing some pretty fine hams for export, and Smithfield ham from Virginia pigs fed on peanuts developed a reputation that still ranks it among the greatest hams of the world.

From the original colonies, across the Appalachians and into the Ohio Valley and Midwest, American settlers moved west and pigs went with them. Cincinnati in the late 1700s became the largest pork processing center in the country, and by 1860 was slaughtering 400,000 hogs a year, which earned Cincinnati the nickname "Porkopolis." It's always, of course, location, location, and the fact that Cincinnati was on the Ohio River enabled packers to quickly and efficiently transport their pork down river to lucrative Southern markets before the development of the railroads. After the Civil War, which prevented river commerce, Chicago displaced Cincinnati and became the "Hog Butcher for the World," as Carl

Sandburg described it. At the hub of the growing railroad system, Chicago meat packers developed highly efficient systems to butcher, cure, can, and then ship pork products by rail from the Corn Belt to the rest of the country.

Pork Taboos

Odds are that if you're reading this book, you're not one of the estimated 1.3 billion people on the planet who eschew pork (approximately 20 percent of 6.5 billion), but a history of the pig would not be complete without a discussion of the many taboos and restrictions regarding its consumption (or, in some instances, even of contact with the animal itself or the swineherd). The largest majority of nonpork eaters are Muslims, but Jews, Hindus, some Buddhists, and even Ethiopian Orthodox refrain from eating the meat of the pig. Early Egyptians had something like a love-hate relationship with the pig. Although the pig was considered sacred and thought to have magical medicinal properties, pigs were also regarded as "unclean," and the people who kept them, the swineherds, were treated like lepers (some even believed that drinking a pig's milk could cause leprosy).

Archaeologists agree that ancient Israelites did eat pork, but after the Torah's injunction against it in Leviticus 11:7, Jews wouldn't go near the stuff and were forbidden to even speak of pigs except indirectly, as in "that beast." Muslims followed the same edict against pork when the Koran was written a millennium later. No one can agree (and there have been thousands of opinions written about the subject) whether there was an underlying rational explanation for the Jewish ban on pork, such as pigs will eat anything (including waste), or pork meat spoils quickly in hot climates, or pigs can be infected with organisms such as trichinosis. Few of those things were known at the time and the best explanation of all simply says that Jews shouldn't eat pork because the Hebrew God says not to. Buddhists and Hindus refrain more from a vegetarian point of view than a belief that pork is inherently dirty or unhealthy or arbitrarily taboo.

> *Like all Jewish girls I left home in order to eat pork and take birth control pills. When I first shared an intimate evening with my husband, I was swept away by the passion (so long dormant inside myself) of a long and tortured existence. The physical cravings I had tried so hard to deny were finally and ultimately sated . . . but enough about the pork.*
>
> —ROSEANNE

Pigs in America Today

While most domesticated farm animals are slaughtered only after they've outlived their useful-ness, pigs are not useful to us until after they're, *ahem,* gone. Sheep, of course, are bred for wool and milk, goats and cows for milk, chickens for their eggs, and cattle are used as laborers, but the pig is bred solely for dinner. Well, that's not entirely true if you consider the truffle-hunting pig, but today we use pigs not just for their meat but also for their by-products. In the United States today, pharmaceuticals are second only to meat in terms of a pig's usefulness: things like insulin, cortisone, skin for burns, and valves for hearts. We also use pig by-products, such as blood (fabric dyes, plywood adhesives, animal feed), bone (glass, enamel, fertilizers), fatty acids (insecticides, lubricants, crayons), and bristles (artist's brushes, insulation, upholstery). Just about all of the pig carcass can be used, as the saying goes, "except for the eyes and the oink."

The bottom line for the pig, though, is that it is bred primarily for its meat, and up until the second half of the twentieth century also for its lard. Pig breeds in the United States are clas-sified as lard, meat, or bacon hogs. Lard pigs, chubby creatures fed on a diet consisting mainly of corn, have a high proportion of back fat. Bacon pigs are bred to have long bodies with quite a bit of belly meat and little back fat. Meat pigs, developed for the American market in the 1930s, have large muscles, big hams, and a moderate ratio of fat to lean. After World War II, when consumers started preferring vegetable fats such as Crisco to lard, the pigs bred specifi-cally for their prodigious quantities of back fat basically disappeared from the market.

Though crossbred or hybrid pigs make up 80 percent of the commercial pork market, of the approximately 300 recognized pure pig breeds in the world now, the 8 most common pure swine breeds used by pork producers in the United States today are the Berkshire, Chester White, Duroc, Hampshire, Landrace, Poland China, Spotted, and Yorkshire. Most of the pure breeds, specifically the Berkshire, Chester White, Duroc, Hampshire, Poland China, and Spotted, were originally bred as lard pigs and have become meat pigs. The Landrace and Yorkshire (which has the least amount of back fat) began as bacon pigs and have also become meat pigs.

How to Use This Book

Master Recipes

When cooking procedures, techniques, and times are essentially the same for a certain cut, I've provided a Master Recipe that explains in detail how to prepare the specific dish. Several variations that use the same methods only with different spices, flavorings, marinades, or other ingredients, typically follow Master Recipes. It's my hope that once you've mastered a Master Recipe you'll feel confident enough to come up with your own variations.

Basic Ingredients

Salt This is the most important flavor ingredient in any recipe in this book. In most cases I let you determine your own amounts, but in recipes where I specify an exact amount I expect you'll use that amount, then taste your dish after cooking and add more, if necessary, to your own taste. This is not true for brine or salami recipes, where the salt amount is strictly determined for the process. You can use any type of salt you wish (kosher salt, table salt, or sea salt), but I've specified kosher salt in each recipe because I've used Diamond Crystal Kosher Salt in all my testing. I prefer this particular brand because it has a couple of properties I like: larger flakes than Morton's Kosher Salt, and Diamond Crystal Kosher dissolves easily in water and on the surface of meat. Diamond Crystal is lighter than table salt or Morton's Kosher, so if you substitute table salt for Diamond Crystal use half as much, and if you use another brand of kosher salt, like Morton's, reduce the amount by one quarter. (For smaller quantities, like a teaspoon or two in a spice rub, I wouldn't bother measuring an exact amount because the difference will be negligible.) I tend to undersalt my recipes, but when a recipe calls for large quantities of salt, as in the brines, you'll definitely want to make the adjustment. Better yet, when making brines, measure your salt by weight rather than by volume: One cup of Diamond Crystal Kosher Salt weighs 5 ounces and one cup of table salt weighs 10 ounces. A final note on salt—I love the many kinds of specialty salts available today, such as *fleur de sel* or Maldon Sea Salt, but because they're expensive I like to use them where I can taste the salt—for instance, sprinkled on finished dishes like salads or sliced roasts where I appreciate the salt's texture and subtle flavor.

Pepper When I say pepper I mean black pepper, freshly ground. If large quantities are needed as in sausage and salami recipes, I find it easiest to grind the whole peppercorns in an electric coffee grinder (I try to grind it coarse). There are many special varieties of peppercorns, such as Tellicherry and Malabar, and each has a unique taste. In recipes that call for large amounts or where the taste of the pepper is an integral flavor component, such as in salami or sausage, you may want to vary the pepper flavor. If so, try some different kinds; they can be purchased from specialty spice purveyors (see Sources on page 318). I never use white pepper, even if I see that a recipe calls for it. I find it has a petroleum taste and substitute black pepper instead.

Cooking Fats and Oils Several recipes call for lard, or mention it as an option. Lard is, of course, the rendered fat of a pig and it's important that you make your own (page 313), buy it fresh from an ethnic market (where they make their own), or get it from a mail-order source (page 318). Never ever use the kind of commercial lard from a supermarket that comes packaged in brick form. It contains stabilizers, antioxidants, and, worst of all, is partially hydrogenated, meaning it has the dreaded and very bad-for-you trans-fatty acids. Even lard sold in tubs can contain hydrogenated fats, so read the label. In recipes that use small quantities of lard for sautéing, you can substitute bacon fat, with the exception of Pork Confit (page 310) and Piecrust (page 238). Most recipes call for olive oil for sautéing or in marinades. I prefer to taste any oil I add, even if it is just for frying, so I always use a good quality extra-virgin olive oil or at least a virgin olive oil (for cooking not the most expensive kind). Many of the Asian recipes use peanut oil, but you can use any mild vegetable oil instead. Recipes that call for sesame oil are referring to the Asian oils that are made from toasted sesame seeds and are highly flavored. They can be ordered online or by mail-order (page 318). Always smell an oil before you use it because eventually oil goes rancid even if stored in a cool, dark place.

Butter Although it's not specified, I always use unsalted butter in my recipes because I think it has a fresher flavor. Salt is used in butter mainly to preserve rather than flavor it. If you do use salted butter in any of my recipes, you may need to decrease the amount of salt that's called for (you can always add more at the end). Never substitute margarine for butter. It, too, is hydrogenated.

Herbs and Spices Most of the recipes that follow call for fresh herbs because I like their taste better than dried. If you do substitute dried for fresh, then use half as much except for sage, which has a stronger taste fresh than it does dried. Use the same amount of dried sage and then adjust to suit your taste. If you don't have fresh rosemary, cilantro, or flat-leaf parsley, don't bother replacing them with dried; just leave them out altogether. Dried herbs and ground spices, such as paprika, lose their flavor after a few months, about six months maximum, so try to buy them in small quantities and keep them stored away from heat and light. (I've never understood why anyone would keep dried spices over the stove, where they turn to gray sawdust.) Using herbs and spices that are fresh is particularly important for sausage-making because they play such a dominant role in the taste of the final product, which will taste dull and muddled if made with old spices. If your store doesn't carry a good selection of fresh herbs, consider growing a little herb garden in a window or on a roof or deck.

Stocks and Broths Homemade stocks are preferred for all my recipes and I've given you an excellent recipe for Dark Pork Stock that uses roasted bones (page 87). (If you like to bone your own meat at home, you'll get a nice collection of bones in your freezer to use for your stock.) Homemade chicken stock or canned chicken broth is always an acceptable substitute. If you use canned broth, make sure you used the low-sodium brands, otherwise your reduced sauces will be too salty. For the same reason, don't use bouillon cubes.

Removing Fat Always trim the external fat from roasts and chops to ¼ inch, and it's important, for both nutrition and appearance, to degrease all of your sauces. When you cook fattier cuts such as country ribs, Boston butts, or pork bellies, after the dish has cooked, remove the meat and let the sauce and meat cool in separate covered containers in the refrigerator overnight. When the fat has congealed on the surface, it can be easily skimmed off (or lifted off) and discarded. In any recipe that is served immediately after cooking, skim off the surface grease as much as possible.

Curing Salts Many of the recipes in the section Preserving Pork (page 245) call for Insta-cure No. 1. This is a mixture of 1 part sodium nitrite to 15 parts table salt and colored pink so as not to confuse it with regular salt. Because such minuscule amounts of sodium nitrite are needed for brine or salami recipes, these quantities are too small to measure with normal scales; you would need a highly sensitive gram scale. As a consequence, the sodium nitrite is mixed with salt to bulk it up into amounts that can be measured with regular scales, measuring spoons, and cups. Insta-cure No. 1 must be used in recipes where the meat is aged or smoked at temperatures above refrigerator temperatures, which are ideal breeding grounds for bacterial growth like botulism. For food safety reasons, do not leave the Insta-cure out of any of these recipes that call for it. Some recipes, such as pâtés, call for Insta-cure as an option only to preserve the pink color of the meat, and, if you wish, you may leave it out. For more on curing and sodium nitrite, see page 249.

Salt and Phosphate-Pumped ("Enhanced") Pork Many national pork producers have come to realize that today's pork has become too lean. Combine that with the fear of trichinosis and the misinformation about how to cook pork (from outdated cookbooks and recipes passed down from Grandma), and what consumers end up with is dry, hard, and inedible meat. To rectify the situation, the producers decided to "enhance" their pork by pumping it with a solution of water, salt, and sodium phosphates so that now pork producers are selling you salted water at meat prices. This is a much more radical solution to the problem than the "flavor-brining" I endorse as a way to make lean pork juicier. Much of this commercial pumped pork is labeled with misleading terms like "flavor-enhanced," "extra-tender," "tender and juicy," "guaranteed tender," and so on. Read the fine print on any pork label, which will say "contains x percent water, salt, and phosphates added." Some pork will have only 10 percent, while others can contain even more added liquid (25 to 35 percent). That's right—you're paying for a big bag of water. Pumping the salt solution directly into the meat causes the muscle fibers to unwind just enough so they can absorb the water and swell in size; the phosphates act to keep the water in the cells during cooking. Consumers may perceive pumped pork as tender because even when it's overcooked the meat stays softer and juicier than it would have. But to me the meat seems rubbery, spongy, and mushy (not unlike today's water-added hams) and I can taste the added salt and phosphates, which have a slightly bitter, acrid taste. Yes, the meat is juicier, but you can get your own excellent results by flavor-brining the meat yourself and you won't have the same amount of added salt or acrid sodium phosphate. Once meat has been "enhanced" (pumped), additional flavor-brining is irrelevant and useless. This also applies to brining for meat preservation, so never use "enhanced" pork to make bacon, ham, or *lonza* (cured and air-dried pork loin; see page 296). In fact, I would avoid "enhanced" meat altogether and rely on proper cooking techniques (with an accurate meat thermometer) and flavor-brining to produce good-tasting pork. Who wants to eat mushy, rubbery meat anyhow? If, however, you absolutely insist on cooking your pork chops, loin roasts, and tenderloins to 170° F or beyond, then I guess pumped meat is for you.

Storage, Leftovers, and Other Bits of Advice

Pork is highly perishable, and once purchased you should use it within three days, otherwise I recommend freezing it. Properly wrapped, frozen fresh pork should be used within three months. Smoked or salted pork, such as bacon, does not keep as long because the salt speeds up rancidity, a process that occurs slowly in frozen meat. Smoked or cured meats can only be kept frozen for up to two months. Ham should not be frozen because it gets too soft, mushy, and watery.

Frozen meat needs to be thawed slowly, so take what you plan to cook out of the freezer 24 hours ahead for smaller cuts, and let it thaw in the refrigerator. That way you will have minimal moisture loss and the best texture. Large roasts will need 48 hours to thaw completely and really large roasts—Boston butt or fresh ham—will need 72 hours, or three full days in the refrigerator.

Part One: Pork Particulars

1
Buying Pork

No matter how good the recipes in this book may or may not be, I would have failed you miserably if I didn't try to help you buy the best pork. Unfortunately, I won't be standing by your side at the meat counter when you're trying to choose from the rows and rows of little Styrofoam trays filled with an assortment of pork cuts, and in most cases there probably won't be a butcher there either.

In the old days you would simply have said to your butcher, "Mr. Shultz, pick me out four of your best chops," and, if Mr. Shultz was worth his salt, he'd do exactly that. You'd go home, cook your dinner, and be happy as a pig in mud, looking forward to your next trip to the butcher so Mr. Shultz could do his thing. But now, unless you are one of those fortunate few who have a knowledgeable person behind the meat case, there's no Mr. Shultz to advise you. You're on your own. Ideally, you need to use three of your five senses, sight, smell, and touch when choosing meat. Sight's not a problem, but it's difficult to touch and smell something sealed in a package. So let's concentrate on sight first.

First Impressions

Appearance Good pork should be pale pink to light red, never purplish-red. The fat, especially on roasts and chops, should be trimmed to ¼ inch and be creamy white, with no dark spots. Lean meat should be moist-looking but never dry on the edges or have dark spots or blemishes. If buying chops or other sliced cuts of pork, look for intramuscular fat called marbling. In most cases, there will be little since the majority of today's pork is extremely lean. If there is any, those are the chops for you. The type of cuts that show the grain are chops or cut roasts and they should have a fine grain, not coarse or stringy. Finer-grained meats tend to hold moisture better and have a firmer mouthfeel.

Once you get your package home, examine the meat using your other senses.

Feel Good pork should be firm to the touch. It should be moist, but never, ever sticky, which is a pretty good indication that it's getting old and spoiled and should be returned to your butcher as soon as possible. It should never be hard and dry, either.

Smell Fresh pork has very little smell. If there are any sour, ammonia-like, or off odors, it means the pork is not fresh. Pork that is sold in vacuum packages, such as pork tenderloins, often have an odor when the package is opened, which is normal when meat is stored airtight and not allowed to breathe. However, once the meat is rinsed briefly under cold running water, the package odor should dissipate. If the meat is sticky to the touch, though, it's a bad sign and probably needs to be tossed or returned the store where you bought it.

Large club stores often offer consumers good buys on whole boneless pork loins, Boston butts, and fresh pork legs. Sold in vacuum packages, they're a great purchase for a large party. Or cut them into smaller pieces, repackage, and freeze them.

Grades of Pork

PSE

Avoid at all costs any pork that is sitting in a pool of light reddish liquid, particularly if it is cloudy, which is a telltale sign that the meat is "off." Even if the liquid is clear, but there's lots of it (there will always be a little bit of liquid in a package), and if the pork is very pale and soft to the touch, then the pork is PSE, which is an acronym for pale, soft, and exudative. Meat that is PSE, no matter how perfectly it's cooked, will be dry, tough, and shrunken—in a word, inedible. PSE meat is from pigs that were highly stressed during the slaughter process. With today's modern slaughterhouse practices, only a minority of pigs become stressed. But when an animal does become stressed, lactic acid is released in the muscles, which in turn lowers the pH and diminishes the ability of the muscle fibers to retain moisture. Unfortunately PSE is not uncommon and some pale, soft, and exudative pork ends up in the meat case. Now you can recognize the inferior products and avoid them. No matter what the meat guy might recommend, tell him to throw the PSE-looking ones out.

Pork is graded differently from beef, where marbling determines the quality and price. Of all beef sold in the United States, USDA Prime is the highest quality, has the most marbling, and commands the highest prices. USDA Select, the lowest grade (there are other grades lower than Select, but they're not usually sold in retail markets), has the least marbling and is often sold to the consumer at lower prices than the higher grade USDA Choice, but not always.

Pork is graded with a numbering system. USDA 1 is the best quality, while USDA 4 is the lowest. The grades are based not on intramuscular fat, but on lean yield, which means the proportion of lean to fat that the carcass produces. So a USDA 1 carcass will have more meat and less fat. Many years ago, when the USDA developed the grading systems, there were some very large pigs available that had thick layers of back fat and less lean meat. These hogs were raised more for the lard they produced than the meat and would have had a lower quality rating of 2, 3, or 4. Today almost all the pork sold by markets and butchers is USDA 1–graded.

Buying the Right Cut

At some point you'll have to go to the store and attempt to buy the correct cut needed to prepare your dish. Throughout the book I have done my best to help you in this process by explaining cuts, telling you my favorites, and how to choose the right cut for your method of preparation. This advice should help you at any market or butcher counter.

You may have to actually talk with the meat guy if he doesn't carry what you want or bring the book along and show him the picture. Meat guys are visual characters (how's that for a stereotype?), but let's face it, how do you verbalize what a Boston butt is? Nomenclature when it comes to meat varies from region to region. If you don't have the book with you, most meat guys have a meat chart that illustrates cuts and uses common names, so you'll be able to use that as your visual reference. If you live in an area with an actual butcher, then give him a try. If he's the real deal, his knowledge and enthusiasm should be treasured, and while you may sometimes pay more, you should get exactly what you want.

When it comes to the naming of specific cuts, there is a lot of confusion. That's because there is no uniform national standard for naming meat cuts. One does exist, published by the National Livestock and Meat Board, but, unfortunately, many in the retail trade don't use it. Tradition, regional differences, and creative merchandising are simply more powerful influences with regard to meat names than a desire to be consistent and less confusing to the consumer.

Fortunately there are fewer multiple names for pork, but there are still enough to cause consumer confusion. What I know as a Boston butt has the long-winded official name of Pork Shoulder Blade Boston Roast but goes under such other names as Boston shoulder, Boston butt roast, Boston-style roast, shoulder butt roast, Boston butt, pork butt, or fresh pork butt. I've done my best to provide you with names I'm familiar with, but I can't guarantee it's complete because new names for cuts are created all the time. What I've done is to offer you pictures of each cut, which are fairly consistent, as well as try to familiarize you with a little bit of pig anatomy (see Butcher's Chart of the Pig, endpapers). Since most of the animal provides tender meat, it won't be a total disaster if you buy the wrong cut. Just try to avoid using any cuts from the loin area (pork chops, center loin roasts, sirloins, or tenderloins) for long, slow, moist-heat cooking, because the result will definitely be dry and not something you'll want to serve or eat, for that matter.

Primal Cuts

In the wholesale world of pork butchery, the meat is sold in primals, large sections of the pig that are either broken down into smaller pieces or are sold as is. The pig carcass is divided into four primal cuts. At the head end is the **shoulder primal cut** (15 to 25 pounds), consisting of the top of the shoulder called the Boston butt, pork butt, Boston butt, or Boston shoulder roast. The foreleg section of the shoulder is called picnic or picnic shoulder. The feet from the front legs are sold separately as pig's feet, or trotters.

The midsection of the pig contains two primal cuts: **The back portion is a primal called pork loin,** while some markets sell the whole loin (15 to 20 pounds), and is usually divided into the center-cut loin, which contains the rib section and the area with the T-bone chops. The shoulder end of the loin is called the blade end (these are often butterflied and sold as country spareribs). The hip end of the loin is called the sirloin end and contains a portion of some of the hipbone.

The other primal from the midsection is called the belly (12 to 14 pounds). The belly provides rib bones for spareribs and the remaining boned belly is usually made into bacon, but

My Favorite Cuts

Boston Butt You can stew it, pot-roast it, or make it into kebabs. It's the best cut for making sausage, pâté, and pork confit, and it ain't bad smoked.

Spareribs Bones, bones, lots of tasty bones, as well as moist succulent meat. I still stain my shirt every time I eat them.

Leg of Pork (Fresh Ham) This makes the most delicious roast and cracklings too, and then there are all those leftovers for pork sandwiches. I'm a ham for ham.

Sausages Hey, with hundreds of varieties how could I ever get bored? I'm not known as the "Sausage King" for nothing.

Bone-on Rib Chops I like these thick-cut and grilled, or pan-fried and sauced.

Fresh Pork Shanks I'm a sucker for bones and long, slow braises.

uncured unsmoked raw belly is gaining in popularity as something to be cooked and enjoyed on its own. You may have to special-order fresh belly or buy it from a website (see Sources on page 318) or ethnic market, but as it gains fans, I predict it will become more widely available.

The fourth primal cut is the ham (15 to 25 pounds). Ham refers both to the fresh leg of pork as well as to the cured and smoked version. The ham area not only contains the leg proper, but some of the meat surrounding the hip. This area is known as the sirloin. The feet from the ham area are also sold separately as pig's feet, or pig's trotters. Smoked hams, sold as whole, boneless, or shank or butt-half, are available year round, but fresh hams are sold mostly around Easter and Christmas. (They can usually be special-ordered from butchers other times of the year.) A fresh ham is well worth searching out since I think it makes an incredible roast pork, and if you feel the same, you may be able to influence your local meat provider to get it on a regular basis. Other primal cuts, such as whole loins, are often sold at club stores, cash-and-carry stores, or old-fashioned butchers, especially those located in Asian, Hispanic, German, or Eastern European neighborhoods.

2
Seasoning and Cooking Pork

Making Pork Flavorful

Throughout this book I constantly remind you of the old axiom "fat is flavor." You'll probably hear it so much that you will be wanting to kick me in my proverbial "ham." The crux of the matter is that the days are long gone (thirty years at least) when you could actually purchase pork chops, loins, and tenderloins, that had ample marbling to give the meat a little flavor. I recently tasted pork from old breeds like Berkshire and Duroc (pages 10, 317), which had enough marbling so that all the meat needed was a sprinkling of salt, pepper, and some fresh herbs. Unfortunately, this is now a very rare occurrence. Next to knowing when the meat is properly cooked, seasoning and flavoring is the most important step to providing a great-tasting piece of pork.

Even fattier cuts like Boston butt and spareribs need additional flavoring to make them taste good. Basically, pork is fairly bland and mild-tasting, which is also its main attribute. Like a blank canvas waiting for the artist to do his thing, that pork roast sitting in the fridge is waiting for you to do your thing or, more likely, for you to use one of the recipes in this book to help you along the way. The range is huge because pork's blandness and slightly sweet undertones mean that it goes well with sweet ingredients like fruits, subtle ingredients like mushrooms, and strong forceful flavors like chili, garlic, ginger, curry spices, and soy sauces.

Pork has one final attribute that separates it from all other red meats. It has an affinity for salt. Because pork tastes so good when combined with salt (this is known as curing), two-thirds of all the pork sold in the United States is cured or processed in some way and because salt is such an important flavoring when it comes to pork, I spend extra time discussing salt, below. I've also devoted the second longest part of this book to preserving pork (sausages, pâtés, cured pork and salami, smoked pork and confit), the world of pork products that owe their flavor to salt.

The cook has three ways to add flavor to meat: Seasoning the meat before it is cooked (this includes dry rubs, salting, wet pastes, marinades, flavor brines, and wrapping the meat in bacon, pancetta, or prosciutto, or stuffing the meat), introducing flavors during cooking (this includes moist-heat cooking, saucing, glazing, and smoking), and adding flavoring after the meat is cooked (this includes condiments and sauces). Often more than one flavor-adding technique is used in preparing a specific dish, and no pork dish should be cooked without at least flavoring the meat before it's cooked.

SALT That means that *no* piece of meat should be cooked without undergoing the minimal step of being sprinkled with salt and usually pepper. (No, I don't expect you to salt your smoked ham steak—it's already salty enough.) And even though you've read cookbooks that tell you *never* to salt your meat before cooking it because salt will draw out the moisture and cause the meat to become dry—that's rubbish. It is true that meat covered with a layer of salt loses moisture—that's how country hams are made—but the process takes at least two weeks or more. And more salt is used on a country ham than anyone would ever dream of sprinkling on a roast or chop.

So why am I so adamant about salting pork before it's cooked? Because I want you to have the best taste experience possible. The browning of the surface of the meat is due to a complex set of chemical reactions between caramelizing sugars, melted fats, and the amino acids that make up the protein combined with salt. The bottom line is that the process of salting and browning meat causes it not only to smell good but also to taste good. If you omit salt entirely or add it after the meat is cooked, the salt won't be incorporated into the whole browning process. The salt accentuates the caramelized taste and rounds out and mellows the flavor profile so that it tastes balanced: not salty but correct. If you salt the meat after it's browned, then you taste a layer of saltiness over the complex flavors that make up the caramelized exterior. If you don't believe me, try a little experiment yourself. Salt half a chop *before* cooking, then compare the taste of it with the half that is salted *after* it's cooked.

OTHER DRY SEASONINGS (DRY RUBS) Pepper is the second most important seasoning for pork. It, too, rounds out the flavors of browned meat but because pepper is highly volatile it changes taste and potency when heated. Pepper still contributes flavor but is less distinct than it would be if freshly ground. So if you like the flavor of freshly ground pepper, grind some on the meat after it's cooked as well as before.

Besides salt and pepper, which are the bare minimum flavor enhancers for all meat, spices and fresh or dried herbs can be rubbed or sprinkled on the meat before and after cooking. When the spices are combined with salt and pepper and put on the meat before cooking, the mixture is referred to as a dry rub. Whether you mix the spices first or sprinkle them individually on the meat, the effect will be the same in terms of final flavor. Usually dry rubs only affect the surface of the meat, but if you apply them a day or two ahead, they can penetrate a little ways in and enhance the flavor more. Sometimes salt is removed from a dry rub when it is applied to meat that has already been flavor-brined or otherwise salted. Dry rubs are very important in slow-roasted meats, like barbecued spareribs and barbecued Boston butt. Some herbs and spices have a particular affinity to pork and are frequently seen in my spice rub recipes. Sage, thyme, rosemary, savory, fennel seed, mustard seed, paprika, garlic, ginger, coriander, cumin, and brown sugar all go well with pork.

WET RUBS Mixtures of spices, fruit purees, oil, chilies, or vegetables such as onions, or garlic when finely chopped or pureed, have a paste-like consistency. The simplest wet rub is made just like a dry rub but has oil, garlic, or a bit of lemon zest added. Wet rubs made from a puree of lime, onion, garlic, spices, and chilies are common flavorings in Latin American cuisines, and pastes made with ginger, cilantro, soy, garlic, and other herbs are commonly used to flavor pork in Asian cooking. Some pastes contain nuts or coconut milk as well. Pastes are usually applied generously, and the meat is left to marinate at least 2 hours at room temperature or, better still, for up to 24 hours in the refrigerator. Wet rubs or pastes enhance the flavor of meat, as do liquid marinades. (A paste is simply a marinade in a more concentrated, less liquid form.) In most cases, a layer of the paste is left on the meat, especially if it is to be grilled or roasted, and the paste then forms a savory crust. Occasionally a paste is added to other liquid ingredients to be made in a sauce, which is then served with the meat after it is cooked.

WET MARINADES There is considerable hocus-pocus and controversy about using wet marinades that contain acidic ingredients to tenderize meat. According to Shirley O. Corriher, who is an expert on how things cook (*Cookwise*, Morrow, 1997), acidic marinades do tenderize moderately tender meat. Harold McGee (*On Food and Cooking*, Scribner, 1984), who also has conducted scientific tests on cooking processes, says that the acidic ingredients in marinades only manage to affect the surface of the meat. For me, tenderizing is really not a goal. I use marinades basically to enhance flavor, and I know from experience that they do that exceptionally well. For the best results, the meat should stay in the marinade for at least 12 hours, and 24 hours is even better (and some pork is marinated for 48 hours). It is possible, however, to overmarinate, especially with marinades using strong flavors like ginger, molasses, or bourbon, so take care not to go beyond 24 hours if your marinades contain these ingredients.

According to Shirley O. Corriher, the ability of any marinade to penetrate into the meat is enhanced if the marinade contains oil with monoglycerides. Extra-virgin olive oil is a monoglyceride and, therefore, is best used in marinades instead of regular pure olive oil.

Once a marinade is combined with meat, it can become contaminated with bacteria (which is destroyed when the meat is cooked). If a recipe specifies using the marinade to make a sauce that will be served with the meat, then you *must* bring the marinade to a boil when you add it to the sauce. Never reuse a marinade or pour a used marinade over cooked meat.

FLAVOR-BRINING This technique, which you'll master the first time out, will change the way you relate to lean pork. Flavor-brining will assure that you'll never cook a dried-out, hard, tasteless pork chop again and your pork loin roasts will be juicy and tender, too. There is one caveat: You still need to make sure not to overcook your lean pork. A final internal temperature somewhere between 145° to 155° F is what you want.

All there is to the flavor-brining technique is to dissolve some salt in water (I usually add sweet ingredients and other flavorings), but salt and water alone will do the trick.

"Flavor" brines use less salt, and the meat is immersed in them for a much shorter time than the "pork-preserving" brines used for bacon and ham. By soaking a piece of lean pork in a mild salt solution, water from the salt solution is absorbed into the meat by a process called osmosis. Salt dissolves into the meat by a process called diffusion. The result is that flavor-brined meat has a net gain in weight. Once the meat is cooked, it then loses less water than it would if it were not brined.

The principle of osmosis is that when two different solutions of dissolved substances and water are separated by a cell membrane, water will flow across that membrane from the solution that has more water molecules per volume (less dissolved substances) toward the solution that has fewer water molecules (more dissolved substances). Flavor brines work because the free water (the water not trapped in the muscle proteins) in the meat cells has a higher concentration of dissolved substances than in the brine, and the water is drawn into the meat cells.

Flavor-Brining Rules

There are several variables that affect brining that you must pay attention to:

1. Saltier brines take less time to penetrate the meat but are much more difficult to control. The saltiness of my flavor-brine recipes allows for the brining process to be slow and controllable.

2. The temperature of the flavor brine affects the process immensely, especially the diffusion of salt into the meat. Diffusion happens more quickly once the temperature is raised. To be consistent and controllable, all flavor-brining should be done at refrigerator temperature, which is less than 45° F. (That also means that the flavor brine must be cooled to 45° F or lower before adding the meat.)

3. The size of the piece of meat affects brining time. Large pieces of meat, like roasts, take an overnight soaking while small pieces, like chops, take only 3 to 6 hours. It is possible to overbrine, which will cause the meat to become too salty.

4. "Enhanced" pork is not an option for flavor-brining. Many of the large pork processors have realized that the ultra-lean pork of today can easily be overcooked, rendering it dry and inedible. Instead of producing richly marbled pork, they have taken a distorted version of my advice about flavor-brining and now sell loins and tenderloins injected and pumped with a salt solution containing phosphates. Do not flavor-brine meat that has been previously brined by the manufacturers (page 14) because this process makes the flavor brine useless.

5. My flavor-brine recipes call for kosher salt and I use Diamond Crystal brand. (See note on Basic Ingredients, page 11.)

Then you ask, why not just soak the meat in unsalted water? It turns out the salt in flavor-brining has a very important role. As the muscle cell absorbs some of the salt, it causes the muscle fibers to unwind and form bonds with some of the water molecules entering the cells. The result is that the muscle fibers swell in size and, most important, the water gets trapped within the protein matrix during cooking and stays there if the meat is not overcooked. Eventually, if the meat is overcooked, the protein fibers will shrink and tighten, forcing water out of the cells onto the bottom of your pan.

Another benefit of flavor-brining is that the swollen muscle cells have a mouthfeel of being more tender as well as juicy. (This only works with moderately tender meat. Brining won't tenderize tough collagen-laden meat.)

I've only discussed water and salt, the two essential ingredients contained in all brines, but flavor brines usually contain a sweetener such as brown sugar and other flavoring agents, such as herbs and spices. These too are carried into the cell in a modest way so that brined meat is seasoned, not just on the outside, but throughout the interior as well and the sweetener rounds out and helps to balance the flavors.

Flavor-Brining Chart

This chart is for lean pork cuts soaked in a brine solution of ½ cup kosher salt (2.5 ounces) per 8 cups (2 quarts) ice water, plus any other ingredients (sugar, spices, herbs and so on).

CUT AND THICKNESS	BRINING TIME
Kebabs 1½-inch cubes	2 hours
Kebabs ¾ to 1-inch cubes	1 hour
Pork chops ½ to ¾ inch	2 hours
Pork chops ¾ to 1 inch	3 hours
Pork chops 1¼ to 1½ inch	4 to 6 hours
Pork tenderloins	4 to 6 hours
Pork tenderloins, butterflied	2 hours
Boneless pork loin roasts	24 hours
Bone-in pork loin roasts	48 hours
Whole bone-in pork leg	3 days
Boneless pork leg (inside), tied and rolled	24 to 36 hours
Boneless sirloin roast	24 to 36 hours
Boneless pork leg (outside) roast	24 to 36 hours
Pork knuckle roast	24 hours
Butt or shank half pork leg	2 days

DO-AHEAD FLAVOR-BRINING STRATEGY If you serve pork chops, pork loin roasts, or pork tenderloins on a regular basis, why not keep some already-made flavor brine in your refrigerator? It keeps for several weeks. It only needs to be a basic brine of salt, sugar, and water, to get the job done. Simply put your meat of choice in a zip-lock plastic bag, add enough brine to cover the meat, and then stick the bag in the fridge for an appropriate time (see Flavor-Brining Chart on page 31). When you're ready to cook, remove the meat, pat it dry, and proceed with the recipe. You can even refrigerate the meat, wrapped, after it's been brined for a day or two or until you're ready to use it. You can also adapt a flavor brine to your own favorite pork recipe; just omit the salt called for in the recipe and taste for salt at the end of cooking.

How to Cook Pork

Because most of the pork we buy today is very lean (particularly the popular and tender cuts such as loin and tenderloin), it starts to dry out and become tough when cooked to temperatures of 160° F and beyond. But overcooking of today's pork is not always the cook's fault. Most of the cookbooks that were written before 1989 tell us to cook pork to internal temperatures of 170° F and even to 180° F, and those old-fashioned metal meat thermometers that are left in the meat instruct us to cook pork above 170° F. Also, many cooks rely solely on roasting tables that give vague cooking times based on minutes per pound. Unfortunately, those tables don't take into consideration variables such as thickness of the meat, temperature of the meat before it goes into the oven, and inaccuracies of home oven thermostats. The best use for timetables is to use them as an approximate guide to know when to begin checking the internal temperature of the meat.

HOW MEAT COOKS When meat cooks, the muscle fibers begin to shrink. By the time the meat exceeds 140° F (medium-rare to medium), the fibers have begun contracting enough to squeeze moisture out of the cells. Shrinking of the muscle fibers continues at a rapid pace between 140° to 160° F as the meat changes from medium to medium-well and once the meat reaches 160° and higher, enough moisture has been squeezed out to make it downright tough and dry. However, when the meat has adequate intramuscular fat, the melting of that fat can counter the loss of water and provide a moist mouthfeel. Lean pork cuts, such as loin, tenderloin, sirloin, and leg, lack this intramuscular fat and will be dry if cooked much beyond 150° F.

Trichinosis (trichinellosis)

There's a reason that Grandma cooked her pork roast to just short of incinerated—fear of trichinosis. American pork fifty years or so ago (this was not an issue with European pork) was occasionally infected with a parasitic worm called trichina, which was the result of pigs being fed table scraps or refuse already infected with trichina. Pork produced in this country today is from pigs no longer fed garbage but a scientifically designed diet of grains, protein, and fat. Essentially, modern methods of pork husbandry have all but eliminated trichina from pork, but because the USDA, the government agency that inspects our meat, does not use microscopic or immunological tests on each and every pig carcass, they cannot guarantee with 100 percent certainty that there is no trichinosis in our pork. Until the USDA uses those tests, which are widely available in Europe, the USDA inspectors, to protect themselves, will continue to treat all pork as if it is contaminated with trichina worms and, therefore, officially recommend that consumers cook pork to 160° F or more. Even if some pork was contaminated (and remember that it is not), there are two simple ways to kill trichina worms: Freeze the meat at −10° F for at least 7 days, or cook the pork to an internal temperature of 137° F and hold that temperature for several minutes. Freezing meat below −10° F works fine for large commercial meat processors, but is not reliable for us with home freezers. Cooking pork to more than 137° F (which is well below my preferred range of doneness) is easy if you use an accurate thermometer such as an instant-read or continuous-read digital thermometer (page 35).

To give you a sense of how effectively trichinosis has been eliminated from our pork supply, there were fewer than 30 documented cases from 1983 to 1989 and only 8 cases since 1997 in the entire United States, compared with 400 cases of trichinosis in 1950, when many unregulated pig farms still fed their pigs garbage. Of the more recent cases most, if not all, were from uninspected pork from homegrown pigs, or from wild boar or bears—wild animals that have been known to raid a garbage bin or two.

Fatty cuts—Boston butt, spareribs, blade-end loin roasts, belly, and shanks—have enough intramuscular fat to keep the meat moist even when cooked to temperatures beyond 180° F. As an example, the Real Barbecued Pork (page 174) is produced when Boston butts are slowly cooked to internal temperatures of 180° F or more, yet there is ample fat to retain succulence. Another factor that helps to combat loss of moisture in well-done meat is collagen. Collagen (connective tissue) is particularly present in tough cuts of meat such as beef brisket, veal shanks, pork shanks, or pork cheeks. When these cuts are cooked slowly with moist heat (techniques like braising and stewing), the collagen is softened and turned into gelatin, which gives these cuts a moist and silky texture. Lean cuts contain another kind of connective protein called elastin, which instead of turning to gelatin turns hard and tough as it cooks. So even if you were to cook a pork loin using moist heat, the meat would still get drier and tougher and eventually fall apart into a mass of dry strings (think jerky). That's why loins and legs are never used to make stews or other dishes that involve long, slow cooking with moist heat.

When Is It Done?

Most recipes in this book use the range of 140° to 145°F to judge doneness for lean pork roasts. This is the temperature the roast should be when it's removed from the heat source. It is **not** the final temperature. The final temperature is achieved once the roast is allowed to rest for at least 10 minutes and up to 30 minutes for large roasts before carving. During its rest, the temperature will rise 5° to 10° F, depending on how hot the heat source was and how large the piece of meat is. In addition, juices in the meat, which have been pushed to the surface, will have time to "settle down" and be reabsorbed into the center of the roast. Pork chops, pork steaks, and other thin cuts such as butterflied pork tenderloins and medallions are also done when they reach an internal temperature of 140° to 145° F and should rest for 5 to 10 minutes for 1½-inch or thicker chops. Other cuts of pork with different doneness temperatures are discussed in the recipes, but you can also consult the doneness chart included on page 36. If you prefer pork that does not have a trace of pink (cooked to the range of 155° to 165° F) and you still want it to be juicy, then you must flavor-brine the meat first (pages 29 to 32).

Without a doubt, the most important tool I can recommend to the home cook who wants to prepare delicious, juicy pork roasts and chops is a good meat thermometer. There are many kinds on the market, and they range in price, accuracy, and ease-of-use.

Dial-Type Instant-Read Thermometers These are the least accurate but are also the least expensive (about $10). One major drawback is that the probe needs to be inserted about 2 inches into the meat, which makes it difficult to use with thin cuts.

Instant-Read Digital Thermometers These are more accurate than the dial-type, slightly more costly ($15 to $40), and have much more sensitive probes, needing only to go into the meat ¼ inch, depending on the model and price. Drawbacks are that they can break if dropped and may have hard-to-find batteries.

Continuous-Read Digital Thermometers Unlike the old-fashioned metal dial mercury thermometers that stay in the meat the whole time it cooks (and take a long time to get a read-out), these new models are extremely accurate. This type has a probe attached by a long cable to a digital read-out. The probe stays in the meat while the read-out can sit on the counter near the oven. (Some models are wireless so you can carry them with you.) The advantage to this type of thermometer is that you can keep track of the temperature of the meat without having to open the oven. Also, they take ordinary pen-light batteries and are reasonably priced in the $30 to $40 range.

Determining Doneness

There are several ways to determine the doneness of meat. The most obvious way is by observing its internal color—pink or reddish-pink for rare, and white or grayish-white for well-done—but in order to do that you have to cut into the meat. Unfortunately, the resulting gash causes loss of juices, which is exactly what you want to prevent. Professional chefs can press a piece of meat with their finger and tell if it's done, but few home cooks have that ability. A less invasive, and much more reliable way is with an accurate meat thermometer (see above).

If you have an accurate thermometer, how do you get the most accurate reading? For large, symmetrical cuts, such as bone-in or boneless pork loins, tenderloins, sirloins, and small roasts cut from the leg, you need to determine the center of the meat by eyeballing it. If

Pork Doneness Chart

Pork Cut	Remove from Heat	Ideal Temp. (after resting)	USDA Recommends
Loin Roast	140° to 145° F	145° to 155° F	160° F
Sirloin Roast	140° to 145° F	145° to 155° F	160° F
Tenderloin Roast	135° to 140° F	145° to 150° F	160° F
Whole Fresh Ham	145° to 150° F	150° to 160° F	160° F
Half Fresh Ham	145° to 150° F	150° to 160° F	160° F
Top Leg (Inside)	140° to 145° F	145° to 155° F	160° F
Bottom Leg (Outside)	140° to 145° F	145° to 155° F	160° F

Pork cooked to this temperature will be faintly pink to pinkish-gray in the center. Juices will be faintly pink. It should be firm but not hard and the grain of the meat will be compact.

Center-cut Chops	140° to 145° F	145° to 155° F	160° F
Leg Steaks (Fresh Ham Steak)	140° to 145° F	145° to 155° F	160° F
Butterflied Tenderloin	140° to 145° F	145° to 155° F	160° F
Sirloin Chops	140° to 145° F	145° to 155° F	160° F
Scaloppini	140° to 145° F	145° to 155° F	160° F
Medallions	140° to 145° F	145° to 155° F	160° F
Kebabs (from Loin, Sirloin, or Tenderloin)	140° to 145° F	145° to 155° F	160° F
Kebabs (Boston Butt or Country-style ribs)	145° to 150° F	150° to 160° F	160° F

Pork cooked to this temperature will be firm and compact in texture (tenderloins will be softer) and have a faintly pink to pinkish-gray color. Juices will be faintly pink.

Fully Cooked Smoked Ham	130° to 135° F	140° to 145° F	160° F
Country Ham	140° to 150° F	145° to 160° F	160° F
Blade Roast	155° to 165° F	160° to 170° F	160° F
Boston Butt	155° to 165° F	160° to 170° F	160° F
Picnic Shoulder	155° to 165° F	160° to 170° F	160° F
Spareribs	155° to 165° F	160° to 170° F	160° F
Country-style Ribs	155° to 160° F	160° to 170° F	160° F
Back Ribs	145° to 155° F	150° to 165° F	160° F
Pork Belly	155° to 160° F	160° to 170° F	160° F
Fresh Sausage	145° to 150° F	150° to 160° F	160° F
Smoked Sausage	135° to 140° F	140° to 150° F	160° F

it's somewhat irregular in shape, you may want to take 2 or 3 readings from different areas. Make sure you wait a few seconds so the thermometer comes all the way up to temperature, before making a determination. For boneless chops and pork steaks, roughly determine the center by using the probe to judge thickness, then insert it halfway. You may find that the temperature continues to inch up after 30 seconds and that's because there is little distance from the center of the chop to the much hotter exterior. The thinner the chop, the more difficulty you will have in determining doneness; aim, therefore, for the lower doneness number in the range so that the chops are not overcooked during this rapid temperature change.

Choosing the Right Cut to Match the Cooking Method

You're probably thinking, "Why do I need to know which cuts to buy to match a method, when you tell me which ones to use in the recipes?" The answer is that I want to educate you so that you can create or adapt your own recipes. I want to provide you with some basic concepts about pork cookery.

There are two kinds of heat used to cook meat: dry heat and moist heat. Dry-heat methods are those cooking methods that do not use any liquid and are ideal for cooking tender cuts of meat. These methods are frying (including deep-frying, pan-frying and pan-broiling, sautéing and stir-frying), grilling, broiling, and roasting (including the slow-roasting method known as barbecuing). Moist-heat cooking uses liquid in the cooking process. The heat is usually applied gently, as in simmering versus boiling, because high levels of moist heat can toughen and shrink the meat. Moist heat is ideal for tough cuts of meat because the moist heat turns tough collagen into gelatin. Moist-heat methods are braising (including pot-roasting), stewing, steaming, poaching, and pressure cooking (high-pressure steaming).

Today's pigs not only come to market bred much leaner, they're slaughtered at a considerably younger age, and because younger animals tend to have less collagen, nearly all the cuts will be tender enough to be cooked by dry-heat methods (assuming, of course, they're not overcooked). Unfortunately, today's pigs also have less intramuscular fat and their meat is easily overcooked. Ideal candidates for dry-heat cooking come from the loin, sirloin, legs, and tenderloins, which are areas of the pig that produce the tenderest meat. Cuts in these areas come in larger pieces, which can be divided into roasts or into small chops, steaks, and cutlets to be grilled, fried, or broiled. The exceptionally tender pork tenderloin can be cooked by any of the dry-heat methods. The Boston butt is the most versatile of all cuts. It's tender enough to be cooked by dry-heat methods and can be roasted, cut into steaks, kebabs, or strips, and grilled or fried, but it is also ideal for moist-heat cooking because it has ample fat to balance the loss of moisture during long cooking times.

Moist-heat cooking is most often reserved for tough cuts because the moist heat turns tough collagen into tender gelatin. Shanks, ribs, cheeks, trotters, picnic shoulder, uncured pork belly, neck bones, smoked ham hocks, tails, ears, and whole heads are those collagen-laden cuts that become juicy and silky-soft from long, slow, moist heat. In addition, Boston butt and blade-end loin (country ribs), which are not particularly tough but do have ample fat, can be cooked with moist heat, and cubes cut from those pieces (often sold as country spareribs) as well as from the picnic shoulder, are the best cuts for stews.

Lean tender cuts—loin, tenderloin, sirloin, or leg—cannot be cooked for any extended time with moist heat. If these cuts are cooked with liquid to an internal temperature much above 155° F, they become overcooked, and because they don't have enough fat to keep them from drying out, they'll become hard and dry even though the meat is sitting in liquid. Eventually, if the meat continues to cook, it will fall apart into dry strings. You can, however, use moist heat for short periods of time to finish pork chops and medallions in pan sauces, as long as the final temperature of the meat stays below 155° F (ideally between 145° and 155° F).

So here is your take-home lesson for choosing the right cut to match the cooking method: Tender cuts are cooked with dry heat; tough cuts with long, slow, moist heat. You'd never broil a pork shank to 145° F (medium) or cook pork tenderloin in a stew for 1½ hours to a final temperature of 180° F (beyond well done). Some pork cuts, like Boston butt, country spareribs, and blade-end loin, are tender but have enough fat to be cooked by either method.

Dry-Heat Cooking for Pork:
Perfection Is in the Details

Several of the dry-heat cooking methods are explained within the recipes. (See, for example, the Master Recipe for Sautéed Pork Chops on page 110.)

BROILING I'm not really a big fan of broiling, which means that meat is cooked by direct exposure to radiant heat. The problem is that most home broilers don't reach high enough temperatures to sear the meat's surface adequately. Often what passes for broiling is only hot enough to pull vital meat juices to the surface, where they quickly evaporate instead of caramelizing. The result is gray, dry, and chewy meat. Commercial restaurant broilers achieve heats of 700° F, while home broilers struggle to achieve 550° F, a temperature not quite hot enough to serve its intended purpose. Pork chops should be ideal candidates for broiling, but because broiling temperatures are hard to control and the chops can be very lean, they can easily dry out. Pan-sautéing, pan-grilling, or outdoor grilling are much better methods for cooking pork chops. Broilers are excellent for browning the surfaces of ribs, chops, or tenderloins that have been almost fully cooked by another method, such as roasting or pan-sautéing. Broiling also works well for caramelizing sweet glazes and barbecue sauces, but care must be taken—it may only take a minute or so to caramelize a sweet glaze and a minute or two longer to create a blackened mess.

ROASTING I like to imagine that the first time meat was roasted was when one of our cave-dwelling ancestors dropped his woolly mammoth drumstick into the campfire and discovered that the crispy fat and caramelized meat was much tastier than the raw chewy stuff he was used to. Perhaps a few centuries later an enterprising fellow or (more likely) madam figured out that you could control the charring of the meat by setting it on sticks slightly away from and out of the fire. Thus was born the primitive spit. For several more millennia, the spit remained the state-of-the-art when it came to roasting. (Some cultures roasted their meats by burying them in hot rock-lined pits.) Even today, spit-roasting, especially of whole animals like sheep, lamb, or small pigs, is the preferred method for Greek weddings or Puerto Rican barbecues and other special events, and many high-end home grills come equipped with motor-driven rotisseries. Spit-roasting cooks by radiant heat, but most meat today is roasted inside closed boxes called ovens that use both radiant and convection heat. All ovens use convection heat, though the heat is enhanced in a "convection oven," which uses a fan to circulate the air and make the process more efficient. Convection simply means the movement of air (which occurs whenever air is heated). Meat is cooked both by its contact with hot dry air and the radiant heat created by the heating of the oven surface. The heat from the hot air is then passed to the object being cooked.

CONVECTION OVENS The air currents and movement of hot air in a static, or conventional oven, is somewhat random and the burners that are heating the air are not necessarily even, so that static ovens tend to have hotter and cooler spots. That's why meat, if not turned occasionally as it roasts, will brown and cook unevenly. Convection ovens alleviate the problem of hot spots by placing a fan in the back of the oven, which forces air to circulate at a much more rapid rate than in static ovens.

Convection ovens, though, offer much more than just even cooking and browning. Because hot air is moving rapidly, it is more effective in transferring heat than slow-moving air. Imagine the wind-chill factor in reverse. Just as rapidly moving air transfers chill better than slow-moving cold air, rapidly moving hot air transfers heat more effectively, which means that meats cook more quickly in a convection oven than in a conventional oven set to the same temperature. But the real bonus, to my way of thinking, is the fact that meats simply brown better. So if you're like me and you love great roasted meats and perfectly browned poultry, you may want to consider adding a convection oven to your kitchen arsenal. That said, all the recipes in this book were tested using a conventional static oven (a huge sacrifice on our part, I might add), but I realize that not everyone has access to a convection oven. If you do own one, when following the recipes for roasting that say to first roast for 15 minutes at 450° F, eliminate this step because the meat will overbrown. Instead, just leave the thermostat set to 325° F for the entire cooking time.

Since convection ovens cook more efficiently, most manufacturers of convection ovens instruct you when following a recipe to reduce the oven temperature by 30° to 50° F. I happen to like the superior browning that foods cooked in a convection oven achieve, as well as the fact that they cook in a shorter amount of time when set at the same temperature as a conventional oven. Except for eliminating the browning step (see above) I don't recommend reducing convection oven temperatures. If you own a convection oven, experiment with oven temperatures to see what works best for you, but keep in mind that convection cooks more quickly and begin monitoring the internal temperature of the meat sooner than the recipe suggests.

When it comes to slow-roasting (see below) in a convection oven, I *do* recommend reducing the thermostat because rapidly moving hot air increases the evaporation of moisture. This is not a concern in the relatively short times of 2 to 3 hours associated with moderate roasting temperatures (300° to 350° F). But in low-temperature roasting, where times can take 5 hours or more, I recommend temperatures of 200° to 225° F for convection ovens instead of the 250° to 275° F called for in static oven slow-roasting recipes.

Roasting Methods

Just as there are lots of ways to skin a cat (not that I ever would), there are several ways to roast a piece of pork (something I've done often). Some of the variables that affect the roasting method you choose are the size and shape of the pork roast, its tenderness, its degree of marbling, your personal taste, and how much time you have to get the job done. As you know by now, to achieve success—a juicy, tasty roast—you need to cook the meat to the correct internal temperature, but how you get it to the correct temperature is a function of how hot your oven is and how long the meat is roasted. You can get to the same internal meat temperature (doneness) quickly with a hot oven, or slowly with a cooler oven, and the results will be very different. If you take two identical roasts and cook one in a hot (450° F) oven it may be well browned but will have lost more liquid than the one roasted in a cool oven (250° F), which will be more succulent but not very brown. In addition, the roast cooked at 450° F will be much more cooked on the circumference, while the slow-roasted meat will be more uniformly cooked across its entire diameter. However, because the slow-cooked roast has less browning, it may have less of the "cooked flavor" that most of us associate with pork. But your choices and preference may be different from mine, so you're welcome to alter any of my recommendations to suit your own tastes.

All that said, for the pork cuts throughout the book, I use three basic roasting methods and one hybrid method, and with each method I recommend why a particular method is best suited for a specific cut.

MODERATE-TEMPERATURE ROASTING (300° to 350° F)

The Cuts This method is best suited to larger cuts such as 8-bone, bone-in pork rib roast, Boston butts, or double-loin roasts, or whole fresh ham. It is also the preferred method for cured smoked ham or stuffed pork belly.

Moderate-temperature roasting is ideal for lean and tender meats, which would dry out if cooked at high temperatures. The steady application of gradual heat keeps the moisture in the meat, and lean roasts will not dry out if overcooked. Roasts cooked in a moderate oven lose less weight overall than pork cooked in a hot oven. Smaller roasts or roasts with small diameters, like pork loins, when cooked in a moderate oven risk not browning because they're not in the oven long enough. Large-diameter roasts like Boston butts or hams do brown well because they take much longer to roast. If you're a lover of well-browned roasts (as I am), then you may want to brown your pork loins first on top of the stove in a hot skillet, or choose the hybrid method that follows.

HYBRID METHOD FOR MODERATE ROASTING **(This is the English method—short searing at 450° to 500° F, followed by 300° to 350° F roasting for the remainder of roasting time.)**

The Cuts This is my preferred method for all pork loin roasts, oven-roasted spareribs, boneless roasts cut from the fresh pork leg, baby back ribs, and any skin-on roast, such as skin-on fresh ham or David's Porchetta (page 178).

The roast is cooked in a hot oven (450° to 500° F) for a short time, 15 to 20 minutes, then the heat is reduced to moderate (300° to 350° F) until the meat is fully roasted. This method results in the full flavor of a well-browned exterior, yet uses moderate heat for the bulk of the cooking time to provide juiciness and easier control of degree of doneness. This hybrid method does cause a little more shrinkage than the straight moderate method, but is still very acceptable, provided you don't overcook the meat.

HIGH-TEMPERATURE ROASTING (425° to 500° F)

The Cuts This method can only be used with the tenderest cuts, which means pork tenderloins. The method can also be used to crisp pork rinds or precooked pork belly.

Because high-temperature roasting does not enhance tenderness, it can only be used with pork tenderloins that are roasted for a very short period of time, less than 20 minutes. I like cooking tenderloins in a hot oven so that they brown nicely; in addition, I start the browning process first on top of the stove in a hot skillet for a few minutes.

Basic Roasting Method

1 Trim the meat if directed to do so in the recipe.

2 Flavor the meat: This may be as simple as just sprinkling it with salt and pepper, or it may be a dry spice rub, spice paste, marinade, or soaking in a flavor brine.

3 Preheat the oven to the desired temperature.

4 Lay the roast, fat-side up, on a roasting rack set in a shallow roasting pan so that hot air can circulate all around the meat.

5 If you're using a continuous-read digital thermometer (highly recommended, see page 35), then insert the probe into the center of the thickest part of the meat and set the temperature alarm to the desired degree of doneness, which is 140° to 145° F for most roasts. Do not plug the wire cable into the monitor yet. Make sure to lower your oven rack so that there is sufficient clearance between the probe and the ceiling of the oven. If not, you can also put the probe in at an angle.

6 If you're not using a continuous-read thermometer, set your oven timer to the shortest time recommended in the recipe to begin monitoring the internal temperature.

7 Put the roast in the oven and if using a continuous-read thermometer attach the cable out of the oven to the read-out monitor.

8 When the roast is done, remove the pan from the oven and tent it loosely with foil. Let the meat rest anywhere from 10 minutes for tenderloins and up to 45 minutes for whole fresh hams.

9 During the resting period, you can transfer the roast to a cutting board and make a pan sauce using the pan juices, if desired.

10 Carve the roast and serve as is, or with the sauce suggested in the recipe.

11 Enjoy!

Remember that when meat is cooked in a hot oven the internal temperature is increasing rapidly and that the surface of the meat is hotter than if it was cooked in a moderate oven. Resting of the meat is imperative so that the external heat can equilibrate and bring the meat up to its final temperature. During this resting period, the internal temperature may rise 10° F or more, so I would remove the tenderloin from the oven when it's in the 135° to 140° F range to prevent overcooking.

SLOW-ROASTING (200° to 275° F)

The Cuts Preferred cuts have adequate fat and are somewhat tough, such as Boston butt, picnic shoulder, spareribs, pork belly, and whole pigs.

When it comes to pork cookery, no method has been practiced longer and with greater success than barbecuing. Barbecuing (as opposed to grilling) means cooking meat at low temperatures (200° to 250° F) with smoke-laden heat for long periods of time. The classic Southern pulled pork, which is made from Boston butt, takes at least 8 hours and up to 14 hours for the meat to get cooked enough to fall apart when teased with a fork or a finger. Even though it's cooked beyond well done, the meat remains moist and succulent. That's partially because of the inherent fattiness of the Boston butt and the fact that the slow-roasting keeps moisture loss to a minimum. Furthermore, it is the perfect temperature to soften collagen into gelatin. The proteins that make up collagen are softened with moist heat in the range of 150° to 175° F, which is pretty much the internal temperature range of slow-cooked Boston butt.

While the smoky, woodsy taste of barbecuing cannot be beat, you can use an indoor oven as well for slow-cooking, especially with the fattier cuts. I am very impressed with the effect of slow-roasting on picnic shoulders, which can be roasted up to 24 hours (page 171), and you can also use slow-cooking for thick slabs of spareribs in any of the roasted rib recipes (pages 145 to 151).

Grilling

I could write a whole book about grilling and, in fact, there are several excellent books out there on that very topic, which are well worth the money, particularly if you have a passion for outdoor cooking. My intent here is, of course, to concentrate on the grilling of pork since that's what this book is all about. In the case of specific and popular cuts for grilling, such as chops, ribs, sausages, tenderloins, and loin, I've provided detailed information within the recipes themselves, so I only want to make a few introductory comments and concentrate here on the setting up of the grill itself.

Barbecue manufacturers have really cashed in on America's love of grilling, which is by far the most popular method for cooking meat, even in fall and winter months. Nowadays there are more choices for grills and barbecues than there are whiskers on a hog's back, and you can spend as little as $4 for a portable hibachi or as much as $10,000 for stainless behemoths that do everything except wash the dishes and put the baby to bed. I'm a Southern California boy who grew up with backyard barbecuing (as we called it then). In those ancient days our grill was nothing more than a couple of stacks of bricks with a rack set across them and my dad, who never prepared anything more than cold cereal, was the grill master at our house, which probably accounts for the fact that for most of my childhood I thought all hamburgers were supposed to be blackened. Anyway, at some point I realized that I needed to rustle the barbecue tongs away from my dear old pop. By the time I was thirteen, I had several inches on the old man and was able to take over the grilling chores. Eventually I learned how to cook meat so it wasn't charred on the outside and raw in the middle. And even though there are now so many choices of charcoal and gas grills on the market, the basic concept remains the same. Successful grilling is all about controlling heat (and I'm not using the word "fire" here on purpose, since an open flame is the enemy of most grilling).

What I can't describe for you here are all the possible idiosyncrasies of the specific grill you own and how to deal with them. That's why the first thing you'll need to do after you purchase your new grill is to become familiar with its instruction manual. (If you already have a grill, you may want to read it again.)

When I grew up all of our grilling was done on open grills. There were no covered barbecues, as we know them today, so all of our cooking was done directly over the heat. But today, with covered grills, you can use them for indirect grilling, which is just another way of roasting (I call it grill-roasting). But unlike indoor roasting, you get to add the elements of wood and smoke, which are particularly great flavoring agents when it comes to pork; it's a technique well worth mastering. Most of my tips relate to charcoal grills, but for those of you who own gas grills (I think you're in the majority these days), my best advice is to keep the flame down for most grilling tasks. Medium-high is about as far as you want to go. While you can use a gas grill for grill-roasting (indirect grilling), when you shut off some of the burners, it is very difficult with most gas grills to get the temperature low enough to use the grill for low-temperature roasting and barbecuing. For that you'll need a water smoker or other low-temperature barbecuing apparatus.

DIRECT GRILLING BASIC METHOD Direct grilling is best done with tender meat that is no more than 2 inches thick. Ideal cuts are pork chops, pork steaks, tenderloins (especially when butterflied), back ribs, sausages, country ribs, pork burgers, precooked belly, and kebabs.

■ The key to successful direct grilling is building a fire that has varying degrees of intensity. This is accomplished by layering the charcoal. Areas with charcoal 3 or 4 layers high will have high heat; areas with 1 or 2 layers will be moderate; and some areas of the grill should have no charcoal at all (this area can be used to slow down the cooking). With gas grills, regulate the burners so you have areas of varying intensity. Your job is to judge whether things are cooking too fast or too slow and to move the meat to the appropriate area to speed up or slow down the cooking. This takes practice and attention. That means you cannot walk away from the grill when you're on duty. Each piece of meat will not finish cooking at the same time so make sure you have a warm platter and some foil ready so that you can keep the cooked meat covered on the platter while you finish cooking the other pieces.

■ To determine how hot the grill is: Once the coals are lit and coated with gray ash, test the heat by placing your hand at the height of the grilling surface. If over the hottest area, it's too hot to keep your hand there on the count of two, you have sufficient heat to begin grilling. You can check the heat in the moderate heat area with the same method with a count of four to six.

■ Put the meat over the high-heat area and immediately cover the grill, leaving the top and bottom vents open. Covering the grill should prevent flare-ups, but move the meat to a less intense area and cover the grill if any flare-ups occur.

- For most cuts, you'll want to sear the meat for 1½ to 2 minutes, flip, and sear the other side. Then move the meat to a less intense area to complete the cooking. For chops that are ½ inch thick or less, they will probably be done after the initial searing. Pieces of meat that are more than ¾ to 2 inches thick will require 3 to 6 minutes per side, depending on thickness to complete cooking. Monitor the internal temperature with a digital instant-read thermometer. Remove the meat from grill as it reaches the desired temperature. Remember, the meat must always rest at least 5 minutes before serving.

- If you want to put a sauce or glaze on the meat, it should be applied right before the meat is finished. Put the meat over the hot part of the grill and make sure the glaze does not burn, 1 to 2 minutes per side is usually ample time.

INDIRECT GRILLING (GRILL-ROASTING) BASIC METHOD The best cuts for grill-roasting are center-cut loin roasts, blade-end loin roasts, sirloin, fresh ham, smoked ham, tenderloins, Boston butt, picnic shoulder, spareribs, back ribs, country ribs, belly, thick chops, and meat loaves.

All the information for roasting (pages 41 to 44) applies to grill-roasting. The basic method for grill-roasting, or indirect grilling, is similar to the moderate-temperature roasting method described on page 42. The best results are with large pieces of meat, but unlike indoor roasting, you can add the elements of wood and smoke. Use small chunks of hardwoods such as hickory, oak, alder, apple, and other fruitwoods. If you can't find chunks, then use wood chips, but they will burn quickly and must be replaced more often. Both wood chunks and chips should be soaked in water for at least 30 minutes, but longer is better. You can also soak the wood overnight. Wood chips are fine for short roasting times, but chunks are best for long times. Most methods for grill-roasting have you place a drip pan in the center of the grill and bank the coals on either side, but I've found that you really only need to place coals on one side of the grill, leaving the other half without coals. You may have to turn the roast from time to time, but this method works well for all but a really large roast like a whole ham.

- Remove the top grate from a covered charcoal grill. Fill a chimney starter with briquettes (40 to 60). Leave all the vents open on the grill and when the coals are covered with gray ash dump them on half of the grill. Put a drip pan on the other half. Add 2 or 3 soaked wood chunks or a handful of chips.

- Replace the grill grate so that the holes are above the coals to allow more coals to be added as needed. For a small roast like tenderloin or thick pork chops, sear it directly over the coals for 2 or 3 minutes, then move to the area without coals. For larger roasts, simply center the roast over the area without coals. Insert a continuous-read thermometer if you're using one, otherwise cover the grill. If your grill is equipped with a thermometer, measure the temperature of the grill, which should be between 300° and 375° F. If the temperature is too high, partially close one of the upper vents. If it's still too hot, then partially close the lower vents. (The vents control the amount of oxygen, which regulates the heat.)

- Adjust the vents to control the heat and add more coals, wood chunks, or chips as needed. (For 2 hours of grill-roasting, you will need 6 to 8 chunks or 3 to 4 cups of wood chips.)

- Begin testing the meat for doneness as directed in the recipe, or preset the alarm on the continuous-read thermometer. If you are applying a glaze or marinade containing any sugar, do so during the last 15 to 20 minutes of cooking to prevent the sugar from burning. Remove the roast from the grill and let it rest as directed in the recipe before serving.

MOIST-HEAT COOKING (BRAISING, STEWING, AND POACHING) Except for shanks, smoked hocks, feet, tails, heads, and ears, most pork is tender enough to be cooked by the various dry-heat methods, but braising and stewing not only tenderize tough cuts, they produce wonderfully savory dishes, such as curries, moles, cassoulet, and other great culinary creations. Pork dishes cooked by moist-heat methods should not be ignored.

Braising, stewing, and poaching are very similar cooking methods. In braising and stewing, the meat is browned first, then the liquid is added. The difference between the two is that stewing uses more liquid than braising, which creates a large amount of sauce at the end (think pot roast). In poaching, the meat is usually not browned first and it's cooked slowly in a great deal of barely simmering liquid.

Moist-heat cooking allows for an exchange of flavors as the meat absorbs some of the cooking liquid and the liquid receives flavor from the meat. Moist-heat dishes are some of my personal favorites in all of pork cookery.

My Top 10 Tips for Grilling Pork

1   Build a fire of varying intensities by layering the coals.

2   Don't grill in sandals or bare feet. Embers can fall through the vents and cause painful burns.

3   A good pair of spring-loaded tongs is a grill chef's best friend—they function like long, heatproof hands.

4   Always season food for the grill *before* you cook it.

5   Heat is good, flame is bad. Grill with the lid down to control flare-ups.

6   Guard against overcooking—the exception is sausage, which needs to be cooked to 160° F. You can also poach sausages first in simmering water for 10 minutes before putting them on the grill.

7   Buy thick chops for grilling (1½ inches is ideal). If the meat is too thin, it's but a minute from perfect to overcooked.

8   If meat is cooking too fast (or charring), flip it and move it to an area of the grill that is cooler. It's better to flip meat frequently than to let it burn.

9   Don't judge a pork chop by its color; use an instant-read thermometer to determine doneness. An accurate instant-read thermometer or continuous-read thermometer is a must for successful grilled meats.

10 Let meat rest before serving so that the juices can be reabsorbed and the cooking process can be completed. Tenderloins and chops should rest 5 minutes, roasts 10 to 15 minutes or more.

Basic Moist-Heat Method

1 Season the meat with a rub, marinade, or spice paste.

2 For most recipes, the meat is browned first (with a few notable exceptions), because the caramelized exterior gives the liquid a rich meaty flavor: Petit Salé of Pork (page 292), braised shanks, Choucroute Garni (page 242), and several other world-class dishes do not brown the meat first.

3 If the recipe calls for browning the meat first: Brown the meat in a heavy skillet or casserole over medium-high to high heat in olive oil, bacon drippings, or lard (not butter, which will burn). Take care that the meat is not crowded in the pan, which causes it to release liquid and steam rather than sear. Turn the meat frequently to prevent burning and sear until the meat is nicely browned on all sides. This step should be done in several batches, if necessary.

4 When all the meat is browned, set it aside. Remove and discard all but 1 or 2 tablespoons of the fat from the pan and reduce the heat to medium. If aromatic vegetables are called for in the recipe, add them to the pan along with any bacon, pancetta, or ham that may be called for. Cover and cook slowly, stirring occasionally, until the vegetables have become soft and aromatic. Add liquid and scrape up any brown bits on the bottom of the pan. Increase the heat to high and bring the liquid to the boil. Return the browned meat to the pan, lower the heat to maintain a simmer, and finish the cooking on top of the stove or in a preheated 325° to 350° F oven. I prefer the oven, which provides a little more even cooking and evaporation and concentration of liquid. Sometimes the liquid must be periodically replenished, but that usually means the lid does not fit tightly on the pan or the heat in the oven is too high.

5 When the meat is almost done (take a taste sample to tell), add any vegetables or other ingredients specified in the recipe. Cook 20 minutes longer for all the flavors to meld or until the vegetables are softened. (You may also cook the vegetables separately and add them to the pot for the last 5 minutes of cooking.)

6 When the meat is done, remove the pan from the oven and degrease the liquid, in one of two ways. If you want to eat the dish immediately, remove the solids with a slotted spoon and skim and discard the fat from the surface of the sauce. If you're making the dish ahead, cool the meat and sauce separately, and refrigerate for a few hours or, better yet, overnight. (Moist-heat dishes actually improve in flavor upon sitting.) When the fat has congealed on the surface of the sauce, scrape it off and discard. Reheat the meat and/or vegetables in the sauce before serving.

7 To reduce the sauce if it's thin, after you've degreased it, boil it over high heat until it is reduced to the desired consistency or intensity (when it's syrupy). Return the meat and vegetables to the pot to rewarm before serving.

Cuts suitable for moist-heat cooking must have sufficient fat; otherwise they end up dry, stringy, and basically unpalatable. In a word, the lean cuts from the loin, tenderloin, sirloin, and fresh ham cannot be braised. Cuts from the pork shoulder are ideal for braising because they have the necessary fat yet are relatively tender, so they'll take less time to cook (about 1 to 1½ hours) than similar cuts of beef.

The Cuts The preferred cuts for moist-heat cooking are Boston butt, picnic shoulder, neck, cheeks, spareribs, country ribs, blade-end loin roasts, fresh belly, smoked belly, shanks, trotters, ham hocks, ears, tails, and whole heads.

Since pork takes so well to sweet flavors, liquids with fruit, sweet wines, cider, and citrus are good partners. Pork also pairs well with strong flavors as in the recipes for Pork Mole Verde (page 222), Burmese Curried Pork (page 225), and Choucroute Garni (page 242).

STEAMING Steaming is a method where food is cooked above a boiling liquid, usually water, in a covered pot. The meat, in this instance, is cooked by being bathed in hot steam. Chinese cooks, whose kitchens often lack ovens, use steamers to cook many dishes, particularly pork-filled dumplings, meatballs, and bits of seafood stuffed with savory pork fillings. Steaming is great for rewarming sliced ham or Petit Salé of Pork, but I don't use this method very often for pieces of pork larger than meatballs. (It is, however, a great way to cook fish, but this is a book dedicated to swine. . . .)

PRESSURE-COOKING Another more intense way to use steam is under pressure in a specially designed pot called a pressure cooker. While pressure cookers make quick work of tough and gnarly meats, it is very easy to miss the mark and wind up with a disintegrated pile of stringy fibers. Because pressure-cooking can take about a third of the time as regular steaming, a pressure cooker is a useful device for cuts like pig's trotters, ears, tails, hocks, and shanks. Consult the manual that comes with your pressure cooker for specific instructions.

MICROWAVING Yes, you can use your "nuker" to make crispy bacon by putting the strips between paper towels (or in one of those infomercial devices), but otherwise forget it for any real cooking. Pork cooked from scratch in a microwave ends up sitting in a pool of its own juices resulting in a gray mass that even my cat won't eat. The microwave, however, is a great help in the kitchen when it comes to rewarming moist-heat dishes, and it works pretty well for rewarming ribs, too.

Part Two: Light Meals and Starters

3

Breakfast and Brunch Fare

I doubt you purchased this book to learn how to make bacon and eggs, ham and cheese omelets, or sausage and waffles, and I'm going to guess that you've been making a very good version of these standard pork-inspired breakfast dishes for years. So my goal in this chapter is to offer breakfast (and/or brunch) fare you may never have made before or simply want to make better (Kirsten's Fried Pork Chops with Country Gravy on page 62). If you just want to stretch out a little and change one of your old standby recipes, such as strata, I've included variations of some of my favorites (page 58).

With homemade bacon, ham, or sausage on hand, I guarantee that you'll begin to look for new breakfast dishes. Why not consider making a ham hash with sweet potatoes, or put bacon in your traditional recipe for red flannel hash (which is actually a traditional ingredient of the classic New England dish)? Turn leftover firm polenta into hash by cutting it into small cubes and combining it with onions, crumbled sausage, or bits of smoked ham. Try adding bacon, crisped and then crumbled, to one of your favorite muffin or biscuit recipes substituting some of the oil or butter called for in the recipe with bacon fat.

I also like to make breakfast sandwiches using homemade ham or bacon. It may be as simple as broiling fontina and ham on a piece of good rye, or as elaborate as putting bacon or ham between two slices of French toast drizzled with maple syrup. Oh, and breakfast burritos made with scrambled eggs and Carnitas (page 210) or Chorizo de Los Angeles (page 265) are truly special. Even if you've purchased some really good ham or bacon from a good mail-order source (see Sources on page 318), get creative: Breakfast will never bore you again.

Shirred Eggs with Canadian Bacon and Piquillo Peppers

Shirred eggs (eggs baked in a ramekin) are wonderful for brunch or lunch and are a nice change from fried or scrambled. Piquillo peppers are sweet and intensely flavored peppers, imported from Spain, found in jars or cans in specialty or ethnic markets. If you can't find them, use a high-quality canned whole pimento instead. SERVES 2

1 Preheat the oven to 350° F. Generously grease 2 ramekins (4 to 5 inches each) with butter. 2 Melt the 2 teaspoons butter in a medium skillet over medium heat. Add the bacon and cook 2 to 3 minutes per side. 3 Lay 2 slices of cooked bacon in each ramekin and scatter pepper strips over it. Gently break 2 eggs into each ramekin, covering the bacon and peppers. Drizzle 1 tablespoon of the cream over the eggs in each dish, then add a few grindings of black pepper and a sprinkling of Parmesan. Set the ramekins on a baking sheet and bake in the middle of the oven for 20 minutes or until the egg whites are set and cooked through but the yolks remain soft when you press on them lightly with your finger. Remove from the oven, garnish with the chives, put each ramekin on a plate, and serve.

CHEF'S NOTES: The eggs in this recipe are not fully cooked. If salmonella in eggs is a potential concern in your area, continue to cook the eggs until the yolks are firm. There are lots of ways to vary this dish. Use ham instead of Canadian bacon, or even leftover roasted pork loin. Instead of piquillo peppers, try fire-roasted mild chilies, such as Anaheim, and top the eggs with jack cheese instead of Parmesan. Serve with homemade salsa. One of my favorite shirred egg preparations uses cooked sausage sliced on the diagonal instead of the Canadian bacon.

2 teaspoons butter, plus more for greasing the ramekins

4 slices Canadian bacon, about ¼ inch thick, either home-cured (page 300) or store-bought

8 piquillo pepper strips (each ½ inch wide)

4 large eggs

2 tablespoons heavy cream

Freshly ground black pepper

2 tablespoons freshly grated Parmesan cheese

1 tablespoon chopped chives or scallion greens, for garnish

Breakfast Strata

This simple but satisfying do-ahead breakfast casserole is a savory version of bread pudding. The ingredients most always include day-old bread mixed with a little pork (sausage, ham, or bacon) and whatever cheese or vegetables are currently lurking in the fridge. The mixture is then layered in a casserole and custard is poured over all and allowed to soak in overnight. It's a perfect dish for guests waiting for a holiday morning brunch. SERVES 6 TO 8

1½ pounds bulk fresh sausage such as Brown Sugar and Sage Breakfast Patties (page 259), Italian-Style Sausage with Rosemary and Grappa (page 260), or Boulevard's Pork and Mushroom Sausage (page 262)

1 cup finely chopped onions

½ cup finely chopped celery

4 large eggs

2 cups milk

Softened butter, for greasing the dish

12 slices day-old French or Italian bread, crusts removed

1½ cups grated cheese, such as sharp cheddar, jack, Swiss, fontina, asiago, Parmesan, or mozzarella

1 In a large skillet, cook the sausage over medium-high heat, breaking it up as it cooks with a fork or spatula, about 5 minutes. Add the onions and celery and cook 5 minutes, stirring frequently. Remove the pan from the heat and set aside. 2 Break the eggs into a medium bowl, whisk to break them up, then whisk in the milk. 3 Butter the bottom and sides of a 2½-quart casserole or shallow baking dish. 4 Put a layer of bread slices (one third) on the bottom of the casserole, and spoon half the sausage mixture over it. Sprinkle with ½ cup of the cheese. Make another layer with more bread, followed by the remaining sausage mixture and ½ cup of cheese. Cover with one more layer of bread and cheese. 5 Pour the egg and milk mixture (the custard) slowly and evenly over the contents of the casserole. Cover and let the bread absorb the mixture for at least 1 hour or preferably overnight in the refrigerator. 6 Preheat the oven to 350° F. 7 Put the casserole on a baking sheet (to catch any overflow) and bake in the middle of the oven for 1 hour or until the top is browned and bubbling.

CHEF'S NOTES: Leftover strata is a gift because it is great rewarmed—simply cover in foil and bake at 350° F for 20 minutes or until the interior is warm (Use your instant-read thermometer to determine the temperature; anything over 130° F is fine.) 🐖 Regarding leftovers: The strata can be served as a side dish to accompany roast pork or pork chops and is not unlike a bread stuffing, except it's a bit lighter and more soufflé-like. You can take the bull by its horns and not wait for leftovers to serve the strata as a side dish. Make a fresh version, using half the amount of the sausage and adding 2 cups of diced cooked butternut squash, sliced mushrooms, cauliflower, or broccoli. The cheese is optional.

Variations for Breakfast Strata Instead of using all raw sausage, do a

combination of raw and smoked sausage. Cajun *andouille* is nice. Dice the sausage into ½-inch cubes and cook together with the raw sausage. You should still use a total of 1½ pounds sausage. 🐖 You can also replace some or all of the sausage with diced ham or bacon. If you eliminate all of the sausage, then reduce the amount of ham or bacon to 1 pound. You may need to pour off some of the fat before adding the vegetables. Once the meat and vegetable mixture is cooked and cooled, add 1 cup finely chopped green onions or chives. I like to use Swiss cheese and sometimes I add chopped fire-roasted sweet peppers to the mixture. 🐖 If you're a smoked food fanatic, make your strata with a combo of fresh and smoked sausage and for the cheese, use smoked cheddar, Gouda, or mozzarella. 🐖 Seafood is a great addition to strata. Cook a combination of fresh and smoked sausage, add the vegetables and once they're cooked, stir in 1 cup cooked shrimp, crab, lobster, or my favorite, oysters. Use a mild cheese like jack, or omit the cheese altogether. 🐖 For a little Italian twist, use Italian-style sausage with Rosemary and Grappa, casings removed (page 260), or Nancy's Artichoke and Piquillo Pepper Sausage (page 264), casings removed but with ½ cup diced pancetta added. After you cook the vegetables, stir in 1 cup cooked Swiss chard, spinach, or kale. (I like black "dinosaur" kale.) Use a good-quality fontina or mozzarella and sprinkle a little Parmesan over the top before baking. 🐖 For a strata from south-of-the-border, use Chorizo de Los Angeles (page 265), casings removed, but cut it back to 1 pound since it is fairly strong. Once the vegetables are cooked, add 1 cup diced mild chilies to the mixture and use *queso* Oaxaca or jack cheese. 🐖 Mushroom lovers can add 2 to 3 cups sliced mushrooms to the onions and celery. My favorite mushrooms would be fresh porcini, chanterelles, or morels, but portobellos, shiitakes, and even plain white or brown domestic mushrooms would be fine. Use fontina or Port Salut cheese.

I think you get the picture—don't be afraid to mix and match. Experiment a little bit.

Scrapple

🐖 Traditional recipes for this Pennsylvanian treat call for boiling pig's head and various scraps until tender, adding cornmeal, and pouring the mixture into loaf pans. Once cooled and set, slices are fried and served with eggs and, for those with a sweet tooth, a little maple syrup. My version is made with a savory blend of breakfast sausage, cornmeal, and onions. It may not be completely authentic, but it sure tastes good and you don't have to go looking for a pig's head. MAKES ABOUT 3 TO 4 POUNDS

1½ pounds bulk fresh sausage, such as Brown Sugar and Sage Breakfast Patties (page 259), or store-bought

1½ cups finely chopped onions

3 cups Dark Pork Stock (page 87), homemade chicken stock, or canned low-sodium chicken broth

1¼ cups yellow cornmeal

½ teaspoon kosher salt

1 teaspoon dried sage

½ teaspoon dried marjoram

1 teaspoon freshly ground black pepper

2 tablespoons lard, olive oil, or bacon drippings

1 In a large, heavy skillet, cook the sausage over medium-high heat for 3 minutes, breaking it up with a spatula or fork. Pour off all but 2 tablespoons of the fat and add the onions. Lower the heat to medium-low, cover, and cook for 5 minutes. Set aside. 2 In a large saucepan, bring the stock to a boil and stir in the cornmeal, salt, sage, marjoram, and pepper. Lower the heat to maintain a simmer and cook, stirring frequently, for about 20 minutes. Stir in the reserved sausage and onion mixture and cook for 5 minutes. Moisten a loaf pan (9 by 5 inches) with water and pour in the scrapple mixture. Allow to cool, then press a piece of plastic wrap directly on top of the scrapple, and refrigerate overnight. It keeps 5 days refrigerated. 3 To serve, unmold the scrapple and slice ½ inch thick. Heat the lard or oil in a skillet over medium heat, add the slices, and fry until nicely browned, about 5 to 6 minutes per side. Serve at once.

Pam's Ham and Apple Breakfast Pie 🐖

My wife's co-executive chef at Boulevard, Pam Mazzola, gave me her family's old recipe for deep-dish breakfast pie, which they've been making longer than she can remember. I agree that it makes a great breakfast and seems no more odd when you think about it than cinnamon rolls or maple syrup-laden pancakes.

Not all of us have baked country ham in our fridge, but Pam says you can use store-bought Westphalian ham or even prosciutto. Buy about 6 ounces of sliced ham. The pie is always served warm. SERVES 6

1 To make the piecrust: Combine the flour and salt in a large bowl. Cut in the butter with a fork or pastry blender until the mixture is the size of small peas. Add the orange juice or water, 1 tablespoon at a time, until the dough comes together in a rough ball. If the dough seems dry, add a little more orange juice or water. (The dough can also be made in an electric mixer or food processor, but because it's such a small quantity, Pam prefers to make it by hand.) Shape the dough into a disk, wrap it in plastic wrap, and refrigerate for 30 minutes or up to 2 days. 2 Preheat the oven to 350° F. 3 To make the filling: Toss the apples, cornstarch, brown sugar, cinnamon, nutmeg, and pepper in a large bowl. Grease a 9-inch deep pie plate or a 7- by 10-inch baking dish with the butter. Cover the bottom of the dish with one third of the apples and top with half of the ham. Repeat with another third of the apples and the remaining ham. Top with the remaining apples. Set aside. 4 Roll the dough out on a lightly floured surface into a circle or rectangle ½ inch larger than the pie dish. Transfer to the pie. Cover the apples, pressing down to seal the dough on the edge of the pie dish. Cut a few slashes in the dough as steamvent. Bake the pie for 50 minutes or until browned. Lay the optional cheese slices on the crust and bake 5 minutes longer or until the cheese is melted. 5 To serve, cut the pie into wedges or rectangles and eat while hot or still warm.

Piecrust

1 cup unbleached all-purpose flour

¼ teaspoon salt

4 tablespoons cold butter, cut into ¼-inch pieces

3 tablespoons cold orange juice or ice water

Filling

6 medium Granny Smith apples, peeled, cored, and thinly sliced

2 tablespoons cornstarch

½ cup firmly packed brown sugar

½ teaspoon ground cinnamon

¼ teaspoon ground nutmeg

Pinch freshly ground black pepper

1 tablespoon butter

1½ cups julienned Westphalian ham or prosciutto (about 6 ounces)

6 thin slices Gruyère cheese or sharp aged cheddar (optional)

Kirsten's Fried Pork Chops with Country Gravy

 Kirsten Goldberg was one of the pantry cooks at Boulevard. One night when I was eating at the counter opposite her station, I asked her if she had a favorite pork recipe to contribute to my book. She didn't hesitate a second and replied, "The pork chops with country gravy my mom served for breakfast."

Most times when I've had fried chops, I've been disappointed because the meat always ends up dry from overcooking. The solution is to give the chops a quick soaking in a simple flavor brine of salt, sugar, and water. If you're serving them for breakfast, brine them the night before for 2 to 4 hours. Remove the chops from the brine and keep them, wrapped, in the refrigerator until you're ready to cook them. Otherwise make breakfast a little later—2 hours in the brine should be enough to make them succulent.

Serve these chops in true Midwestern style with warm biscuits—some folks spoon the gravy over the biscuits as well as the chops—and fried or poached eggs. If you're really feeling like going "whole hog," serve up a mess of grits, too. SERVES 4

Basic Brine

3 cups cold water

¼ cup kosher salt

¼ cup sugar

2 cups ice cubes

6 bone-in pork rib chops
(each ½ inch thick) or
6 boneless pork chops

1 To make the brine: Put the water in a large bowl and stir in the salt and sugar until the sugar is dissolved. Add the ice cubes and cool the mixture to at least 45° F. Submerge the pork chops in the brine. Refrigerate for 2 hours or up to 4. Remove the pork chops from the brine, pat dry, and wrap in plastic wrap. Store in the refrigerator until ready to cook. 2 To make gravy: In a large skillet, cook the sausage over medium heat, breaking it up with a spatula or fork. Pour off all but 2 tablespoons of the fat and discard. Reserve the fat in a cup for cooking the chops.

3 Sprinkle the flour over the cooked sausage in the skillet; stir to coat. Gradually stir in the half-and-half, nutmeg, and Worcestershire. Cook, stirring, until the sauce thickens, scraping up any browned bits from the bottom of the pan. Add more half-and-half if the sauce becomes too thick. Season to taste with salt, pepper, and Tabasco. Cover the skillet and set aside while you cook the chops. 4 Sprinkle the chops generously with pepper. Dredge them in the flour, shaking off any excess. 5 In a large, heavy skillet, heat the reserved fat plus additional oil to a depth of ⅛ inch over medium-high heat. Put the chops in the pan, as many as will fit without crowding, and fry until golden brown, about 2 or 3 minutes. Turn and cook the other side, 2 to 3 minutes. If you're cooking more than one batch of chops, keep the fried chops warm in a preheated 250° F oven. 6 To serve, put one chop on each diner's plate (you will have 2 remaining for second helpings) and spoon the gravy over them. Serve extra gravy on the side to pour over biscuits or grits.

Country Gravy
MAKES ABOUT 2 TO 2½ CUPS

½ pound bulk fresh sausage, such as the Brown Sugar and Sage Breakfast Patties (page 259) or store-bought

2 tablespoons all-purpose flour

2 cups half-and-half, plus additional if needed

Freshly grated nutmeg

¼ teaspoon Worcestershire sauce

Kosher salt

Freshly ground black pepper

Tabasco sauce

Freshly ground black pepper

½ cup all-purpose flour

Sausage fat or bacon fat, lard, or canola or safflower oil

Glazed Smoked Pork Loin

Some lazy Sunday morning, when you have a little extra time to prepare breakfast, you may wish to try baking and glazing a smoked pork loin (also called Canadian bacon) or smoked pork shoulder. The presentation will elicit "oohs and aahs" at the table, and the freshly carved slices will be much juicier than if you just sliced and then sautéed them in a pan. If you've gone the extra mile and made your own Maple-Cured Canadian Bacon (aka Smoked Boneless Pork Loin on page 300), this is a great way to show off your work. The same can be said for homemade Molasses-Cured Pork Shoulder Bacon (page 299). If you're using a store-bought smoked loin or smoked shoulder, it's still an impressive breakfast. Store-bought shoulder bacon may be sold as cottage ham, smoked pork butt, or smoked Boston butt. SERVES 6

¼ cup grape or red currant jelly

2 teaspoons cider vinegar

1 tablespoon brown sugar, maple syrup, or molasses

1 tablespoon Dijon mustard

¼ teaspoon ground allspice or ground cloves

1 (2-pound) piece smoked pork loin or smoked pork shoulder (if using pork shoulder, it should be cut to roughly the same dimensions as a boneless loin, about 2 inches thick by 3 inches wide)

1 Preheat the oven to 350° F. 2 Put the jelly, vinegar, sugar, mustard, and spice in a small saucepan and bring to a boil over high heat. Lower the heat to maintain a simmer and cook, stirring occasionally, until syrupy, about 5 minutes. Remove from the heat and set aside. 3 Line a roasting pan with foil. (This makes quick cleanup as the glaze tends to burn on the bottom of the pan.) Put the pork, fat-side up, directly on the foil. Put the pan in the oven and bake the loin for 15 minutes and the shoulder for 35 minutes, then brush with the glaze. Continue basting every 10 minutes or so until the pork loin reaches an internal temperature of 140° to 145° F on an instant-read thermometer (about 35 to 40 minutes) and the pork shoulder reaches a temperature of 150° to 155° F (about 45 to 60 minutes). The meat should be a little sticky and have a shiny appearance. If not, brush with the glaze and increase the oven temperature to 450° F. Bake for 5 minutes longer. 4 Let the meat rest 10 minutes before slicing.

CHEF'S NOTE: I like to serve this glazed smoked pork loin with sweet potato hash browns or chunks of peeled yams or sweet potatoes tossed in melted butter and roasted in a hot oven. Add some cornbread muffins and eggs cooked the way you like them, and you have one fine breakfast or brunch.

4

Hors d'oeuvres, Appetizers, and Salads

So immense is the global variety of appetizers, hors d'oeuvres, and salads that include pork, I could devote an entire book to the subject. In the interest of brevity however, I've culled my recipe files to find my favorites, the ones that I turn to time and again when I'm looking for something to serve as a nibble, snack, light lunch, or simple first course. I realize, though, that the few I've included here barely scratch the surface. From Greek *meze* to Spanish *tapas,* from Chinese *dim sum* to Italian *antipasto,* from French *charcuterie* to American bar snacks, just about every cuisine contains a course of small savory dishes to whet the appetite, and pork, because of its versatility, is often featured in both supporting and starring roles. Pork is also a frequent visitor to cold plates and salads. What would a wilted spinach salad be without its bits of crispy bacon? Imagine a platter of antipasto without sliced prosciutto and salami, a bistro frisée salad without some pork confit or a slice of pâté, and throughout Asia pork is used to add flavor and substance to salads of cold noodles, crispy vegetables, and even seafood.

Crostini with Shrimp, Andouille, and Red Bell Pepper

Think of *crostini* (little toasts) as miniature open-faced sandwiches. I particularly like this combination of briny shrimp, spicy andouille, and sweet bell peppers, but you might also consider topping crostini with pâté or rillettes. This recipe makes a great starter to a New Orleans–style party or as a snack with beer.

In a rush, you can make simple crostini by topping the toasts with a slice of the cooked sausage, a strip of bell pepper, and a squeeze of lemon or dollop of Dijon. MAKES 24, SERVING 6 TO 8

1 Preheat the oven to 375° F. 2 To make the crostini: Brush both sides of all the baguette slices with the olive oil and arrange in one layer on a baking sheet. Bake until the slices begin to turn golden on the edges, about 7 minutes. Turn and bake 5 minutes more or until golden and crisp. Remove from the oven and let cool. (The crostini may be made up to 2 days ahead and stored at room temperature in a zip-lock plastic bag.) 3 Heat the olive oil in a large skillet over medium-high heat. Add the sausage and cook until browned, about 2 minutes. Using a slotted spoon, transfer the sausage to a bowl or plate and set aside. Add the shallots to the skillet and cook for 3 minutes. Add the shrimp and cook, stirring, until opaque, about 3 minutes. Off the heat, stir in the peppers, parsley, thyme, mustard, and the reserved sausage. Season to taste with salt and pepper. 4 To serve, put the crostini on a platter and top each one with a little of the shrimp/andouille mixture. Garnish each with a lemon wedge.

CHEF'S NOTES: You can vary this recipe by changing the sausage. Use store-bought *andouille,* Smoked French Country Sausage (page 266), or a good-quality store-bought smoked country sausage. Nowadays there are many other interesting varieties of sausages on the market so give them a try. 🐖 Instead of shrimp, you can make these with scallops or calamari, which need even less cooking (about 1 minute). If mustard is too strong a flavor, then substitute mayonnaise or try a mixture of half mustard and half mayonnaise. 🐖 Serve the crostini with pâté or rillettes as well.

Crostini

24 pieces (each ½ inch thick) baguette, sliced on the diagonal

2 to 3 tablespoons olive oil

1 tablespoon olive oil

½ cup chopped *andouille* (see Chef's Notes)

¼ cup finely diced shallots or red onion

6 ounces shrimp, peeled, deveined, and coarsely chopped

¼ cup diced fire-roasted red bell peppers, fresh or jarred

2 tablespoons chopped Italian flat-leaf parsley

1 tablespoon chopped fresh thyme

1 tablespoon Dijon mustard

Kosher salt

Freshly ground black pepper

24 small lemon wedges, for garnish

Warm Pita Stuffed with Turkish Meat Patties in Tomato Sauce

Though pork is not common in Turkish cuisine because the country is predominantly Muslim, there is another great religion with a large following in Turkey: Russian Orthodoxy. These meat patties are a good example of how well traditional Turkish spices marry with the sweet and subtle flavor of pork. (The patties are excellent made with lamb or beef as well.) I like to serve them with cocktails in small pita breads, but you can put two of them in larger pitas for lunch. SERVES 8

Meat Patties

1½ pounds lean ground pork

½ cup fresh bread crumbs

1 large egg

½ cup minced white onion

1 teaspoon minced garlic

1 teaspoon chopped fresh marjoram

¼ cup chopped fresh mint or
2 tablespoons dried

½ cup chopped cilantro or parsley

½ teaspoon cayenne pepper

2 teaspoons ground cumin

¼ teaspoon ground allspice

1 tablespoon fresh lemon juice

1½ teaspoons salt

1 teaspoon freshly ground
black pepper

2 tablespoons olive oil

1 To make the patties: Combine the pork and all of the remaining patty ingredients in a large bowl. Knead and squeeze the mixture to combine. Cover and refrigerate for at least 2 hours or overnight. 2 Form the meat mixture into 24 small oval patties, each about 1½ inches wide by 2 inches long and ⅜ inch thick. 3 Preheat the oven to 350° F. 4 Heat olive oil in a large skillet over medium-high heat. Add the patties in batches and fry until lightly browned, about 3 to 5 minutes. Turn and fry on the other side for 3 to 5 minutes. The patties should be faintly pink to gray on the inside. Remove the patties to a plate as they are done. 5 To make the sauce: Pour off all but 2 tablespoons of the fat in the skillet. Reduce the heat to medium and add the onions and garlic. Stir and cook until the onions are soft, about 7 minutes. Add the tomatoes, lemon juice, and allspice. Bring the liquid to a boil, scraping any browned bits from the bottom of the pan. Stir in the pomegranate syrup and add the pork patties. Cover and simmer for 10 to 15 minutes. Stir in the

green onions and taste for salt and pepper. Add a little Tabasco, if desired. 6 While the sauce is cooking, wrap the pita breads in foil and heat in the oven for about 10 minutes. 7 To serve, cut each pita in half. Open up the pocket and place 1 pork patty in each half. Spoon in some of the tomato sauce. Drizzle yogurt over the top and eat out of hand.

CHEF'S NOTE: Instead of patties you can form the pork mixture into small meatballs, which can be served in the sauce as an hors d'oeuvre or first course. Or serve the meatballs as a main course spooned over basmati rice. (This recipe will easily feed 4.)

Tomato Sauce

1 cup finely chopped onions

1 tablespoon minced garlic

2 cups canned whole tomatoes, chopped

2 tablespoon fresh lemon juice

¼ teaspoon ground allspice

1 tablespoon pomegranate syrup (also called pomegranate molasses)

½ cup chopped green onions

Kosher salt

Freshly ground black pepper

Tabasco sauce

12 miniature pita breads (3 to 4 inches in diameter)

Whole milk yogurt

Crispy Pork "Chips"

No, they're not really chips, but rather patties of ground pork, crispy on the outside, juicy on the inside. I call them chips because they share one attribute of potato chips—you can't eat just one. Serve the hors d'oeuvres version with lemon wedges or with Gribiche and the larger patties as a light entrée or lunch on a bed of lightly dressed baby lettuces, garnished with capers or a dollop of Gribiche. The large patties are also delicious with Lisa's No-Fuss Tomato Sauce (page 277).

MAKES 16 PATTIES, ENOUGH FOR 4 TO 6 PEOPLE AS AN HORS D'OEUVRE
OR 4 PATTIES AS AN ENTRÉE

---

2 slices coarse-textured white bread, such as French, Italian, or country bread, crusts trimmed and torn into pieces, soaked in ¼ cup milk for 15 minutes

1½ pounds boneless pork loin, cut into 1-inch pieces

1 teaspoon kosher salt

2 tablespoons heavy cream

1 tablespoon finely chopped shallot or green onions (white part only)

1 teaspoon minced garlic

2 tablespoons sun-dried tomatoes, packed in oil, chopped (optional)

1 tablespoon finely chopped capers

½ teaspoon freshly ground black pepper

2 teaspoons lemon zest

1 tablespoon chopped fresh basil

2 cups fresh bread crumbs of same bread as soaked

Olive oil for frying

1 Squeeze the bread to remove the excess milk. Set the soaked bread aside. 2 Spread the diced pork on a plate and chill in the freezer for 10 minutes. Put half of the pork and ½ teaspoon of the salt in the bowl of a food processor fitted with the metal blade. Pulse until the mixture forms a paste, about 1 minute. Transfer to a bowl and repeat with the remaining pork and salt. (If you have a large processor, you may be able to process the pork in one batch.) Return all the ground pork to the processor and add the soaked bread, cream, shallot, garlic, sun-dried tomatoes, capers, pepper, lemon zest, and basil and pulse until the mixture is just combined. 3 Moisten your hands with cold water and form the mixture into 16 oval patties, 2 to 3 inches long, 1 to 2 inches wide and ½ to ¾ inch thick. (For 4 entree patties, form into ovals 4 to 5 inches long and 3 to 4 inches wide and ½ inch thick.) Put the bread crumbs in a shallow bowl and coat the patties well with the crumbs, then set aside on a plate. 4 Heat olive oil to a depth of ⅛ to ¼ inch in a large skillet or sauté pan over medium heat. When the oil begins to shimmer, add the patties (in batches if necessary) and cook until golden brown, about 3 to 4

minutes. Turn and cook until browned on the other side, about 3 minutes. Cut into a patty to make sure it shows no sign of pink in the center. Transfer the patties to paper towels to drain. Serve hot with the suggested garnishes.

Sauce Gribiche

Gribiche, a French sauce similar to American tartar sauce, is basically homemade mayonnaise that is garnished with chopped hard-cooked eggs, mustard, cornichons, capers, tarragon, chervil, chives, and parsley. If you don't want to go to the trouble of making your own mayonnaise or if you're concerned about the health effects of raw eggs, by all means use a good-quality commercial brand of mayo. Any extra sauce can be kept in the refrigerator for up to 3 days and is great with roast pork sandwiches, chicken, or seafood. MAKES ABOUT 1¾ CUPS

1 In a medium bowl, whisk together the egg yolks with the salt and mustard. Slowly add the olive oil, drop by drop, whisking continuously. Add 1 tablespoon of the vinegar and continue to add oil slowly until the mixture is emulsified and thickened. (Or begin with commercial mayonnaise and skip this step.) Add 1 tablespoon more of vinegar to taste. 2 Stir in the remaining ingredients and adjust for taste. Refrigerate until serving.

Garnishes

Lemon wedges

Capers

Sauce Gribiche (recipe follows)

2 large egg yolks

1 teaspoon kosher salt

1 teaspoon dry mustard

1 cup olive oil

2 tablespoons champagne or tarragon white wine vinegar, or lemon juice

1 tablespoon capers, drained and finely chopped

1½ tablespoons finely chopped cornichons

3 hard-cooked eggs, finely chopped

½ small red onion, finely chopped (about ½ cup)

½ bunch chives, minced

Leaves from ½ bunch Italian flat-leaf parsley, minced

¼ cup fresh minced chervil or 2 tablespoons chopped fresh tarragon

1 garlic clove, minced

1 salt-packed anchovy fillet, rinsed and finely chopped, 1 teaspoon anchovy paste, or 1 teaspoon Worcestershire sauce

Freshly ground black pepper

Thai Seafood and Pork Dumplings 🐷

The seafood and pork mixture that's used to fill these dumplings is infinitely versatile and is a sausage mixture on its own. In addition to using it to fill dumplings, I've also stir-fried it and served it simply in lettuce leaves with thinly sliced cucumbers, carrots, and red onions. It could also be part of a substantial soup of chicken stock, sautéed eggplant, and green beans. Another option is to put the mixture in pork casings, then grill and serve as part of a mixed grill platter with fish or seafood.

For seafood choices, use cooked crabmeat, cooked lobster meat, raw shrimp, raw rock shrimp, or raw scallops. Be careful though, this mixture is very perishable; you must use pristinely fresh seafood, make the mixture the same day you purchase it, and eat within a day or two of making it. Add 2 teaspoons of Thai green curry paste to start as brands vary in heat intensity and saltiness. Taste, then add more, if desired. MAKES 30 TO 36 DUMPLINGS

3 to 4 tablespoons peanut oil

1 tablespoon minced fresh ginger

2 teaspoons minced garlic

2 tablespoons finely chopped green onion

1 teaspoon finely chopped jalapeño (optional)

1 pound boneless Boston butt with some fat

2 to 3 teaspoons Thai green curry paste, store-bought or homemade

½ cup chopped cilantro leaves

1 tablespoon chopped fresh mint

1½ tablespoons chopped fresh basil

2 tablespoons Asian fish sauce

1 tablespoon soy sauce

2 teaspoons fresh lime juice

1 Heat 1 tablespoon of the peanut oil in a small skillet over medium heat and add the ginger, garlic, green onion, and optional jalapeño. Stir and cook for 2 minutes. Set aside. 2 Grind the meat in a meat grinder fitted with a ¼-inch plate into a large bowl. Add the reserved ginger mixture and all the remaining ingredients except the wonton wrappers and stock. Knead and mix until well blended. 3 In a small skillet, cook a small patty, taste, and add more green curry paste or soy sauce, if desired. The mixture can be refrigerated several hours ahead until you're ready to make the dumplings. (You cannot, however, make the dumplings ahead of time because the wrappers will soften and become gummy.) 4 To make the dumplings: Press a wonton wrapper into the curved palm of your hand. Scoop about 1½ tablespoons of the filling into the small cup in the center of the wrapper. Using the fingers of both hands, gently gather and fold the sides of the wrapper to make natural

pleats. Squeeze the top and sides of the wrapper together to make sure it forms around the filling. Tap the dumpling on a flat surface so that it can stand upright. Repeat until all the wrappers and filling are used. 5 Heat remaining peanut oil in a large nonstick skillet over medium-high heat. Add the dumplings, as many as will fit comfortably without crowding, and cook until they're golden brown on the bottom, about 3 to 5 minutes. (If you're cooking more than one batch, transfer the cooked dumplings to a baking sheet. Add them back to the pan to finish cooking in the stock.) When all the dumplings are browned, drain and discard the oil. Return any dumplings already fried to the pan with the stock. Bring to a boil, cover, and cook until the dumplings are firm to the touch, about 1 to 2 minutes. 6 Transfer the cooked dumplings to a platter and serve with the spicy dipping sauce.

1 cup (6 ounces) coarsely chopped raw shrimp or other seafood (see headnote)

30 to 36 round wonton wrappers

1 cup homemade chicken stock or canned low-sodium chicken broth

Spicy Asian Dipping Sauce (page 75)

CHEF'S NOTES: The dumplings can be steamed in an Asian steamer, covered, for 10 to 15 minutes or until firm to the touch. Use the stuffing to fill wontons for a soup made with chicken stock, ginger, cilantro, and green onions. Garnish the soup with cilantro sprigs.

Pearl Balls with Spicy Asian Dipping Sauce 🐷

This wonderful Asian appetizer gets its name from the grains of rice adhering to the surface of the pork, which look like tiny white pearls. They're easy to make ahead and can be steamed at the last minute when your guests arrive. Serve them warm or at room temperature, never cold. They also reheat nicely.

MAKES 24 MEATBALLS, SERVING 6, WITH OTHER HORS D'OEUVRES

1 cup glutinous rice or other medium-grain rice (see Chef's Note opposite)

1 pound ground pork, preferably from the shoulder or boneless country ribs

1 large egg, lightly beaten

1 teaspoon minced fresh ginger

½ teaspoon brown sugar

1 tablespoon soy sauce

½ teaspoon Asian sesame oil

¼ teaspoon freshly ground black pepper

2 green onions, white and green parts finely chopped

½ teaspoon kosher salt

¼ cup finely chopped fresh or canned water chestnuts or jícama

1 Put the rice in a medium bowl and fill with cold water. Swish the rice around, then, using a strainer to catch the rice, drain and discard the water. Repeat the procedure several times until the water runs clear. Put the rice in the bowl and cover with cold water. Set aside for 2 hours or overnight to soak. Drain the rice and spread it out in a shallow bowl or on a rimmed baking sheet; pat dry with paper towels. 2 Put the pork and all of the remaining ingredients in a bowl. With moistened hands, knead and squeeze the mixture until well combined. Roll into 1-inch meatballs, then roll each meatball in the rice so that the grains are embedded in the meat. Arrange the pearl balls in one layer on a heatproof dish that will fit in your steamer. (You may need 2 dishes depending on the size of your steamer.) You can refrigerate the pearl balls, covered, for up to 8 hours before steaming. 3 Set up a steamer with water and bring to a boil. Put the dish with the pearl balls on it in the steamer and steam over boiling water for 20 minutes or until the rice is translucent and tender. If you have a stacking steamer, you can steam more than 1 dish at a time. 4 Serve the hot pearl balls at once with spicy dipping sauce.

Spicy Asian Dipping Sauce 🐷 MAKES ABOUT ¾ CUP

Stir the soy, vinegar, sesame oil, brown sugar, and green onions together in small bowl until the sugar is dissolved. Stir in the optional cilantro and add chile sauce to taste.

CHEF'S NOTE: Glutinous rice is also known as sticky rice or sweet rice because of its gluey texture. It's sold at Asian food stores or by mail order (see Sources on page 318). If you can't find it, use medium-grain white rice from California, such as Cal-Rose or Hinodi.

⅓ cup soy sauce

2 tablespoons rice vinegar

½ teaspoon Asian sesame oil

½ to 1 teaspoon brown sugar

2 tablespoons minced green onions

¼ cup chopped cilantro leaves (optional)

1 to 2 teaspoons Asian chile sauce, such as Chinese chili garlic paste, Thai chili sauce (*sriracha*), or crushed red pepper flakes

Master Recipe: Pork-Filled Turnovers 🐖

With a great pastry like our cream cheese dough and a variety of pork sausages in the fridge, the sky's the limit on how many different and delicious turnovers you can make for hors d'oeuvres. We like the cream cheese dough because not only is it rich and buttery, but it's also almost foolproof and can be rolled out repeatedly without becoming tough. However, you can use layers of store-bought filo dough or Jeff's Lard Piecrust (page 238) to make excellent turnovers as well. Another plus to these pastries is that they can be put together, frozen on sheet pans, bagged, and then baked at a later time. You can always have some on hand. MAKES 16 (4-INCH) TURNOVERS

Cream Cheese Dough

6 ounces cream cheese, at room temperature

16 tablespoons (2 sticks) butter, at room temperature

2¼ cups all-purpose flour

½ teaspoon salt

Mushroom-Sausage Filling

1 tablespoon butter

½ cup finely chopped onion

½ pound Boulevard's Pork and Mushroom Sausage (page 262), casings removed

¼ cup heavy cream

¼ cup freshly grated Parmesan cheese

2 large egg yolks, lightly beaten

2 tablespoons chopped Italian flat-leaf parsley

Egg wash made with 1 egg lightly beaten with 1 tablespoon cream, milk, or water

1 To make the dough: Put the cream cheese, butter, flour, and salt in the bowl of a food processor fitted with the metal blade. Pulse until the mixture just comes together in a ball. Remove the dough from the bowl and form into 2 disks. Wrap each well in plastic wrap and refrigerate for 1 hour or up to 24 hours. 2 To make the filling: Heat the butter in a medium pan over medium heat. Add the onions and cook until soft, about 5 minutes. Add the sausage, break it up with a fork or spatula, and cook until no longer pink, about 5 minutes. Add the cream, increase the heat, and boil until the cream has been almost completely absorbed. Remove the pan from the heat and stir in the cheese, egg yolks, and parsley. Transfer the filling mixture to a bowl and refrigerate until chilled (50° or less). 3 To assemble the turnovers: roll out one of the dough disks on a lightly floured surface to a thickness of ⅛ inch. If the dough is too hard to roll, let it warm at room temperature for 10 to 15 minutes. Using a 4-inch biscuit cutter, cut the dough into 8 rounds. (You will probably need to gather the scraps and reroll it for 8 rounds.) Repeat with the remaining dough disk so that you have 16 dough rounds in all. 4 Place 1 heaping tablespoon of the cooled filling on one half of a dough round, then fold the other half over to make a half-moon shape. Seal the edges with

the tines of a fork and continue making turnovers with the remaining dough rounds and filling. 5 Preheat the oven to 450° F. 6 Put all the turnovers on one large baking sheet (or 2 sheets to avoid crowding) and brush the tops with the egg wash. Bake until the turnovers are golden, about 20 minutes. Remove from the oven and let cool slightly before serving.

Other Fillings for Turnovers

Artichoke and Piquillo Pepper Sausage Filling

1 tablespoon olive oil

8 ounces Nancy's Artichoke and Piquillo Pepper Sausage (page 264), casings removed

¼ cup frozen or jarred artichokes, drained and chopped

¼ cup chopped fresh or canned tomatoes

½ cup grated fontina cheese

2 large egg yolks, lightly beaten

2 tablespoons chopped fresh basil

Spicy Chorizo Filling

1 tablespoon olive oil

½ cup finely chopped onion

¼ cup finely chopped carrot

8 ounces Chorizo de Los Angeles (page 265), casings removed

½ cup cooked sweet potatoes, cut into ¼-inch cubes (optional)

¼ cup chopped fresh or canned tomatoes

2 large egg yolks, lightly beaten

¼ cup chopped cilantro leaves

Smoked Sausage and Hominy Filling

1 tablespoon butter

½ cup finely chopped onion

6 ounces *andouille* or Smoked French Country Sausage (page 266), finely chopped

¼ cup fire-roasted fresh green chilies or canned green chilies, chopped

½ cup canned hominy, drained

¼ cup chopped fresh or canned tomatoes

½ cup grated sharp cheddar cheese

2 large egg yolks, lightly beaten

2 tablespoons thinly sliced green onions

Tigelle (Pork-Stuffed English Muffins) 🐖

The first time I met the late cooking teacher Loni Kuhn, she was giving a party for Bert Greene, a well-known cookbook writer. I walked into her house and was immediately seduced by the aromas wafting from her kitchen. There was Loni, grilling English muffins over an enormous cast-iron griddle. The muffins looked like grilled cheese sandwiches, but smelled very porky indeed. Before I could say a word, she handed me one, which I ate gingerly (they were quite hot). Loni, ever the teacher, explained she had just returned from Emilia-Romagna and that these little appetizers, known as *tigelle,* were her take on a snack served by the wives of the grape pickers who worked high in the mountains between Emilia-Romagna and Tuscany.

Twenty years later I was on a press trip learning about *balsamico,* Parmigiano-Reggiano, and the other great foods of the Emilia-Romagna region and our group was having lunch at an inn high above Modena. Sure enough, I was served what looked like a stuffed English muffin that was similar to the *tigelle* that Loni had served. They were little bubble-holed muffins toasted on a griddle over an open flame, then split open and smeared with a paste of pancetta, rosemary, and Parmesan cheese. Real *tigelle* are made of dough similar to English muffin dough that are baked sandwiched between a hot disk and a terra-cotta hearthstone. When duplicating Loni's recipe, I too found that a good-quality English muffin will work in place of the homemade *tigelle.* But, if you like to bake, by all means make your own. MAKES 32 PIECES

2 garlic cloves

½ pound pancetta (page 293), diced

1 tablespoon chopped fresh rosemary

1 cup freshly grated Parmigiano-Reggiano or good-quality domestic Parmesan-style cheese

8 English muffins (I like Thomas's), fork-split in half

¼ cup lard or olive oil

1 With the motor running, drop the garlic through the feed tube of a food processor. Stop and scrape down the sides of the bowl and add the remaining ingredients except the muffins. Pulse until the mixture forms a paste. Spread the paste on one side of each split muffin and re-form to make 8 sandwiches. (The sandwiches can be assembled up to 6 hours ahead.) 2 To cook the *tigelle:* Heat ⅛ inch of melted lard or olive oil in a large skillet (preferably cast iron) over medium heat. Add 3 or more muffins (or as many as will fit without crowding) and cook on one side until lightly browned, 3 to 5 minutes. Turn and cook on the other side until lightly browned. Drain on paper towels. Transfer to a platter and cut into 4 wedges. Serve hot or warm, but not cool.

Mexican Cracklins

If you're lucky enough to have access to an ethnic market that sells pork skin, or you've got some skin that you've trimmed off a large cut of pork (though I love skin-on pork roasts and bellies), this recipe is the ultimate in crackling, crunchy snacks. It's particularly good served in front of the TV with a few cold beers.

MAKES ENOUGH FOR 4 SNACKERS

1 Put the pork skin a large saucepan, cover with the water, and add the baking soda and salt. Bring to a boil over high heat, then reduce the heat to maintain a simmer and cook until the skin is soft, about 1 hour. 2 Preheat the oven to 425° F. 3 Remove the skin and discard the water. Pat the skin dry and put fat-side down on a rimmed baking sheet. Bake for 20 to 30 minutes or until the skin is bubbling and crisp. 4 Remove the skin from the oven and let cool. Serve with a sprinkling of salt and hot sauce to taste. Store in an airtight container in the refrigerator for up to 1 week.

1 pound pork skin, cut into
1-by 4-inch strips

2 cups water or more

4 teaspoons baking soda

1 teaspoon kosher salt

Tabasco or Mexican bottled
hot sauce

Lisa's Chopped Grilled Vegetable Salad with Grilled Pork Medallions

My co-author, Lisa Weiss, has a way with salads and this recipe is one she frequently made for lunch while we were testing recipes for this book. While the ingredient list seems lengthy, the beauty of this dish is that it's quite flexible and you can use it as a springboard for improvisation. Instead of cooking pork medallions, you could use leftover cooked pork loin, scaloppini, or sliced ham. Use whatever vegetables you can find that are fresh and in season. SERVES 8

---

2 pork tenderloins (12 to 16 ounces each), cut crosswise into ¾-inch slices

Lemon-Soy Marinade

¼ cup freshly squeezed lemon juice

½ cup soy sauce

½ cup olive oil

3 tablespoons brown sugar

2 tablespoons Dijon mustard

Vinaigrette

¼ cup white balsamic vinegar or white wine vinegar

¼ cup freshly squeezed lemon juice

2 teaspoons Dijon mustard

1 tablespoon kosher salt

1 cup extra-virgin olive oil

1 Put the pork medallions in a zip-lock plastic bag. 2 To make the marinade: In a small bowl, stir together the lemon juice, soy sauce, olive oil, brown sugar, and mustard. Pour the marinade over the pork and marinate in the refrigerator for 4 hours or overnight. (Omit this step if using leftover pork roast, scaloppini, or ham.) 3 To make the vinaigrette: Whisk together in a small bowl the white balsamic vinegar, lemon juice, mustard, and salt. Slowly add the olive oil, whisking constantly. Set aside. 4 To prepare the vegetables: Toss the zucchini, squash, and asparagus in a bowl with the olive oil and herbs. Skewer the fennel and radicchio wedges. Blanch the green beans in a large pot of boiling water until crisp-tender, about 4 minutes. Drain and immediately plunge into a bowl of ice water to prevent further cooking and preserve the color. Drain, pat dry with paper towels, and set aside.

5 To grill the vegetables and pork: Prepare a charcoal grill. Grill the zucchini, squash, asparagus, and onion slices over a medium-high heat until nicely marked and crisp-tender. Set aside. 6 Brush the fennel and radicchio skewers with the vinaigrette and grill, turning once, until the radicchio is softened but crisp around the edges and the fennel is golden on both sides. Sprinkle the optional corn with salt and pepper and grill, turning often, until lightly browned in spots, about 10 minutes. Grill the pork medallions until medium done, 2 to

3 minutes per side. (Omit this step if using leftover pork roast, scaloppini, or ham.)

7 To assemble the salad: Cut the grilled vegetables and the blanched green beans into ½-inch pieces and put in a salad bowl. Cut the grilled corn, if using it, off the cob and add to the bowl. Dice the avocado right before serving and add to the bowl. Gently toss with about ½ cup of the vinaigrette. Season to taste with salt and pepper. 8 In a separate bowl, toss the romaine with some of the remaining vinaigrette. Place a bed of romaine on each of 8 dinner plates and top with a portion of the chopped salad and 2 medallions of grilled pork. Drizzle with the remaining vinaigrette.

Vegetables

8 small zucchini, cut in half lengthwise

8 small yellow crookneck squash, cut in half lengthwise

1 pound asparagus, woody ends removed

¼ cup olive oil

1 tablespoon fresh or dried herbs, a mixture or all one kind (dried herbes de provence are particularly nice)

1 fennel bulb, trimmed and cut into wedges

1 large head radicchio, cut into wedges

½ pound green beans, ends trimmed

1 large red onion, sliced into ½-inch rings

2 ears fresh corn, husks removed (optional)

Kosher salt

Freshly ground black pepper

Salad

2 avocados

Romaine lettuce, washed and torn in bite-size pieces

Warm Pork Confit and Frisée Salad 🐖

Having some pork confit stored away in the fridge means that you can throw together a quick luncheon salad or first course for a special dinner party at a moment's notice. I have adapted this classic bistro salad, which is usually made with duck confit, substituting pork for the duck.

In addition to frisée or curly endive, you could also use mesclun mix or escarole in the salad, and instead of the honey vinaigrette, try a traditional red wine vinegar and mustard one.

SERVES 4

---

1 tablespoon peanut oil

½ cup walnut halves

1 tablespoon lard or fat from pork confit

1 cup coarsely shredded Pork Confit (page 310)

Honey Vinaigrette

1 tablespoon sherry or champagne vinegar

2 teaspoons semi-dry sherry

2 teaspoons honey

1 teaspoon Dijon mustard

3 tablespoons olive oil

Kosher salt

Freshly ground black pepper

3 cups frisée or curly endive, washed, dried, and torn into pieces

1 Heat the peanut oil in a small skillet over medium heat and add the walnuts. Shake the pan occasionally until the nuts are lightly browned and give off a nutty aroma, about 5 minutes. Transfer to a bowl. Set aside. 2 Heat the lard in a medium nonstick skillet over medium-high heat and add the shredded pork confit. Cook the pork until the edges begin to brown and crisp, 2 to 3 minutes. Set aside. 3 To make the vinaigrette: Whisk all of the ingredients together in a small bowl. Season to taste with salt and freshly ground black pepper. 4 In a salad bowl, toss the frisée with the vinaigrette and divide the salad among 4 plates. Top each with some of the warm pork confit and sprinkle with the walnuts. Grind a little fresh pepper over each salad before serving.

CHEF'S NOTES: In place of the pork confit, use slices of Pickled Pigs' Feet Terrine (page 286). Simply top the frisée with a slice of the cold terrine and garnish with a little bit of chopped cornichons or capers. 🐖 Another option: slices of crisp fried John Desmond's Blood "Puddy" (page 268).

Sausage, Vegetable, and Potato Salad 🐷

I love this salad for its versatility and often make it for a quickie lunch. The idea is to use any leftover combination of cooked vegetables and any flavor of sausage I may have in the fridge or freezer. If I don't have any cooked potatoes, then I leave them out and substitute homemade croutons. I always include eggs, which I cook at the last minute so they're still warm when I put them in the salad. If you have the time, you can make the salad with freshly cooked and still warm vegetables, which ain't bad either. SERVES 4 TO 6

1 Spread lettuce over the bottom of a large, shallow salad bowl. Arrange the potatoes, green beans, tomatoes, eggs, and olives in an attractive pattern over the lettuce. 2 Cook the sliced sausage in a nonstick skillet over medium-high heat for 3 to 5 minutes per side, until nicely browned. Remove with a slotted spoon and scatter over the salad. 3 Make the dressing immediately. In the same nonstick pan you used to cook the sliced sausage, add the chopped sausage or bacon and 1 tablespoon of the olive oil. Cook and stir for 1 minute. Off the heat, stir in the mustard and vinegar, then whisk in the remaining oil. Drizzle all the dressing generously over the salad and serve at once.

CHEF'S NOTE: Other sausages that work well in this salad are Nancy's Artichoke and Piquillo Pepper Sausage (page 264), and Toulouse Sausage (page 261). You may also use a high-quality store-bought sausage, particularly the varieties that have an Italian flavor profile, such as those containing fennel seed, sun-dried tomatoes, or artichokes.

4 cups assorted lettuce leaves, washed, dried, and torn

6 small red potatoes, halved, boiled until tender, about 15 minutes, and drained

½ pound green beans, cut into 2-inch pieces, boiled until tender, about 5 minutes, and drained

1 cup cherry tomatoes, washed

4 hard-cooked eggs, quartered

½ cup niçoise or Kalamata olives

3 links hot or mild Italian sausage, sliced into ½-inch-thick rounds, or any other fresh sausage of your choice

Warm Sausage Dressing

¼ pound smoky *andouille*, finely chopped, or 2 ounces bacon, chopped

2 tablespoons extra-virgin olive oil

2 teaspoons Dijon mustard

2 tablespoons sherry or wine vinegar

Johnson and May Koo's Burmese Shredded Pork Ear Salad

Henry Joe Peterson, a fellow barbecue enthusiast, gave me this much-loved family recipe, which came from his wife Cindy's parents, Johnson and May Koo. They moved from Rangoon, Burma, to San Francisco in the 1970s. Burmese cuisine is often overshadowed by the cuisines of Burma's neighbors, India, China, Thailand, and Vietnam, but this dish is a wonderful and authentic example of a proud culture. As Henry told me, shredded pig's ears are a popular ingredient in Burma and add both flavor and a distinct crunch to this simple but tasty salad. SERVES 4 TO 6

3 raw pig's ears

1 teaspoon kosher salt

1½ cups thinly sliced red onions

1½ cups roughly chopped cilantro leaves and stems

1 serrano or jalapeño chili, seeded and thinly sliced (optional)

Dressing

2 tablespoons peanut oil

½ teaspoon minced garlic

¼ cup Asian fish sauce

¼ cup freshly squeezed lime juice

1 teaspoon sugar

1 teaspoon Asian sesame oil

1 Put the pig's ears in a large saucepan and add water to cover generously. Add the salt and bring to a boil over high heat. Reduce the heat to maintain a simmer and cook until a chopstick can easily be pushed through the ears, 2½ to 3 hours. (The ears should be soft but still retain a little crunch when you bite them.) Drain and set aside to cool. (The ears may be prepared 1 day ahead and refrigerated, but the ears and the salad should be served at room temperature.) 2 To serve, slice the ears into strips no wider than ⅛-inch. Put in a salad bowl with the onions, cilantro, and optional chili. 3 Whisk the dressing ingredients together in a small bowl and pour over the salad. Toss well and serve at room temperature.

CHEF'S NOTE: If you live near an Asian community, such as the San Francisco Bay area where I live, you can often find pig's ears raw or even already cooked. If you find them cooked, omit the first step in the recipe.

5

Soups

There are few kitchen endeavors I find more satisfying than making soup, for several reasons: Soups are easy to prepare in quantity, I don't have more than one dirty pot to clean afterward, I can get creative with the odds and ends in the fridge, and, best of all, I love to eat soup. To me, a large bowl of soup, some crusty bread, and a ripe tomato and onion salad are about as good as a meal gets. And since I always make enough to feed an army, there's enough for tomorrow, and the next day, and the day after that. I love the versatility of soup and pork products enhance that quality.

All good soups start with a good stock or broth, and I've included a recipe for a basic stock made with roasted meaty pork bones (page 87). Any of the recipes in this chapter, though, can be built on a chicken stock base as well.

In addition to being a major flavor base and component of soups, pork products, especially ham and bacon, can also be used to great effect as a garnish. Tasso can be diced and served atop a gumbo, and chorizo can be crumbled into a tortilla soup. Crispy bacon bits make a perfect garnish for cheese soups as well as vegetable soups, like cauliflower, broccoli, winter squash, tomato, leek, potato, spinach, and mushroom. Small dices of ham sautéed in butter are wonderful sprinkled on bowls of corn chowder or pureed English pea soups. One thing I like to do that's a little different is to put medium-thin slices of Serrano ham or prosciutto in a low oven (about 200° F) for about 2 hours until dry and crisp and use them to garnish Spanish shellfish or bean soups. The ways pork can be used in soups are endless and the recipes in this chapter barely scratch the surface. So put on your creative culinary thinking cap and fashion some of these suggestions to create your own soup improvisations.

Dark Pork Stock ·🐖 Jeff Bergman, a great cook who often likes to

warm up dreary Seattle days with homemade soup, provided this recipe.

Dark stocks get their color and rich flavor from meaty bones that have been roasted until golden before being added to the stock pot. An extra step, yes, but one that gives you a lot of bang for your buck. Use dark stock in any of my soup recipes—and braises and stews as well—for extra depth of flavor. MAKES ABOUT 6 CUPS

1 Preheat the oven to 475° F. 2 Put the pork shank bones in a large roasting pan and sprinkle lightly with salt and pepper. Put the pan in the preheated oven and roast until the pork is golden brown, about 45 minutes. Turn the bones once or twice so that they brown evenly. 3 Transfer the pork to a large soup or stock pot and add water to cover them by about 2 inches. Drain and discard the fat from the roasting pan, then put the pan over medium heat. Add 1 cup water and scrape up the brown bits on the bottom of the pan. Add this deglazing liquid to the stock pot. Bring the water to a boil over high heat, then reduce the heat to maintain a simmer. Skim and discard the fat and foam that rises to the surface. Add the onion, celery, carrot, bay leaf, and thyme sprig to the pot and continue to simmer for 2 hours, adding additional water as necessary to keep the pork covered. 4 Strain the stock through a fine-mesh sieve into a large storage container; discard the solids. Set the stock aside to cool completely, cover, and refrigerate for 5 days or freeze for up to 3 months. (You can also transfer the stock to smaller containers for freezing.)

4 pounds pork shanks, sawed into large pieces, or 4 pounds neck bones, or a combination of any meaty bones

Kosher salt

Freshly ground black pepper

1 large yellow onion, unpeeled and quartered

1 celery stalk, cut into 2-inch pieces

1 large carrot, cut into 2-inch pieces

1 bay leaf

2 sprigs fresh thyme

Italian Pork and Greens Soup

On a visit to Campania, the province that includes Naples, in Italy, we had several stellar meals at a spectacular restaurant, Oasis, in a nondescript town called Vallesaccarda. The cook's name is Lena Fischetti and she and her brothers own the restaurant. We began our lunch with a soup of various wild and domestic greens flavored with pork shoulder. To accompany the soup, we were given a rustic hot water cornbread made with pork cracklings. I could have been in the back country of North Carolina: Great-tasting and almost identical peasant food can be found the world over. SERVES 6 WITH LEFTOVERS

3 tablespoons olive oil

2 pounds boneless Boston butt, cut into 2-inch chunks

Kosher salt

Freshly ground black pepper

3 quarts (double recipe) homemade Dark Pork Stock (page 87), homemade chicken stock, or canned low-sodium chicken broth

2 bay leaves

3 sprigs fresh thyme tied together with twine

6 garlic cloves, unpeeled

1 medium onion, chopped

1 carrot, chopped

2 cups firmly packed chopped collard green leaves, stems removed and discarded

2 cups firmly packed chopped turnip green leaves, stems removed and discarded

1 cup firmly packed chopped watercress

1 Heat 2 tablespoons of the olive oil in a large pot over medium-high heat, add the pork, sprinkle with salt and pepper, and cook, turning occasionally, until browned on all sides, about 10 minutes. Add the stock, bay leaves, thyme bundle, and garlic. Bring to a boil over high heat; then reduce the heat to maintain a simmer, skimming occasionally to remove any foam and fat on the surface. Cover and cook for 1½ to 2 hours, until the pork is very tender. Remove the pork with a slotted spoon and discard the bay leaves, thyme, and garlic and degrease the soup. 2 In a medium skillet, heat the remaining 1 tablespoon olive oil, add the onion and carrot, and cook until soft and just beginning to color, about 10 minutes. Add to the soup. When the pork is cool enough to handle, dice or shred it into bite-size pieces and set aside. 3 Add all the greens to the soup and simmer for 12 to 15 minutes, until just

tender. Return the pork to the pot and cook for 2 minutes. Season the soup to taste with salt and pepper. 4 Ladle the soup into bowls and sprinkle with the cheese. Serve with the cornbread, if desired, and encourage diners to dip the bread into the soup.

2 cups roughly chopped Swiss chard leaves, stems removed and discarded

½ cup freshly grated Parmesan cheese

Hot Water Skillet Cornbread with Cracklins (recipe follows, optional)

Hot Water Skillet Cornbread with Cracklins

MAKES ONE 9-INCH ROUND BREAD

1 Preheat the oven to 375° F. 2 Heat the lard or olive oil in a 9-inch cast-iron or other heavy ovenproof skillet over medium heat, add the pancetta, and cook until the fat has rendered and the pancetta has crisped, about 5 minutes. Transfer the pancetta with a slotted spoon to paper towels to drain and set aside. (Omit this step if using cracklings from lard rendering.) Reserve 3 tablespoons of the fat in the skillet and discard the rest. 3 In a medium bowl, whisk together the cornmeal, sugar, and salt. Add the boiling water, stirring constantly to prevent lumps. Stir in the reserved pancetta (or cracklings) and let rest for 10 minutes. 4 Heat the skillet with the fat over high heat, then scrape the cornmeal batter into it, spreading it out with a spatula to smooth and level the top. Place the skillet in the oven and bake for 25 minutes or until the top is browned and the center is dry when pierced with a skewer. Unmold the cornbread on a rack and let cool for 10 minutes before cutting into thin wedges. Serve warm.

1 tablespoon lard or olive oil

4 ounces pancetta, cut into ¼-inch dice, or ½ cup cracklings from lard rendering

1½ cups stone-ground cornmeal

1 teaspoon sugar

1 teaspoon kosher salt

2¼ cups boiling water

CHEF'S NOTES: While I used four types of greens, you can use many other combinations from a list that includes: mustard greens, green cabbage, Savoy cabbage, spinach, beet greens, radish tops, arugula, bok choy, pea shoots, various kales, and wild greens. Instead of pancetta or cracklings you can use an equivalent amount of smoked bacon.
If you're not up to making the cornbread, serve the soup with any peasant-style bread or store-bought croutons.

El Profé Pozole Blanco 🐖 In most Mexican restaurants,

pozole is a mixture of pig's feet, neck bones, chunks of hominy, and other odds and ends, floating in watery broth. By the time you add the ample garnishes of shredded cabbage, chopped white onions, sliced radishes, oregano, and lime juice, this humble dish becomes an inexpensive and satisfying meal. But me, I'm always looking for the meat. Then I had the *pozole blanco* at El Profé, a bustling little restaurant not far from the airport at Zihuatanejo on the Pacific coast of Mexico. We had heard that on Thursdays, El Profé served *carnitas* that were the best in the whole area, so when we arrived we ordered the *pozole* as a kind of appetizer to take the edge off our hunger while we waited for the *carnitas*. As it turned out, the *carnitas* were the appetizers, served on a large platter with *taquitos* (cheese rolled inside tortillas and fried), sliced avocados, and shredded cabbage. The *carnitas* were indeed delicious, and when our *pozole* arrived we scarcely had any appetite left. However, the *pozole* that was presented was extraordinary, a rich broth packed full of meaty shredded pork, with lots of hominy, served with a tray of fresh garnishes. Our appetites piqued once again, we finished the lot. Upon returning to our casita on the beach, we spent the rest of the afternoon and evening in our hammocks, full and satisfied. Here's my attempt to re-create the *pozole* served at El Profé. SERVES 8 TO 10

Stock

5 to 6 pounds pork picnic shoulder with partial skin attached, or
5 pounds meaty pork neck bones, plus 3 pounds boneless country ribs

2 carrots, sliced

2 onions, sliced

6 garlic cloves

3 bay leaves

12 whole black peppercorns

1 tablespoon kosher salt

1 To make the stock: Put the meat in a large soup pot with at least 3 quarts water. If necessary, add more water to cover the meat. Bring to a boil over high heat and reduce the heat to maintain a simmer. Skim and discard any fat and foam from the surface. Add the carrots, onions, garlic, bay leaves, peppercorns, and salt. Cook, uncovered, until the meat is quite tender, about 1½ to 2 hours. Remove the meat and set aside to cool. Strain the stock through a fine sieve into a container and set aside to cool. Discard the solids. 2 Remove the meat from the bones, discarding the gristle, fat, and skin, and coarsely shred the meat. Set aside.

3 Wipe out the soup pot, and in it heat the olive oil with the chopped onion over medium-high heat. Cook, stirring frequently, until softened, about 5 minutes. Add the garlic, chilies, oregano, cumin seeds, and cilantro stems. Add the reserved stock, increase the heat to high, and bring to a boil. Add the hominy and reduce the heat to maintain a simmer. Cook for 20 minutes. Add the reserved shredded meat. Season to taste with additional salt and pepper. The *pozole* can be served at this point but will develop flavor and is easier to degrease if you let it cool and refrigerate it overnight.

4 Remove and discard the fat from the surface of the chilled *pozole* and rewarm it over low heat. To serve, ladle into large soup bowls and let diners add their own garnishes.

3 tablespoons olive oil

1 onion, finely chopped

3 garlic cloves, minced

2 poblano chilies, fire-roasted, peeled, and diced

1 jalapeño chili, seeded and chopped

1 teaspoon dried Mexican oregano

2 teaspoons cumin seeds

½ cup finely chopped cilantro stems

6 to 7 cups canned hominy, drained (about four 15-ounce cans)

Kosher salt

Freshly ground black pepper

Garnishes

Bottled Mexican hot sauces

2 cups shredded cabbage

1 cup chopped cilantro leaves

1 cup diced white onion

½ cup thinly sliced radishes

1 avocado, thinly sliced

4 limes, cut into wedges

Whole dried Mexican oregano

Albóndigas Soup with Chili Broth and Cilantro Salsa

Pretty much every little Mexican restaurant my family ate at in Los Angeles served a soup of *albóndigas* (Mexican meatballs) as a prelude to the various combination plates that followed. Some of these soups were good, but most were fairly bland, not much more exciting than canned chicken soup with some mushy meatballs thrown in. Reboso's was different. This was a special place that took the care and time to make things right. The tortillas were hand patted, the chips fried with fresh oil, the chilies freshly roasted, and the *sopa de albóndigas* was spicy and satisfying. I visited Reboso's often, usually late on a Saturday night after a botched blind date or movies with my high school pals. While a cup of it was included with the meal, I liked the soup so much I would persuade the *mamacita* to sell me a big bowl, which I ate with warm tortilla chips and freshly made guacamole. It was usually an effort to make room for the tamales and enchiladas that I too hastily ordered in my hunger-induced enthusiasm.

Reboso's didn't garnish its soup with cilantro pesto but served lime wedges instead as the lone condiment. I think the salsa gives the soup a burst of bright flavors that makes it truly special. SERVES 8

Meatballs

2 tablespoons olive oil

Kosher salt

Freshly ground black pepper

1 cup finely chopped onions

1 teaspoon ground cumin

2 teaspoons New Mexico chili powder or Hungarian paprika

2 slices country-style white bread (such as Italian, French, or Pepperidge Farm White Bread), crusts removed, torn into pieces, and soaked in ¼ cup milk for 15 minutes.

1 pound ground pork

1 large egg, lightly beaten

1 To make the meatballs: Heat the olive oil in a small skillet over medium heat. Add the onions and a pinch of salt and pepper, and cook, stirring frequently, until the onions become translucent, about 5 minutes. Stir in the cumin and chili powder and cook 1 minute until the spices become fragrant. Scrape the mixture into a medium bowl. Squeeze the liquid out of the bread and discard. Add the softened bread to the onions. Add the meat, egg, oregano, mint, optional cilantro, salt, and pepper. Using your hands, mix the ingredients until well blended, but take care not to overmix, which can make the meatballs dense and heavy. (Wet your

hands occasionally to prevent sticking.) Chill the meatball mixture for at least 20 minutes. Roll the meat mixture into 1-inch balls. (You should have 45 to 50 meatballs.) 2 To make the broth: Heat the olive oil in a large soup pot over medium heat and add the onions and garlic. Cook, stirring, until the onions are soft and translucent, about 7 to 8 minutes. 3 Drain the chilies and reserve the soaking liquid. Stem and seed the soaked chilies and puree in a blender or food processor with ¼ to ½ cup of the soaking liquid. (The puree should have the consistency of heavy cream.) Add the chili puree and tomatoes to the pot with the onions and cook and stir for 1 minute. Stir in the stock and bring to a boil over high heat. Reduce the heat to maintain a simmer and add the carrots and reserved meatballs. Cook for 10 to 15 minutes or until the meatballs are cooked through. Add the zucchini and cook for 3 minutes. Add salt and pepper to taste. Skim and discard the fat on the surface. 4 While the soup is cooking, make the salsa: Place the cilantro, mint, optional chili, and salt in a small food processor. Pulse until the mixture is finely chopped. With the machine running, pour in the lime juice and olive oil, add the cumin, and and process until smooth. 5 To serve, ladle broth and some of the vegetables into 8 soup bowls. Place 5 or 6 meatballs in each bowl and top with a spoonful of the cilantro salsa. Serve hot.

1 teaspoon dried oregano, preferably Mexican

1 tablespoon chopped fresh mint

2 tablespoons chopped cilantro leaves (optional)

Chili Broth

2 tablespoons olive oil

1 cup finely chopped onions

2 teaspoons minced garlic

2 dried ancho chilies, soaked in boiling water for at least 30 minutes

4 ripe tomatoes, peeled, seeded, and diced, or 1 cup canned tomatoes, drained and chopped

6 cups homemade Dark Pork Stock (page 87) or canned low-sodium chicken broth

1 cup diced carrots

1 cup diced zucchini

2 teaspoons kosher salt

1 teaspoon freshly ground black pepper

Cilantro Salsa

1 cup tightly packed cilantro leaves

6 fresh mint leaves

1 jalapeño chili, seeded and chopped (optional)

½ teaspoon salt

¼ cup freshly squeezed lime juice

3 tablespoons olive oil

½ teaspoon ground cumin

Split Pea Soup Van Leeuwenhoekhuis

In my former life as a scientist, I spent a cold and gray fall in Amsterdam as a visiting biologist at the Van Leeuwenhoekhuis, the Dutch National Cancer Institute. Since I had little money at the time, I ate most of my lunches in a small canteen subsidized by the lab. Most of the food was pretty grim except on Fridays when the cook turned out a very respectable pea soup, called *ertesoupe*. *Ertesoupe* is a national dish of Holland and every self-respecting cook has his or her own variation. It always contains both fresh and smoked pork, which can vary from ham, ham hocks, bacon, or smoked pork chops. Depending on how much meat and other goodies are packed into the pot, it can either be a soup course or satisfying main dish. I found that *ertesoupe* made those cold and dreary days and nights in Amsterdam much more tolerable. Even now, when the weather turns dark, I still make *ertesoupe* to lift my spirits, but I vary it according to what's in my fridge. Having some leftover baked ham and a ham bone around always inspires me to make this soup. By the way, in case you're wondering about the origin of the name of this dish, Antoni van Leeuwenhoek was a seventeenth-century Dutch clockmaker who invented the microscope. He became an important biologist and the cancer lab was named for him. SERVES 6 WITH LOTS OF LEFTOVERS

1½ pounds *leftover* ham, fat trimmed and chopped, meat cut into ½-inch dice (about 3 cups)

1 pound boneless country-style ribs or pork shoulder meat, cut into ¾-inch dice (about 2 cups)

Kosher salt

Freshly ground black pepper

1 cup chopped onions

1 cup chopped fennel bulb (optional)

1½ cups chopped celery

1½ cups chopped leeks, white part only

1½ cups chopped carrots

2 cups chopped Savoy or napa cabbage

1 In a large soup pot or Dutch oven, heat the chopped ham fat over medium heat. Cook until the fat is rendered. Pour off all but 3 tablespoons and discard the rest. (If there's not enough fat in the pan, then add bacon fat, lard, or olive oil to equal 3 tablespoons.)

2 Add the diced fresh pork, season with a generous pinch of salt and pepper, and fry until the meat is nicely browned on all sides. Add all the vegetables, cover the pot, and cook until the vegetables have begun to soften, stirring from time to time, about 10 minutes. Add the stock, split peas, diced ham (if you have a ham bone, throw it into the pot as well), sage, thyme, cumin, and bay leaves. Bring to a boil, reduce the heat to a simmer, cover,

and cook until the peas are falling apart, about 1 hour. Taste for salt and pepper and remove the bay leaves. 3 Serve at once, garnished with chives or, better yet, refrigerate overnight (see Chef's Notes). The next day, rewarm over gentle heat, and serve. Let diners add their own Tabasco to taste.

CHEF'S NOTES: If you don't have enough fat when you trim the ham, then use bacon drippings, lard, or olive oil. 🐷 Ham stock is the liquid left over from poaching a ham. You can make a very good stock using ham hocks. Cover 4 meaty ham hocks with 4 quarts cold water. Throw in a whole onion, 2 bay leaves, a carrot, and a celery stalk. Bring to the boil, reduce to a simmer, and cook, covered, for 2½ to 3 hours or until the meat is quite tender. Let cool. Once cooled, you can separate the meat, skin, and fat. Use the meat and fat instead of the ham to make the pea soup. 🐷 Pea soup is always best made ahead and refrigerated. It tends to thicken upon standing so add more stock or water when you reheat it.

8 cups ham or chicken stock, or a combination of both (see Chef's Notes)

1 pound green split peas (about 2 cups)

1 ham bone (optional)

1 teaspoon chopped fresh sage
or ½ teaspoon dried

1 teaspoon chopped fresh thyme
or ½ teaspoon dried

½ teaspoon ground cumin

4 bay leaves

½ cup finely chopped chives, for garnish

Tabasco sauce

Soto Daging Babi (Spicy Indonesian Pork Meat Soup)

Back in the mid-seventies, I worked as a guest scientist in Amsterdam. Dutch cooking is simple and good, but lacking in spice. I discovered that all I needed to satisfy my spice craving was to head to one of the many Indonesian restaurants that literally and figuratively peppered Amsterdam. I offer this fondly remembered pork and noodle soup. If you double the amount of pork, it's substantial enough to serve as lunch; it would be perfect as one of several courses in a *rijsttafel*. SERVES 6 TO 8

2 medium onions, chopped

1 (2-inch) piece fresh ginger, peeled

2 red or green fresh chilies (such as serrano or jalapeño), seeded and finely diced

6 curry leaves or 1 teaspoon curry powder

2 garlic cloves, crushed

¼ cup macadamia nuts

1½ tablespoons ground coriander

1 teaspoon shrimp paste (see Chef's Notes) or anchovy paste

1 teaspoon turmeric

2 teaspoons ground cumin

½ teaspoon ground fennel

½ teaspoon freshly ground black pepper

½ teaspoon ground nutmeg (see Chef's Notes)

2 tablespoons Asian fish sauce

2 teaspoons brown sugar

2 tablespoons peanut oil

1 pound boneless country ribs, cut into ¾-inch cubes

1 Put the onions, ginger, chilies, curry leaves, garlic, macadamia nuts, coriander, shrimp paste, turmeric, cumin, fennel, black pepper, nutmeg, fish sauce, and brown sugar in a blender and process until the mixture forms a smooth paste. 2 Heat the peanut oil in a large, heavy soup pot or Dutch oven over medium heat. Using a spatula, scrape in the spice paste and cook and stir for 3 to 5 minutes or until the mixture begins to color and give off a fragrant aroma. Stir in the pork cubes and continue to stir until the meat is well coated with the spices. Add the stock and cook at a simmer for 45 minutes. Stir in the lime juice, coconut milk, and soy sauce and cook for 15 minutes or until the pork is tender. Taste and add more soy sauce if desired. 3 While the soup is cooking, put the rice noodles in a large pot of boiling water. Shut off the heat and let the noodles soak until soft, 5 to 10 minutes. Drain and divide the

noodles among 8 large heated soup bowls. Top with sliced cucumber, hard-cooked egg, and green onions. Ladle the hot soup over the noodles and let guests add their own fried garlic, potato chips, *sambal oelek,* and additional lime.

CHEF'S NOTES: Like soy sauce in China and Japan, fish sauce is a staple in Southeast Asia. It's made of brined and fermented fish (usually anchovies or mackerel) and is called *nam pla* in Thailand, *nuoc mam* in Vietnam, and fish gravy or *patis* in Indonesia. I prefer the mild Thai fish sauces. Shrimp paste, a staple in Southeast Asia, is sold in Asian markets as Thai *kapee* and Indonesian *terasi*. Anchovy paste is an acceptable substitute. *Sambal oelek* is a spicy Indonesian condiment that is used at the table as well as in the kitchen and contains a mixture of chilies, vinegar, and salt (see Sources on page 318).

6 cups homemade Dark Pork stock (page 87) or canned low-sodium chicken broth

2 tablespoons fresh lime juice

1 can (14 ounces) coconut milk

2 tablespoons soy sauce, or to taste

8 ounces cellophane noodles (rice noodles)

Thinly sliced cucumbers

Sliced hard-cooked eggs

Green onions, thinly sliced white and green parts

Garnishes

Fried garlic slices

Crumbled potato chips

Sambal oelek (see Chef's Notes)

Lime wedges

German Goulash Soup

I first encountered goulash soup, not in Hungary, but in Germany when I was a college student doing Europe under serious budgetary constraints. In order to stay within my allotted $5 a day (this was forty years ago), I ate many meals in *Gasthöfe* (simple peasant restaurants) and student cafeterias. Goulash soup, both cheap and filling, was ubiquitous on the menus. Later, when I learned to make this dish at home, both diced pork shoulder and/or beef chuck worked well and allowed me to make the soup regularly on my modest budget. SERVES 6 TO 8

2 tablespoons lard or olive oil

1½ cups chopped onions

2 garlic cloves, minced

2 to 3 tablespoons sweet Hungarian paprika

2 teaspoons hot Hungarian paprika (optional)

1¼ pounds boneless Boston butt or boneless country ribs, cut into 1-inch cubes

Kosher salt

Freshly ground black pepper

2 quarts (double recipe) Dark Pork Stock (page 87), homemade chicken stock, or canned low-sodium chicken broth

2 teaspoons caraway seeds

2 teaspoons fresh marjoram or 1 teaspoon dried

2 cups diced peeled Yukon Gold or other high-starch potatoes

1 cup diced carrots

¾ cup diced red bell pepper

3 tomatoes, peeled, seeded, and diced, or ⅓ cups canned tomatoes, drained and chopped

Sour cream, for garnish

1 Heat the lard or olive oil in a Dutch oven or large soup pot over medium heat. Add the onions and garlic and cook, stirring occasionally, until softened and golden brown, about 20 minutes. Add the sweet paprika and optional hot paprika, and stir until the onions are well coated. Stir in the meat, a little salt, and a few grinds of pepper. Add ½ cup of the stock, increase the heat to medium-high, and cook until the liquid is almost evaporated. Add the remaining stock and the caraway seeds, bring to a boil, and reduce the heat to maintain a simmer. Cover and cook for 1 hour or until the meat is almost tender. Skim and discard the fat on the surface. Add the marjoram, potatoes, diced carrots, red pepper, and tomatoes. Cook for 20 minutes or more, until the potatoes are tender. Season to taste with salt, pepper, and paprika. 2 To serve, ladle into warmed soup bowls and garnish each with a dollop of sour cream.

Part Three: Main Courses

6

Chops and Steaks, Scallops and Cutlets, and Medallions

About Chops and Steaks

One of the best pork chops I ever ate was at a greasy-spoon breakfast joint in Oakland that specialized in gargantuan breakfasts. That pork chop (actually there were two) was dusted with flour and lots of black pepper. They were crispy on the outside and thoroughly overcooked, but still juicy and quite delicious. Unfortunately, more than thirty years later, that type of fatty pork is long gone. Today's pork comes from svelte porkers—real lean, mean machines. While that's great news for our waistlines and arteries, it also means that we run the risk of dry, hard, tasteless pork chops. But with a little extra attention paid to preparation and cooking, the versatile pork chop can once again be easy and fun to make, and succulent too.

Quality and Selection

Before I offer a few suggestions about putting flavor and juiciness back into your pork chops, I will mention how to choose good chops.

First, see First Impressions, in Buying Pork (pages 20 to 21).

Pork chops are all cut from the loin, a strip of meat about two feet long that runs from the hip to the shoulder. Slices of pork cut from the shoulder are called "steaks" and have names such as blade steaks and include a bit of the blade bone. Steaks from the Boston butt are called Boston butt steaks or shoulder butt steaks.

Starting at the hip are chops called **sirloin chops.** These usually contain some of the hipbone and consequently have a higher percentage of bone than most chops, but they are usually cheaper. I would only buy these if there was a big sale and I was trying to save money. The chops from the lower back come next and are called **loin chops** or **center-cut loin chops** and are recognized by the characteristic T-shaped bone. They contain some meat from the tenderloin. These are the leanest and least flavorful of the pork chops but can be improved immensely by flavor-brining and rubbing the surface with a mixture of spices called a dry rub. Further up toward the head are T-bone chops that have no tenderloin. These are called **top-loin chops** and are the pork equivalent of a New York steak.

As we move up the back toward the head of the pig the next cut of pork chops is called **rib chops** or **center-cut rib chops** and come from the rib section. This is the porcine equivalent of beef prime rib. These are my favorite chops because they have a little more fat, which means more flavor, and they have a great bone to gnaw on (these are the very same rib bones that are sold in slab form as "baby back ribs"). Both the rib chop and loin chop area are also referred to as **center-cut pork loin chops.**

As the pork loin extends into the shoulder area, a bit of the shoulder blade begins to appear. These chops are called **blade chops, pork loin blade chops,** or **blade-end pork loin chops.** Most often they're split into two pieces or butterflied and are sold as **country spareribs.** Sometimes the bone is removed and they are called **boneless country spareribs.** They have the most fat of any loin pork chop and great flavor, but have more gristle and bone. These chops have enough fat so they can be cooked with long, slow, moist heat and still not dry out.

Not all chops are sold on the bone. Boneless pork chops come from anywhere on the entire pork loin. The boneless pork loin has been cut away from the ribs, back, and hipbones, leaving a single oval-shaped eye of meat. Without the distinguishing bones, it is difficult to judge where on the loin the chop is cut from, but if you have a friendly butcher to consult with, tell him you'd like chops cut from the blade or rib areas, which have a little more fat and a bit more flavor.

Pork cutlets can come from the loin, sirloin, leg, or shoulder and because they lack a bone, it is hard to tell from where they came. (Find a friendly butcher again.) I prefer pork cutlets cut from the sirloin or upper leg area. Thin slices of pork cutlets consisting of a single muscle cut from the sirloin, leg, or even the boneless loin are often sold as **pork scallops** or **scaloppini.** Sometimes whole slices are cut from the leg, which include some of the round leg bone and are called **fresh ham steaks.** These are hard to come by. All markets sell **smoked ham,** cut into slices as **ham steaks,** which can be sautéed and served with a pan sauce, especially a sweet pan sauce. Don't overlook **smoked pork chops,** which are fully cooked and great grilled or pan-fried. Because these chops are already brined as part of the curing and smoking process, they can be braised or baked without becoming too dry (see Choucroute Garni on page 242). For best results use smoked pork chops from the rib or blade area and not from the T-bone loin area.

Grilling Pork Chops

Charcoal, gas, direct heat, indirect heat, covered or uncovered; there is a lot to consider when grilling pork chops. For best results, I grill with a covered kettle-type charcoal grill or a covered gas-fired grill. Covered grills allow for better heat regulation and flare-ups are damped when the cover is on. See Direct Grilling Basic Method, page 46.

HOW TO PUT FLAVOR AND JUICINESS INTO GRILLED PORK CHOPS Grilled pork chops need a little help to make them flavorful and juicy. The simplest way to ensure juicy chops and boost flavor is with a "flavor brine," which is nothing more than a solution of water, salt, and a sweetener such as brown sugar or molasses and sometimes herbs and spices. (Read about Flavor-Brining on pages 29 to 32.) By bathing chops for 4 hours or more in a brine solution, the meat soaks up liquid and the muscle fibers swell and become firmer. The result is juicy pork even when slightly overcooked. More flavor can be added to brined chops by then coating them in a spice rub. Even unbrined pork chops are improved by a rubbing with salt, pepper, and various spices. This coating is also called a dry marinade, or dry rub.

Wet marinades also enhance the flavor of pork chops. They contain oil, spices, and an acidic ingredient such as yogurt. While pork chops left for several days in a marinade can become overtenderized, an overnight marination (16 to 24 hours) is ideal for adding extra flavor.

Pastes are a hybrid between a wet marinade and a dry rub. Oil or another liquid is added to a dry rub to just moisten, not liquefy it. The paste is generously spread over the meat, and like a marinade imparts additional flavor. Grilled Thin Pork Chops in Spanish Adobo on page 109 is a good example of this flavoring technique.

Master Recipe: Grilled, Brined, Fresh Herb–Coated Pork Chops 🐖 SERVES 4

1 To make the brine: Pour the water into a large bowl or plastic storage tub. Stir in the salt and continue stirring until the salt dissolves. Stir in the brown sugar and molasses and continue stirring until they dissolve. Add the ice cubes and stir to chill the mixture down. It should be 45° F or colder on an instant-read thermometer. Add the pork chops, cover, and refrigerate for 4 to 6 hours. Remove the pork chops and discard the brine. Pat them dry with paper towels, and either proceed with the recipe or cover the chops with plastic wrap. They can be kept in the refrigerator for up to 2 days before being cooked. 2 To make the fennel and herb rub: Fit a food processor with the small bowl and add all the ingredients. Pulse several times to blend well. Scrape the rub mixture into a small bowl. Coat each brined chop generously on both sides with the rub. Set the chops aside while you prepare your fire. 3 To grill the chops: Build a charcoal fire but spread the coals on only half of the grill. Heat to medium-high. Lay the chops directly over the hot coals. If flaming occurs, move the chops to an area without coals. Sear the chops over the hottest fire for 1½ minutes per side. Then transfer the chops to an area without coals. Cover the grill and continue cooking for 8 to 10 minutes more. The chops are done when they are firm to the touch and an instant-read thermometer inserted in the center registers 140° to 145° F. 4 Transfer the chops to a warm platter and let them rest for 5 minutes so that the juices can be reabsorbed and the chops complete their cooking.

Brown Sugar and Molasses Flavor Brine

3½ cups water

¼ cup kosher salt

¼ cup dark brown sugar

1 tablespoon dark unsulphured molasses

1 cup ice cubes

4 bone-in rib pork chops (each 1¼ to 1½ inches thick; about 3 pounds total)

Fennel Seed and Fresh Herb Rub

1 tablespoon crushed fennel seeds

1 tablespoon chopped garlic

1 tablespoon chopped fresh sage

1 tablespoon finely chopped fresh rosemary

2 teaspoons coarsely ground black pepper

1 tablespoon olive oil

CHEF'S NOTES: Substitute any one of the Flavor Brines that follow for the brown sugar and molasses combination. 🐖 If you prefer a spicier chop, substitute one of the spice rubs for spareribs that follow for the Fennel Seed and Fresh Herb Rub. The rub for the Real Barbecued Pork (page 174) is particularly good.

Flavor Brines and Rubs for Grilled Pork Chops

Each flavor-brine recipe below is meant to be combined with the rub that follows it. As in the Master Recipe, add the pork chops to the brine, cover, and refrigerate for 4 to 6 hours. Remove the pork chops after they've brined, pat them dry with paper towels, then coat each chop generously on both sides with the herb rub before grilling.

Mexican Chili Brine

1 tablespoon cumin seed

2 teaspoons Mexican oregano

3 garlic cloves, crushed

Zest from 1 lime

3½ cups Mexican or light-bodied beer, or water

¼ cup kosher salt

¼ cup sugar

2 tablespoons chipotle chilies in adobo (use chilies and sauce)

1 cup ice cubes

Lime-Oregano Rub

¼ cup freshly squeezed lime juice

1 tablespoon olive oil

2 teaspoons minced garlic

1 teaspoon dried Mexican oregano

2 teaspoons freshly ground black pepper

Spanish-Style Brine

3½ cups water

¼ cup kosher salt

¼ cup sugar

¼ cup sherry vinegar

1 cup ice cubes

Spanish-Style Rub

2 teaspoons minced garlic

2 tablespoons Spanish or sweet Hungarian paprika

1 teaspoon chopped fresh sage

1 teaspoon chopped fresh thyme

1 teaspoon freshly ground black pepper

2 tablespoons olive oil

2 teaspoons sherry vinegar

Coffee and Molasses Brine

2 cups water

1½ cups chilled strong brewed coffee

¼ cup kosher salt

3 tablespoons dark brown sugar

2 tablespoons molasses

1 tablespoon Worcestershire sauce

1 cup ice cubes

Bruce's Spice Rub for Pork BBQ

2 tablespoons paprika, preferably Hungarian

2 tablespoons chili powder

2 teaspoons cayenne pepper

2 tablespoons granulated garlic
or garlic powder

2 tablespoons brown sugar

1 tablespoon ground cumin

1 tablespoon ground coriander

1 tablespoon Colman's dry mustard

2 teaspoons dry sage

2 teaspoons dried oregano

3 tablespoons freshly ground black pepper

⅓ cup kosher salt

Chinese Five-Spice Brine

3½ cups water

¼ cup kosher salt

3 tablespoons dark brown sugar

2 tablespoons soy sauce

2 tablespoons Chinese five-spice powder

1 cup ice cubes

Hong Kong Spice Rub

1½ tablespoons paprika

2 tablespoons brown sugar

1 tablespoon ground fennel seeds

1 tablespoon Chinese five-spice powder

1 tablespoon kosher salt

2 teaspoons minced garlic

Lemon-Tarragon Brine

8 sprigs fresh tarragon or 1 tablespoon dried

Zest from 2 lemons

3½ cups water

¼ cup kosher salt

¼ cup sugar

1 cup ice cubes

Fresh Tarragon Rub

1½ tablespoons chopped fresh tarragon
or 2 teaspoons dried

2 teaspoons freshly ground black pepper

2 tablespoons olive oil

¼ cup freshly squeezed lemon juice

Orange Brine

Zest from 1 orange

1 cup water

2 cups orange juice

¼ cup kosher salt

2 tablespoons brown sugar

2 tablespoons soy sauce

2 cups ice cubes

Orange-Thyme Rub

¼ cup orange juice

1 tablespoon olive oil

2 teaspoons chopped fresh thyme

2 teaspoons freshly ground black pepper

Grilled Yogurt-Marinated Pork Chops

 Yogurt-based marinades are a wonderful way to impart flavor and tenderness to meat, but you need to plan in advance because the yogurt needs at least 8 hours to work its magic; up to 24 hours is even better. Though you'll most often see yogurt marinades with lamb and chicken, I find it works really well with pork. These Middle Eastern–spiced pork chops are terrific served with a cucumber-yogurt salad, couscous, and your favorite salsa. SERVES 4

Yogurt Marinade

1½ cups plain yogurt

3 tablespoons minced white onion

2 teaspoons minced garlic

¼ cup chopped cilantro

3 tablespoons freshly squeezed lemon juice

1 teaspoon ground cumin

1 teaspoon turmeric

¼ teaspoon saffron threads

2 teaspoons ground coriander

1 tablespoon sweet Hungarian paprika

1 teaspoon dried marjoram

1 tablespoon salt

1 teaspoon freshly ground black pepper

4 bone-in rib pork chops (each 1¼ to 1½ inches thick; about 3 pounds)

1 Combine all the ingredients except the pork chops in a nonreactive bowl and stir until well blended. 2 Place the chops in a shallow nonreactive bowl. Spread them with the marinade, then toss, making sure each one is well coated with the marinade. Cover and marinate overnight in the refrigerator. The next day, remove each chop from the marinade and scrape off most of it. Place the chops on a platter and set aside while you prepare the fire for grilling. 3 Spread the coals so that they are on only one side of a covered grill. When the fire is medium-hot, place the chops directly over the coals. Grill for 2 minutes per side, then move them to the part of the grill with no coals. Cover the grill and cook the chops 8 to 10 minutes more or until an instant-read thermometer reaches 140° to 145° F. Transfer the chops to a platter and let them rest for 5 minutes so that the juices can reabsorb and the chops complete their cooking.

Grilled Thin Pork Chops in Spanish Adobo

I learned to make this sweet paprika and vinegar–based spice paste from a gypsy butcher, Anzonini, who came to Berkeley to sing Flamenco songs. Not only was he a wonderful singer, he was also a skilled butcher and superb cook. SERVES 4

1 Combine all of the ingredients except the pork chops in a small bowl and whisk to form a smooth paste. Smear the paste generously over both sides of each chop. Place the chops on a platter, cover, and marinate at room temperature for 45 minutes while you prepare the fire for grilling. Build a charcoal fire and spread the coals so that some areas are stacked higher than others. When the higher layer of coals is medium-hot, the fire is ready. 2 Using your fingers, scrape off some of the adobo paste, leaving on a thin coating. Set the chops directly over the flame. Grill for 2 to 3 minutes per side. If flaming occurs, move the chops to a cooler part of the fire. The chops are done when they're firm to the touch. If necessary, cut into a chop near the bone to check for doneness. The center should be faintly pink. Transfer the chops to a platter and let them rest for 2 to 3 minutes so that the juices can reabsorb and the chops complete their cooking. 3 Serve 2 chops per person.

Spanish Adobo Paste

1 tablespoon minced garlic

1 teaspoon salt

1 teaspoon freshly ground black pepper

¼ cup Spanish or sweet Hungarian paprika

1 teaspoon dried oregano

¼ cup red wine vinegar

1 tablespoon olive oil

8 boneless pork loin chops (each ½ inch thick; about 3 pounds total)

CHEF'S NOTE: To pan-fry the chops, leave a coating of the paste on the chops, then dredge them in flour. Pan-fry in ½ inch moderately hot olive oil for about 2 to 3 minutes per side. Serve at once.

Master Recipe: Sautéed Pork Chops with Pan Sauce

Sautéing or pan-frying pork chops is by far the most common way to cook them. The method is simple, but overcooking or inadequate browning can easily ruin the chops. If you carefully follow this master recipe, you'll quickly be able to become a wiz at sautéing chops.

Chops served with just a sprinkling of salt and pepper or embellished with a spice rub are tasty, but try expanding your flavor horizons by adding a pan sauce. A basic pan sauce is made (after the chops are cooked and removed) by adding a little liquid such as stock or wine to dissolve the caramelized juices stuck to the bottom of the pan. From there the basic procedure can be varied in countless ways: You can add herbs and spices, or flavorful liquids such as apple juice, or cream, or liquor. Vegetables such as garlic, onions, shallots, mushrooms, tomatoes, and sautéed leafy greens, or fruits such as apples, prunes, cherries, peaches, and raisins, or jams, jellies, and marmalades are all complementary additions to pork pan sauces.

For the leanest of all pork chops cut from the lower part of the loin (T-bone loin chops), or any boneless loin chops (you can't really tell where they're from), I think flavor-brining is essential (see Flavor-Brining on pages 29 to 32). One and a quarter to 1½-inch-thick chops need 4 to 6 hours in the brine, which can be done a day ahead, and the chops removed from the brine, wrapped, and refrigerated. One half to 1-inch chops need only 2 to 3 hours in brine.

Choosing Chops for Sautéing

Choose the tender chops cut from the center-cut pork loin. The center-cut loin consists of the ribs and the T-bones. The rib chops have a little more fat and a lot more flavor than the T-bone loin chops, but both can be used. Rib chops can be sautéed without brining, but T-bone chops should be flavor-brined first. You may also use boneless chops, but these will have less flavor than chops with the bone. For the best results, boneless chops should also be flavor-brined first. Purchase chops ideally at least 1¼ to 1½ inches thick so that there is less risk that they become overcooked.

1 For the Flavor Step: Make the Basic Fresh Herb Rub: Combine the herbs, salt, and pepper. Sprinkle over both sides of all the chops. You can continue with the recipe, let the chops sit an hour at room temperature to absorb the seasoning, or wrap the chops in plastic wrap and refrigerate for up to 24 hours. The longer the chops sit with the seasonings, the more flavor they will have. 2 Alternatively, you can immerse the chops in the Basic Flavor Brine (this is my preferred treatment for lean center-cut pork chops, both boneless and T-bone) and refrigerate them. After 4 to 6 hours, remove the chops from the brine, pat dry, and proceed with the recipe; or wrap the brined chops in plastic wrap for up to 2 days before cooking. The brined chops can be just sprinkled with pepper before sautéing, or given a little extra flavor by combining the herb rub (sans salt) and rubbing it onto the chops. 3 To sauté the chops: Heat the oil over medium-high heat in a heavy skillet large enough to hold the chops without overcrowding. When the pan is hot enough to sear the chops but not burn them, add the chops. They should make a gentle hissing sound when they hit the oil, not an "explosive sputter," which will happen if the chops are wet. Adjust the heat if the pan seems too hot, or remove the pan from the heat for 30 seconds or so (count this time as part of the overall cooking time). Sear the chops on one side for 1 to 2 minutes, or until the chops begin to brown lightly. Turn the chops and sear for 1 or 2 minutes more. 4 Reduce the heat so that the chops continue

FLAVOR STEP

Basic Fresh Herb Rub

1 teaspoon chopped fresh thyme

1 teaspoon chopped fresh sage

1 teaspoon kosher salt

1 teaspoon freshly ground black pepper

or

Basic Flavor Brine

3½ cups cold water

¼ cup kosher salt

¼ cup sugar

1 cup ice cubes

4 bone-in rib pork chops, T-bone loin chops, or boneless center-cut loin chops (each 1¼ to 1½ inches thick; 2 to 3 pounds)

1 tablespoon olive oil, bacon fat, or lard

Pan Sauce

4 garlic cloves, peeled

½ cup Dark Pork Stock (page 87), homemade chicken stock, or canned low-sodium chicken broth

½ cup dry white wine

1 teaspoon Dijon mustard

1 to 2 tablespoons crème fraîche or heavy cream

Kosher salt

Freshly ground black pepper

to sizzle. Do not turn the heat so low that there are no more sizzling sounds; if the heat is too low, the chops will sweat and the juices will exude from the meat and leave it dry. Cover the pan and cook for 3 to 4 minutes more on the other side. The chops are done when the meat is firm but not hard when pressed with a finger. Better yet, test them with an instant-read thermometer—the meat should be 140° to 145° F. Transfer to a platter or plate and let rest to catch the juices, covered loosely with foil, for 5 minutes or so before serving. After resting the chops should be 145° to 150° F. (If the chops have been brined, they can even be removed from the pan at a temperature as high as 155° F and still be juicy.) 5 While the chops are cooking, start the pan sauce: Cover the garlic with the stock in a small microwaveable container and microwave on the highest setting for 2 to 3 minutes or until the garlic is soft enough to mash. Pour off and reserve the stock and mash the garlic with a fork. (This step can be completed a couple of hours ahead.) 6 When the chops are done and are resting, pour off and discard all but 1 tablespoon of the fat in the skillet, leaving the browned juices on the bottom of the pan. Put the pan back on the stove over medium-high heat and add the wine. As the liquid comes to a boil scrape up the browned bits from the bottom of the pan, then reduce the liquid by half. Whisk in the reserved stock, mashed garlic, mustard, crème fraîche, and any juices from the resting chops. Continue to whisk until the sauce is smooth and thickened lightly. Remove from the heat, taste, and season with salt and pepper if necessary. Return the chops along with any juices to the pan and turn them several times in the sauce to coat and rewarm them (this should only take 30 seconds to 1 minute). Serve immediately on heated dinner plates or a warm platter.

Sautéed Pork Chop Variations

All these variations are suitable for sautéing or for braising pork chops (page 116).

Old-Fashioned Pan Gravy

1 Flavor and sauté the chops as directed in the Master Recipe (page 110). Remove the chops from the pan and pour off and discard all but 1 tablespoon of the fat. 2 Make the pan sauce: Add the onion to the pan and cook over medium-high heat until soft and translucent. Add ¼ cup of the stock and continue to cook, scraping up any browned bits from the bottom of the pan until the onion begins to turn golden. Add the remaining 1¼ cups stock, juices from the resting chops, and Worcestershire sauce. Bring the liquid to a boil, then reduce it by half. Stir in the cream and cook 30 seconds more. Taste for salt and pepper and adjust if necessary. Combine the cornstarch with 1 tablespoon of water and stir into the sauce until it thickens and becomes syrupy. Add more cream if it becomes too thick. Stir in the optional herbs (or reserve to sprinkle them over the chops as a garnish). Return the chops along with any juices to the pan and turn them several times in the sauce to coat and rewarm them. Serve immediately on heated dinner plates or a warm platter.

FLAVOR STEP: See Master Recipe (page 110).

Pan Sauce

¼ cup finely chopped onion

2 cups Dark Pork Stock (page 87), homemade chicken stock, or canned low-sodium chicken broth

½ teaspoon Worcestershire sauce

2 tablespoons heavy cream, or more as needed

Kosher salt

Freshly ground black pepper

2 teaspoons cornstarch

1 teaspoon chopped fresh herbs such as sage, thyme, savory, marjoram, rosemary, or mint (optional)

Sweet Red Pepper Pan Sauce

FLAVOR STEP

Hungarian Rub

1 teaspoon chopped fresh marjoram
or ½ teaspoon dried

2 teaspoons Hungarian paprika

1 teaspoon kosher salt

1 teaspoon freshly ground
black pepper

Pan Sauce

3 tablespoons chopped shallots
or red onion

1 teaspoon Hungarian paprika

¼ cup dry white wine

¼ cup Dark Pork Stock (page 87),
homemade chicken stock, or canned
low-sodium chicken broth

½ cup heavy cream

½ cup fire-roasted red bell peppers
or pimentos, fresh or jarred

Kosher salt

Freshly ground black pepper

1 teaspoon chopped fresh marjoram

1 Flavor and sauté the chops as directed in the Master Recipe (page 110). Remove the chops from the pan and pour off and discard all but 1 tablespoon of the fat. 2 Make the pan sauce: Add the shallots to the pan and cook over medium-high heat until soft and translucent. Stir in the paprika and when the vegetables are coated, add the wine and stock and bring the liquid to a boil, scraping up any browned bits from the bottom of the pan. Reduce by half. Stir in ¼ cup of the cream and continue to reduce until the liquid is thickened and almost syrupy. Meanwhile, put the remaining ¼ cup cream and the bell peppers in the bowl of a food processor or blender and puree. Add the puree to the pan sauce. Taste for salt and pepper and adjust if necessary. Return the chops along with any juices to the pan and turn them several times in the sauce to coat and rewarm them. Serve immediately, sprinkled with the fresh marjoram.

Prune or Fig Pan Sauce

1 Flavor and sauté the chops as directed in the Master Recipe (page 110). 2 Make the pan sauce: While the chops are cooking, put the prunes or dried figs in a small microwave container and add the port to cover (omit this step if using fresh figs). Cover and microwave on the highest setting for 3 minutes; set aside. Remove the chops from the pan and pour off and discard all but 1 tablespoon of the fat. Add the shallots and cook over medium-high heat until soft and translucent. Add the wine and bring to a boil, scraping up any browned bits from the bottom of the pan. Add the microwaved dried prunes or figs or fresh figs, port, and bay leaves and reduce the liquid by half. Add the stock and thyme and continue to reduce until the liquid is thickened and almost syrupy. Taste and adjust for salt and pepper if necessary, removing and discarding the bay leaves. Return the chops along with any juices to the pan and turn them several times in the sauce to coat and rewarm them. Serve immediately with the prunes or figs on the side.

FLAVOR STEP

Sage, Herb, and Mustard Rub

½ teaspoon chopped fresh thyme

½ teaspoon chopped fresh sage

½ teaspoon dry mustard

1 teaspoon kosher salt

1 teaspoon freshly ground black pepper

Pan Sauce

16 pitted prunes or 16 small fresh or dried Mission figs

½ cup tawny port

2 tablespoons chopped shallots or red onion

½ cup dry red wine

2 bay leaves

½ cup Dark Pork Stock (page 87), homemade chicken stock, or canned low-sodium chicken broth

1 teaspoon chopped fresh thyme

Kosher salt

Freshly ground black pepper

Master Recipe: Braised Chops

The technique for braising chops is very similar to the one for sautéing (see Sautéed Pork Chops with Pan Sauce—Master Recipe page 110). The difference is braised chops are partially cooked by searing, removed while a sauce is made, then returned to the pan to gently finish cooking in the liquid. Once the chops are braised, they're removed from the pan to rest while the pan sauce finishes its cooking. If the completion of the pan sauce takes more than 5 minutes, then the chops are returned to the pan to rewarm, otherwise the braising sauce can be spooned over the chops and served. The benefit of letting the chops return to the braising liquid is that they absorb even more flavor as they simmer and rewarm. The problem is that lean chops cut from the center-cut loin cannot stay in the braising sauce for long or they'll dry out. This can be partially alleviated by using a basic flavor brine (see Sautéed Pork Chops, page 110), or by using thick chops for braising. The cooking time naturally will increase if you use thick chops (at least 1¼ inches or, better still, 1½ inches thick) so that they can cook longer with less risk of overcooking. Since chops cut from the rib area have a little more fat than the T-bone loin chops, they work better in braised dishes, but the best chops of all for braising are cut from the blade end of the loin. These have ample fat and because they have a little more connective tissue, they actually benefit from longer cooking times and can even be cooked beyond 155° F to 170° F and remain juicy. Other good candidates for braising are country spareribs (remember, these are actually butterflied blade chops), shoulder steaks, blade steaks, Boston butt steaks, and fresh ham steaks. All these cuts will remain juicy even when cooked beyond 155° F but not more than 170° F.

Since the braising times and doneness temperatures are so different for the lean center-cut pork loin and rib chops, and the fattier blade chops and pork steaks, I'll discuss the methods separately.

Braising Method for Lean Pork Chops

1 For the Flavor Step: Combine the herbs, salt, and pepper and sprinkle over both sides of the chops. You can continue with the recipe, let the chops sit an hour at room temperature to absorb the seasoning, or wrap the chops in plastic wrap and refrigerate for up to 24 hours. Basically, the longer the chops sit with the seasonings, the more flavor they will have. Alternatively, you can immerse the chops in the Basic Flavor Brine (this is my preferred treatment for lean center-cut pork chops, both rib and T-bone) and refrigerate them. After 4 to 6 hours, remove the chops from the brine, pat dry, and proceed with the recipe; or wrap the brined chops in plastic wrap for up to 2 days before cooking. The brined chops can be seasoned as recommended in each recipe. 2 To sauté the chops: Heat the oil in a heavy skillet large enough to hold the chops without overcrowding over medium-high heat. When the pan is hot enough to sear the chops but not burn them, add the chops. Sear the chops on one side for 2 to 3 minutes, or until nicely browned. Turn the chops and brown the other side, about 3 minutes more. Transfer the chops to a plate or platter and set aside while you make the sauce. 3 Make the pan sauce: When the chops are browned, pour off and discard all but 1 tablespoon of the fat in the skillet, leaving the browned juices in the pan. Put the pan back on the stove over medium-high heat and add the liquid and/or vegetables, scraping up any browned bits on the bottom. Return the chops to the pan along with any accumulated juices. Decrease the heat to maintain a simmer and cover the pan. After 3 to 4 minutes, turn the chops and cover the pan. Cook 3 to 4 minutes more. Check the internal temperature of the chops: It should be 140° to 145° F. If the chops have gotten away from you a little bit and the internal temperature has reached 150° or even 155°, don't worry; they'll be a bit overcooked but still won't be dry or hard, and if you flavor-brined them first, they're even more forgiving of slight overcooking. 4 Transfer the chops to a warm plate or platter, cover loosely with foil, and finish the sauce: Skim off and discard any fat from the surface if necessary, reduce the sauce to thicken it slightly, add any last-minute ingredients like sour cream or butter, and taste for seasonings (salt, pepper, lemon juice, Tabasco, etc.). All the final steps are individual to each braising recipe and your own preferences. 5 Before serving the chops, you can rewarm them briefly in the sauce, or simply serve them with the sauce spooned over.

4 rib chops (each 1¼ to 1½ inches thick, my preference), T-bone loin chops, boneless loin chops, or sirloin chops, or fresh ham steaks

Seasonings (See Flavor Step in Sautéed Pork Chops Master Recipe on page 110.)

or

Basic Flavor Brine (page 106)

1 tablespoon olive oil, bacon drippings, or lard

Pan Sauce

See Sautéed Pork Chop Variations (page 113).

Braising Method for Fattier Pork Chops and Pork Steaks 🐷

4 (each 1¼ to 1½ inches thick) blade pork chops (when butterflied also called country spareribs), blade steaks, shoulder steaks, or Boston butt steaks

Seasonings (See any of the Flavor Steps in Sautéed Pork Chops Master Recipe on page 110.)

1 tablespoon olive oil, bacon drippings, or lard

Pan Sauce

See Sautéed Pork Chop Variations (page 113).

1 The method for seasoning and browning fattier pork chops and steaks is the same as for braised lean pork chops. Once browned, the chops or steaks are removed and set aside while the pan sauce is made, as instructed in the individual recipes, then the meat is returned to the pan to finish cooking in the sauce. While you can serve these cuts when they reach 155° F, you can also cook them longer, because fattier cuts tend to be chewier than the leaner ones and will benefit from a longer braising time, say 45 minutes to an hour in a covered pan, until the internal temperature is well above 170° F, or until the meat is falling off the bone. (You may need to add more liquid to compensate for evaporation.) 2 Once these fattier cuts are done braising, transfer them to a warm platter and finish the sauce as directed in the individual recipes. The method is the same as for braised lean pork chops, but the sauce will probably need to be skimmed of fat before serving.

Pan Sauces for Longer Braising 🐷 These variations

below are ideal for tougher, fattier cuts like blade chops, country spareribs, shoulder steaks, blade steaks, and Boston butt steaks, that need a longer period of time in the pan to cook and more opportunity to exchange and absorb flavor from the sauce.

Beer and Mustard Braising Sauce

1 For the Flavor Step: Combine the herbs, paprika, mustard, salt, and pepper and sprinkle over both sides of all the chops. You can continue with the recipe, let the chops sit an hour at room temperature to absorb the seasoning, or wrap the chops in plastic wrap and refrigerate for up to 24 hours. The longer the chops sit with the seasonings, the more flavor they will have.

2 To sauté the chops: heat the oil in a heavy skillet large enough to hold the chops without overcrowding over medium-high heat. When the pan is hot enough to sear the chops but not burn them, add the chops. Sear the chops on one side for 2 to 3 minutes, or until nicely browned. Turn the chops and brown the other side, about 3 minutes more. Transfer the chops to a plate or platter and set aside while you make the sauce.

FLAVOR STEP

Savory Mustard Rub

½ teaspoon chopped fresh thyme

½ teaspoon chopped fresh sage

½ teaspoon chopped fresh savory or rosemary

1 teaspoon sweet Hungarian paprika

1 teaspoon dry mustard

1 teaspoon kosher salt

1 teaspoon freshly ground black pepper

1 tablespoon olive oil, bacon drippings, or lard

Pan Braising Sauce

2 cups thinly sliced onions

½ cup diced carrot

½ cup dark beer

**1 cup Dark Pork Stock (page 87),
homemade chicken stock, or canned
low-sodium chicken broth**

1 tablespoon balsamic or cider vinegar

1 tablespoon coarse-grained mustard

½ cup crème fraîche or sour cream

Kosher salt

Freshly ground black pepper

3 Make the pan braising sauce: When the chops are browned, pour off and discard all but 2 tablespoons of the fat in the skillet, leaving the browned juices in the pan. Add the onions and carrot and cover the pan. Cook over medium heat, stirring frequently, for 10 minutes or until the onions are very soft. Add the beer and stock, scraping up any browned bits from the bottom of the pan. Stir in the vinegar and mustard. Return the chops and any juices to the pan, cover, and lower the heat to maintain a simmer for 20 minutes or until the chops have reached the desired doneness. Slice a small bit and taste to see if they're tender. Transfer the chops to a warm plate or platter and cover loosely with foil.

Skim off and discard any fat from the sauce and reduce if necessary until thickened and almost syrupy. Remove the pan from the heat and stir in the crème fraîche. Season to taste with salt and pepper. 4 Before serving, you can rewarm the chops briefly in the sauce, or simply serve them with the sauce spooned over them.

Moroccan-Inspired Braising Sauce

FLAVOR STEP

Moroccan Rub

½ teaspoon ground ginger

1 teaspoon sweet Hungarian paprika

1 teaspoon turmeric

½ teaspoon ground cumin

½ teaspoon ground coriander

1 teaspoon kosher salt

1 teaspoon freshly ground black pepper

1 tablespoon olive oil

1 Season and sauté the chops as directed in Braising Method for Fattier Pork Chops and Steaks (page 118). Remove the chops.
2 To make the pan braising sauce: Add ½ cup of the chicken stock to the pan and bring to a boil, scraping up any browned bits on the bottom of the pan. Put the remaining ½ cup chicken stock, onions, ginger, preserved lemon, garlic, cilantro, tomatoes, lemon juice, and spices except salt and pepper in a blender and puree until smooth. Add the puree to the pan, bring the liquid to a boil, then reduce the

heat to maintain a simmer for 10 minutes. Return the chops to the pan and add the olives. Cover and simmer for 20 minutes or until the chops have reached the desired doneness. Slice a small bit and taste to see if they're tender. Transfer chops to a rimmed plate. Skim off and discard any fat from the sauce and reduce if necessary until thickened and almost syrupy. Season to taste with salt, pepper, lemon juice, and/or Tabasco. Return the chops and any juices on the plate to the pan to warm through, then transfer to the warm rimmed platter (there will be lots of juices). Garnish with the chopped mint leaves. Serve with couscous or basmati rice.

CHEF'S NOTE: Preserved lemons are preserved in salt. Jars can be purchased in Middle Eastern stores and by mail order (see Sources on page 318).

Pan Braising Sauce

1 cup homemade chicken stock or canned low-sodium chicken broth

1 cup coarsely chopped onions

1 teaspoon minced fresh ginger

2 tablespoons chopped preserved lemon (see Chef's Note) or 1 tablespoon chopped lemon zest

3 garlic cloves

½ cup cilantro stems and leaves

½ cup chopped canned tomatoes

2 tablespoons freshly squeezed lemon juice

1 tablespoon paprika

½ teaspoon ground coriander

½ teaspoon ground cumin

1 teaspoon turmeric

⅛ teaspoon ground cinnamon

½ teaspoon cayenne pepper

½ cup pitted green olives

Kosher salt

Freshly ground black pepper

Lemon juice and/or Tabasco sauce

1 tablespoon chopped fresh mint leaves, for garnish

Baked Buttermilk-Brined Pork Chops

My wife, Nancy, combines salt and buttermilk to make fried chicken flavorful and juicy. She tried the brine on pork and found the results equally delicious. The brine helps to keep the chops moist and flavorful during baking, which may otherwise dry them out. Make sure to use chops that are at least 1¼ to 1½ inches thick. SERVES 4

Buttermilk Brine

3 cups buttermilk

⅔ cup kosher salt

1 tablespoon lemon zest

2 teaspoons chopped fresh rosemary

2 teaspoons chopped fresh sage or 1 teaspoon dried

4 T-bone or rib pork chops (each 1¼ to 1½ inches thick and 8 to 12 ounces)

2 teaspoons freshly ground black pepper

Flour for coating

3 tablespoons olive oil, melted lard, or bacon drippings

1 To brine the pork chops: Pour the buttermilk into a plastic storage container or stainless-steel bowl and stir in the salt until completely dissolved. Add the lemon zest, rosemary, and sage. Add the pork chops, making sure they are completely immersed in the brine. Cover and refrigerate for 3 to 4 hours. 2 Preheat the oven to 400° F. 3 Remove the chops from the brine and rinse off the buttermilk. Pat dry, season generously with the black pepper, and dredge each chop in the flour, shaking to remove the excess. Set the chops aside. 4 In a nonstick ovenproof skillet large enough to hold all the chops, heat the oil over medium-high heat. Put the chops in the pan and cook for 2 to 3 minutes or until nicely browned. Turn and cook 3 minutes more. Transfer the skillet to the oven and bake the chops for about 15 minutes or until they are firm to the touch or register 145° F on an instant-read thermometer inserted into the middle of a chop. 5 Remove the chops to a platter and let rest for 5 minutes before serving. Serve as is or with chutney.

CHEF'S NOTES: Instead of baking these buttermilk-brined chops, grill them. Omit the rinsing and flour dredging steps and grill over a medium-hot fire until nicely colored. Use chops that are at least 1¼ inches thick for the best results. The buttermilk brine is also excellent for a 3-pound boneless pork loin roast, which will need an overnight soak. The next day, remove the loin, rinse it, and bake it to an internal temperature of 140° to 145° F, about 45 minutes. Let rest for 10 minutes before slicing and serving. Pork loin roast can also be seasoned with black pepper and fresh herbs (dill is particularly good) after it is rinsed.

Stuffed Molasses-Brined Pork Chops

If you've been ambitious and have some homemade sausage in your fridge, this is a wonderful family dish to showcase your efforts. It's simple and satisfying, and the brined pork chops play perfectly against the sausage filling. Serve the chops on a plate with a salad of endive, frisée, and sliced apples tossed in a light vinaigrette. SERVES 4

1 To brine the pork: pour the water into alarge bowl or plastic storage tub. Add the salt, brown sugar, molasses, and vanilla. Stir until the salt and sugar dissolve. Stir in the ice cubes to chill the mixture to 45° F or less. Add the pork chops, cover, and refrigerate for 4 to 6 hours.

2 Preheat the oven to 400° F. 3 Remove the pork chops from the brine and pat them dry with paper towels. At this point you can either proceed with the recipe or wrap the chops in plastic wrap. They can be kept in the refrigerator for up to 2 days before being cooked. 4 Combine the sausage and bread crumbs. 5 Cut a pocket in each chop parallel to the cut surface and fill with the sausage mixture. Sprinkle both sides of the chops with ground pepper. 6 In a large skillet, heat the olive oil over medium-high heat. Add 2 chops and sear on both sides until golden brown, about 2 to 3 minutes per side. Remove and sear the remaining chops in the same manner. Place the chops in a baking dish (you could also use the same skillet if it has an ovenproof handle and can hold all the chops in one layer) and bake in the preheated oven for 10 minutes. Turn the chops and cook for another 10 to 15 minutes or until the internal temperature of the sausage filling reaches 150° F on an instant-read thermometer. Remove the pan from the oven, put the chops on a platter, and let rest for 10 minutes before serving.

Molasses Brine

3½ cups water

¼ cup kosher salt

3 tablespoons dark brown sugar

2 tablespoons molasses

¼ teaspoon pure vanilla extract

1 cup ice cubes

4 bone-in rib pork chops (each 1¼ to 1½ inches thick; about 3 pounds total)

½ pound homemade bulk fresh sausage (see Chef's Note) or store-bought bulk sage sausage

¼ cup fresh bread crumbs

Freshly ground black pepper

2 tablespoons olive oil

CHEF'S NOTE: You may also use Brown Sugar and Sage sausage (page 259), Italian-Style Sausage with Rosemary and Grappa (page 260), Toulouse Sausage (page 261), or Nancy's Artichoke and Piquillo Pepper Sausage (page 264) to stuff the chops.

Smoked Pork Chops with Sour Cherry Brandy Sauce

For a long time the folks of Traverse City, Michigan, kept their wonderful dried sour cherries a secret; at least I had never tasted them here in California. Then, in the early 1980s, innovative chefs began to cook with a broad range of indigenous American products. Suddenly I began to see dried cherries popping up all over menus everywhere. I sampled sour cherries with duck, chicken, venison, pork, and even salmon (bad idea), but I like the taste of the cherries best with smoked pork chops or ham. If you don't want to use brandy or kirsch, you can just use plain water, cranberry juice, or even grape juice—no matter. You'll still have a delicious sauce to add to your repertoire. SERVES 4

⅔ cup dried sour cherries

½ cup brandy or kirsch

1 tablespoon olive oil

4 smoked rib pork chops
(each 1 inch thick)

½ cup finely diced shallots

1 tablespoon chopped garlic

2 juniper berries, ground

1 teaspoon chopped fresh thyme

½ teaspoon freshly ground
black pepper

½ cup port

2 cups Dark Pork Stock (page 87),
homemade chicken stock, or canned
low-sodium chicken broth

1 tablespoon sour cherry jam
or red currant jelly

Kosher salt

Freshly ground black pepper

1 In a small bowl combine the dried sour cherries with the brandy or kirsch. Let soak for 1 to 4 hours or overnight, stirring occasionally, 2 In a large skillet, heat the olive oil over medium-high heat. Add the pork chops and brown well, about 3 minutes per side. Remove the chops to a platter and set aside. Remove and discard all but 1 tablespoon of the fat from the pan. Reduce the heat to medium and add the shallots, garlic, juniper, thyme, and pepper and cook for 5 minutes or until the shallots are lightly golden. Add the port and reduce by half. Add the stock, bring the liquid to a boil over high heat, then reduce the heat and cook at a low simmer for 15 minutes. Add the jam and the soaked sour cherries, including the brandy, increase the heat to medium-high, and reduce until the liquid becomes syrupy, about 3 minutes. 3 Return the chops to the pan, cover, and cook over low heat for 5 minutes. Add salt and freshly ground black pepper to taste. Serve the chops with the sauce poured over them.

CHEF'S NOTES: This sauce is also good with unsmoked pork chops. They should cook a little longer when added to the sauce, about 8 minutes, or until the temperature is 145° F on an instant-read thermometer. You can also make this sauce for ham steaks. The cooking times should be about the same for a ½-inch-thick steak. 🐖 Cook the sauce separately and serve it with a baked ham. The sauce is so good you could just pour it over waffles, pancakes, French toast (or the back of your hand) for a really indulgent brunch. 🐖 If you can't find dried sour cherries, then use dried cranberries, often marketed as craisins. 🐖 Dried sour cherries can be purchased from Zingerman's website (see Sources on page 318).

Panko-Crusted Pork Cutlets (Tonkatsu) with Tangy Japanese Dipping Sauce and Braised Green Onions

Tonkatsu, or Japanese fried pork cutlets, are cousins of the European breaded *schnitzel* and, in fact, originated in the West. *Tonkatsu* has become almost as ubiquitous in Japan as tempura and you can now find it served in neighborhood cafes all over the country. The dipping sauce served alongside the pork cutlets also originated in the West, and its two dominant ingredients, ketchup and Worcestershire, are thought to be uniquely Western. However, while some might think that ketchup is an American invention meant to accompany French fries, its origin is probably Indonesian, from *kecap manis*; Worcestershire is a tamarind-based concoction brought to England from the East. The recipe for this delightful sauce comes from Mick Vann and Art Meyer, two robust chefs and cookbook writers from Austin, Texas. SERVES 4

Tangy Japanese Dipping Sauce

½ teaspoon dry mustard

1 tablespoon hot water

¼ cup ketchup

½ teaspoon minced fresh ginger

1 garlic clove, minced

1 tablespoon sake

4 teaspoons soy sauce

4 teaspoons Worcestershire sauce

4 teaspoons sugar

4 teaspoons white vinegar

½ teaspoon ground allspice

1 To make the dipping sauce: Mix the mustard with the hot water in a small bowl, then whisk in the remaining ingredients. Set aside or refrigerate for up to 1 month. (Makes about ¾ cup.) 2 To prepare the pork cutlets: First line up 3 shallow wide bowls on the counter top. Put the flour in the first bowl, the beaten eggs in the second, and the panko in the third. Have ready a wire rack set over a baking sheet. 3 Season both sides of the pork cutlets generously with salt and pepper. Dip each cutlet first in the flour, shaking off any excess, then the eggs, and finally in the panko, patting both sides to make sure they're well coated with the crumbs. Set the coated cutlets on the rack over the baking sheet. When all the cutlets are breaded, refrigerate for 30 minutes or up to 6 hours.

4 To cook the cutlets: In a 12-inch skillet, heat enough peanut oil to cover the bottom by ⅛ inch over medium-high heat until a little bit of panko dropped into the oil bubbles rapidly. (Or heat ¼ inch peanut oil in a large skillet.) Add 2 of the pork cutlets and cook until golden brown on both sides, about 3 to 4 minutes total. Drain on paper towels. Repeat with the remaining cutlets. 5 Serve immediately with the dipping sauce drizzled over the cutlets and the braised green onions alongside, or serve Japanese-style over a bed of steamed rice.

Japanese Pork Cutlets (Tonkatsu)

¼ cup all-purpose flour

2 large eggs, beaten

2 cups panko (see Chef's Notes)

4 (each ½-inch-thick) boneless pork loin chops, pounded ⅛ to ¼ inch thick

Kosher salt

Freshly ground black pepper

½ to 1 cup peanut oil

Braised Green Onions (recipe follows)

Braised Green Onions

Trim the green onions of their roots and any wilted pieces. Cut the tops so that 4 inches of green and all of the white remain. Whisk together the soy, mirin, and sugar in a medium skillet. Heat over medium-high heat until the liquid boils. Reduce the heat to a simmer and add the green onions. Cook until just wilted, about 3 minutes. Remove with a slotted spoon and set aside until serving. Some of the braising liquid may be served over a side dish of rice, if desired. The rest can be refrigerated for up to 1 week.

2 bunches green onions

⅓ cup soy sauce

¼ cup mirin

2 tablespoons sugar

CHEF'S NOTES: In Japan you'll find *tonkatsu* served over either a bed of shredded cabbage or a huge bowl of steamed rice with the sauce generously spooned over the top. I prefer to moisten my bowl of rice with a little of the onion braising liquid (see above) and a few of the braised green onions. Then I place a cutlet on top and spoon some of the tangy sauce over the cutlets, with the remaining sauce served alongside for dipping. As far as I'm concerned, panko, Japanese bread crumbs, are the best thing ever to be invented next to sliced bread. Found in all Asian markets, and now in most grocery stores, these dry crumbs guarantee that anything you fry will turn out beautifully golden and crispy. The trick is to flavor your meat well first, or add seasonings to the panko, because the panko alone are almost flavorless.

Pounded slices of tender pork from the boneless loin, tenderloin, sirloin, or leg are ideal for quick cooking. Because these thin pieces of meat (called scallops, scaloppini, or cutlets) cook in a flash, I like to give them a protective coating, which helps to lock in juices as well as provide a crisp, flavorful exterior that insulates the meat from overcooking. Since the meat is so thin, you must rely on time and feel to determine if the scallops are done, but if you're unsure you can make a small discreet cut to check; the meat should be faintly pink.

I prefer to coat my scallops in fresh bread crumbs from day-old bread. I never use dried store-bought bread crumbs, which to me taste like the cardboard box they come in. Japanese bread crumbs, called panko, are also good because they provide a nice, crispy crust. Another favorite coating is made simply with egg and flour. Called *doré* (page 130), it provides the pork scallops with a softer, eggy-flavored exterior.

Make sure that when you pound the pork you start with a single eye of muscle, because if the slice is made up of more than one muscle it can fall apart after it's pounded.

Pork Cutlets Milanese

I first saw Milanese-style pork cutlets in a country restaurant outside of Milan. The name and location of that restaurant is long gone. But I will never forget those chops. I whiffed the aromatic cutlets (and the olive oil in which they were fried) before I even saw them. What the waiter placed before me was a crispy, golden rib pork chop with the bone attached, the meat pounded so thin and large that it hung over the edge of the plate. But it was nearly hidden under an enormous mound of wild arugula, fennel, and shaved Parmigiano-Reggiano. I was in heaven and returned to the restaurant again the next night to indulge in those cutlets one more time before leaving Milan. While you can make these cutlets with bone-in rib chops, they are trickier to pound out with the bone still attached so in this recipe I use boneless meat. If you want something a little more authentic, buy 8- to 10-ounce rib pork chops, cut 1¼ to 1½ inches thick with the chine bone removed, and carefully working around the rib bone, pound them out so that they are as big as a plate. You'll be rewarded with a dish that will be as memorable as the one I had in Milan. SERVES 4

1 To prepare the pork cutlets: Season both sides of the meat generously with salt and pepper. Line up 3 shallow wide bowls on the countertop. Put the flour in the first bowl, the beaten eggs in the second, and stir together the bread crumbs, Parmesan, ½ teaspoon salt, and ¼ teaspoon pepper, and the rosemary in the third. Have ready a wire rack set over a baking sheet. Dip each cutlet first in the flour, shaking off any excess, then the eggs, and finally in the crumb mixture, patting both sides to make sure they're well coated. Set the coated cutlets on the rack over the baking sheet. When all the cutlets are breaded, refrigerate for 30 minutes or up to 6 hours. 2 To cook the cutlets: Add enough olive oil to a large skillet to cover the bottom by ¼ inch. Heat over medium-high heat until the oil starts to shimmer or a few bread crumbs dropped into the oil bubble around the edges. Add 1 pork cutlet (or two if they fit) and cook until golden brown, about 1½ to 2½ minutes per side. Drain on paper towels. Repeat with the remaining cutlets. If you're cooking one chop at a time, you may want to keep the cutlets warm in a 250° F oven until all are done. Serve with lemon wedges.

4 (each 5 to 6 ounces) boneless pork loin chops, pounded ⅛ inch thick

Kosher salt

Freshly ground black pepper

¼ cup all-purpose flour

2 large eggs, beaten

2 cups bread crumbs made from day-old bread

½ cup freshly grated Parmesan cheese

½ teaspoon finely chopped fresh rosemary

½ cup (or more) extra-virgin olive oil (see Chef's Notes)

Lemon wedges, for serving

CHEF'S NOTES: Top the cutlets with a salad of arugula, shaved fennel, cherry tomatoes, and shaved Parmesan tossed with extra-virgin olive oil and freshly squeezed lemon juice. This is such a simple dish it demands high-quality ingredients. In most cases I would not recommend cooking with extra-virgin olive oil, but here the fruity flavor of the oil really comes through. Also, make sure your Parmesan is fresh, good, and from Italy. To turn these cutlets into a classic pork Parmesan: Place the cooked cutlets in a baking dish large enough to fit all of them in one layer. Top the cutlets with some homemade tomato sauce (see Lisa's No-Fuss Tomato Sauce on page 277) and a slice or two of mozzarella. Bake in a 375° F oven for 10 minutes or until the cheese has melted and begun to brown. Garnish with fresh basil.

Pork Scaloppini Doré

Sometimes simplicity leads to perfection. That's how Lisa and I feel about this embarrassingly simple way to cook pork scallops and best of all, it only takes about 10 minutes to prepare. We added two other variations as well (see Chef's Notes), but the basic version is pretty hard to beat. The only real skill is in knowing when to turn the scaloppini so they come out lightly golden and succulently juicy. And the simple garnish of fried sage and capers gives just enough zing to balance the light and eggy coating on the pork. One of these also makes a great warm sandwich on toasted country bread slathered with mayonnaise and chopped capers. SERVES 2

---

4 boneless pork loin slices
(4 ounces each)

Kosher salt

Freshly ground black pepper

2 large eggs

½ cup all-purpose flour

3 tablespoons olive oil

12 to 16 fresh sage leaves,
stems removed

2 tablespoons capers, drained
and chopped

4 lemon wedges (optional)

1 To prepare the pork: Place each slice between 2 sheets of plastic wrap and pound lightly with a meat mallet to enlarge and spread to an even thickness of ⅛ to ¼ inch. Repeat with all the pork slices. 2 To cook the scallops: Season both sides of the scallops with salt and pepper. Put the eggs in one shallow wide bowl and the flour in another. Beat the eggs lightly. Heat the olive oil in a 10- to 12-inch nonstick skillet over medium-high heat. Dip a scallop first in the flour, then coat completely with the egg. Drain off any excess egg, then put the scallop in the skillet. Fry in batches of 2 scallops at a time. After about 2 minutes, check to see if the scaloppini are lightly golden. Turn and cook on the other side for 2 minutes more. Transfer to a warm large plate and repeat with the remaining scallops. 3 When all the scallops have been cooked, add the sage leaves to the hot oil and stir and fry until the leaves darken and begin to curl. Add the capers and stir and cook a minute more. Spread some of the fried sage leaves and capers over each scallop and serve accompanied with the lemon wedges, if desired.

CHEF'S NOTES: My friend Robert Miller's mother-in-law, Mrs. Angela Barbagelatta, whose ancestors are Italian, has her own family variation of scaloppini doré. To enhance the flavor of the scallops, she first marinates them for an hour in a mixture of ¼ cup milk, ½ cup vermouth, 2 teaspoons chopped garlic, 2 teaspoons chopped fresh sage, and ½ teaspoon each salt and pepper. Once the scallops are marinated, she drains them and proceeds with the sautéing. Mrs. Barbagelatta serves her scaloppini, which she calls "infusione," with a squirt of lemon juice, and some briefly warmed capers. Our pork scaloppini doré can easily be turned into a classic scaloppini variation called pork piccata. After cooking the scallops, remove them from the pan and add ½ cup dry white wine, the juice of ½ lemon, and 2 teaspoons chopped capers to the pan. Deglaze the pan and reduce the sauce to a syrup. Add a couple of tablespoons of chopped fresh parsley and a teaspoon of lemon zest. Pour the pan sauce over the scaloppini and serve at once.

Involtini (Roasted Pepper and Cheese–Stuffed Pork Rolls) *Involtini*

are individual rolls of meat, often veal that is stuffed with a variety of fillings. Here, I've embellished a ricotta stuffing with a little bit of roasted red pepper and some Parmesan cheese and used it to fill thinly pounded pork tenderloin medallions. I think these make an unusual hors d'oeuvre when cut into bite-sized pieces and served with a tangy-sweet tomato vinaigrette. They would also be delicious served as an entrée for two topped with a warm homemade tomato sauce. If you are serving them as an hors d'oeuvre, you will need to make the vinaigrette an hour in advance. SERVES 4 TO 6 AS AN HORS D'OEUVRE, 2 AS A MAIN COURSE

1 Place the pork medallions between 2 sheets of plastic wrap and using a meat mallet or pounder, pound out the medallions so that they form approximate 3- by 5-inch oval scallops, taking care not to tear the meat. 2 In a small bowl, mix together the ricotta, peppers, bread crumbs, and Parmesan. Place a rounded tablespoon of filling on each medallion and spread it out thinly to within ¼ inch of the edge of the scallops. Roll up lengthwise (like small jelly rolls) and secure with toothpicks, making sure the toothpicks are parallel to the long edge of the rolls. 3 Sprinkle the rolls with salt and pepper. In a large skillet, melt the butter with the oil over medium-high heat. Add the rolls and cook, turning, until lightly browned on all sides,

1 pork tenderloin (12 to 16 ounces), cut into 1-inch-thick medallions

½ cup whole-milk ricotta

1½ tablespoons chopped fire-roasted red bell or piquillo peppers, or sun-dried tomatoes

1 tablespoon fresh bread crumbs

2 tablespoons freshly grated Parmesan cheese

Kosher salt

Freshly ground black pepper

1 tablespoon butter

1 tablespoon olive oil

Tomato Vinaigrette (recipe follows)

about 6 minutes. Remove to a plate and let rest for 5 minutes. Remove the toothpicks and serve whole for a main course or slice the *involtini* crosswise into 1-inch pieces as an hors d'oeuvre. Arrange on a platter and drizzle with the tomato vinaigrette. Serve warm or at room temperature.

CHEF'S NOTE: *Involtini* can also be grilled. Thread 3 or 4 crosswise on each skewer; brush with olive oil and grill for 6 to 8 minutes over medium-high heat. Serve 3 rolls per person as a main course, or cut up as described above for hors d'oeuvres.

Tomato Vinaigrette

Drain the tomatoes in a small strainer or colander, pressing lightly on them to remove all the liquid. In a medium bowl, stir together the tomatoes, shallots, and vinegars. Whisk in the olive oil until the mixture has thickened slightly. Stir in the basil and season to taste with salt and pepper. Set aside for 1 hour for the flavors to meld. Whisk again just before serving.

3 ripe tomatoes, peeled, seeded, and chopped

2 tablespoons minced shallots

1 tablespoon balsamic vinegar

1 tablespoon red wine vinegar

½ cup extra-virgin olive oil

1 tablespoon chopped fresh basil

Kosher salt

Freshly ground black pepper

Pork Medallions with Sweet-and-Sour Riesling Sauce

I'm always attracted to any dish that has sweet and sour in its name, and it seems to me that just about every culture has some kind of combination it calls sweet and sour or hot and sour. Food historians believe that sweet/sour dishes evolved when people discovered that sugar could help balance the extreme tartness of acid used as a food preservative. Eventually, the sweet/sour flavor juxtaposition became a favorite pairing in its own right. Italians have their *agrodolce* and the French their *aigre-doux*. The Germans are famous for their *sauerbraten* and the Hungarians their *paprikash*. The Russians have *borscht*, the Chinese have many sweet-and-sour dishes, and think of all the pickles, chutneys, and preserves that use sweet-and-sour flavor components. I have to admit that in this dish I used pork as an excuse to create a sweet-and-sour sauce. SERVES 4

1 Season both sides of the medallions with salt and pepper, then dredge lightly in the flour, shaking off the excess. Set aside. In a large skillet, melt 2 tablespoons of the butter over medium-high heat. Add the onions and cook until softened and just beginning to color, about 5 minutes. Add the garlic and cook, stirring, for 2 minutes. Remove to a plate. Add 1 more tablespoon butter and the 1 tablespoon of the olive oil to the skillet. Add half the pork medallions and cook over medium-high heat for 2 minutes or until browned. Turn and cook for 2 minutes more. Remove the medallions to a plate and tent loosely with foil. Repeat with remaining medallions and a tablespoon of the butter and remaining olive oil. 2 Return the onions to the skillet and add the Riesling, stock, raisins, and vinegar. Increase the heat to high and bring the liquid to a boil, scraping up any browned bits from the bottom of the pan. Reduce the liquid until lightly thickened. Return the medallions with any accumulated juices to the skillet and heat to finish their cooking, about 3 minutes. Remove the medallions to a warm platter, reduce the heat to medium, and stir in the thyme and the remaining 3 tablespoons butter. Taste for salt, pepper, and additional vinegar. Pour the sauce over the pork and serve at once.

2 pork tenderloins (each 12 to 16 ounces), cut into 1-inch-thick medallions

Kosher salt

Freshly ground black pepper

¼ cup all-purpose flour

7 tablespoons butter

1½ cups thinly sliced onions

1 teaspoon minced garlic

2 tablespoons olive oil

½ cup sweet Riesling

½ cup Dark Pork Stock (page 87), homemade chicken stock, or canned low-sodium chicken broth

⅓ cup golden raisins

3 tablespoons white balsamic vinegar, or more to taste

1½ teaspoons minced fresh thyme

7
Kebabs and Ribs

About Kebabs

Kebabs are common to many different cuisines—they make good use of small bits of meat and can be flavored quickly with a large range of marinades, each with a distinct flavor profile. Kebabs can be served as appetizers, sandwiches, first courses, or main courses and they can be embellished with a wide variety of ingredients. I love them because they allow me to mix and match lots of different types of ingredients, from fresh and dried fruits to vegetables, and bread. I also love to alternate brined or marinated cubes of pork with chunks of bacon, sausage, and pancetta, or even mix sausages or meat with seafood such as shrimp, lobster, or scallops.

Kebabs make a great theme for a skewer party (the meat, not the guests). Put out several bowls containing cubes of marinated pork, cubes of flavor-brined pork, cubed onions, various sweet or spicy peppers, chunks of sausage, chunks of summer squash, peppers, eggplant, soaked prunes, soaked figs, mushrooms, wedges of fennel and radicchio, and chicken livers wrapped in pancetta, then supply your guests with some skewers so they can put together their own combinations. One piece of advice: Instead of alternating meats and vegetables on the same skewer, spear them on separate skewers because meat and vegetables often take different times to cook.

For main course kebabs, I cut the pork into 1½-inch cubes; for appetizer skewers, smaller cubes, say ¾ to 1 inch, are preferable because they're easier to eat at a cocktail party.

Boston butt is the best cut to use for kebabs because of its great flavor and ability to stand up to 36 hours in a marinade without becoming soft and pasty. Pork loin, particularly from the rib or blade area (sold as country spareribs), is also a good choice for kebabs. Pork tenderloin is another good option. If you use an acidic marinade with tenderloin, however, cut its marinating time to 2 hours at room temperature or 16 hours in the refrigerator. Pork cut into cubes is ideal for flavor-brining—just make sure everything is at refrigerator temperatures and soak the meat in the brine for about 2 hours.

Just about any marinade or paste recipe in the book works on kebabs, as do all the Flavor Brines. One final word: If you're using wooden or bamboo skewers, don't forget to soak them at least 30 minutes in warm water so they don't burn on the grill. Or soak them while the meat is marinating or brining.

Master Recipe: Grilled Pork Kebabs 🐷 Serves 4

1 To make the marinade: Combine all of the ingredients in a bowl. 2 Put the pork cubes in a 1-gallon zip-lock plastic bag and pour in the marinade. Seal the bag and refrigerate for 16 to 24 hours, turning the bag from time to time to redistribute the marinade. 3 To prepare the kebabs: Remove the meat from the bag, discard the marinade, and pat the meat dry. 4 Set up a charcoal or gas grill with a medium-hot fire. Thread the meat on skewers and the apples and onion pieces on separate skewers. 5 Combine the lemon juice and olive oil and brush the mixture all over the fruit and onion kebabs. Grill the skewers until the pork is firm to the touch and the apple and onions are lightly colored and beginning to soften. Turn the kebabs frequently to prevent burning. The meat skewers will take about 10 to 12 minutes and the apple and onion skewers about 7 to 10 minutes, but remember that time and temperatures vary a great deal, so pay attention to the visual cues. If you're not sure if the meat is done, remove one piece and cut into it. It should be faintly pink. If not, cook a minute or two longer. 6 To serve, remove the apples and onions to a platter and lay the pork kebabs on top.

Apple Cider Marinade

2 tablespoons minced red onion or shallot

¼ cup apple cider or apple juice

1 tablespoon cider vinegar

1 teaspoon chopped fresh sage or 1 teaspoon chopped fresh thyme

2 tablespoons Calvados or other apple brandy or regular brandy

¼ teaspoon ground cinnamon

3 tablespoons soy sauce

1 tablespoon olive oil

or

Marinade or Flavor Brine of your choice

1½ pounds Boston butt, blade-end loin (also called country spareribs), or rib loin, cut into 1½-inch cubes

2 Granny Smith apples, cored and cut into 1-inch cubes

1 cup (1-inch) squares red onion

2 tablespoons freshly squeezed lemon juice

1 tablespoon olive oil

or

Fruit and vegetables of your choice

Grilled North African Marinated Pork Kebabs on Couscous with Apricot Sauce

🐖 North Africa, especially Morocco, is home to both non-pork-eating Muslims and Christians who do cook with pork. The flavors and spices of that region influence this recipe, which would work equally well with lamb or chicken. My favorite cut for kebabs is Boston butt, though blade-end loin, boneless country spareribs, pork tenderloin, and boneless rib center-cut loin would work fine. SERVES 4

North African Marinade

2 small garlic cloves

½ cup chopped cilantro leaves

2 tablespoons fresh mint

⅓ cup freshly squeezed lemon juice

1 tablespoon olive oil

1 teaspoon kosher salt

1 teaspoon freshly ground black pepper

½ teaspoon cayenne pepper

2 teaspoons sweet Hungarian paprika

1 teaspoon ground cumin

1 teaspoon turmeric

1 teaspoon ground fennel seed

Pinch ground cinnamon

2 pounds boneless pork, cut in 1½-inch cubes, or 4 (1½-inch-thick) rib pork chops

16 dried apricots, soaked in hot water for about 5 minutes and drained

1 red onion, cut into 1½-inch chunks

1½ cups instant couscous

½ cup dried currants or raisins

½ teaspoon salt

1 To make the marinade: Put all of the marinade ingredients in a blender and process until the mixture forms a wet paste. 2 Rub the mixture over the pork cubes and marinate for 2 hours at room temperature or overnight in the refrigerator. 3 Set up a gas or charcoal grill for medium-hot heat. Remove meat from marinade. Reserve ¼ cup of marinade and discard the rest. Thread the pork cubes onto 4 separate skewers, alternating them with the apricots and chunks of onion. Grill the skewers about 4 to 5 minutes on one side, turn, and grill 4 to 5 minutes more. Set the skewers aside to rest for 5 minutes while you make the accompaniments. 4 Combine the couscous, currants, salt, and 2½ cups boiling water in a heatproof bowl and cover. Let stand for 5 to 10 minutes while you make the sauce. 5 To make the sauce: Combine the reserved marinade, apricot jam, and stock or in a small saucepan. Bring to a boil and simmer until the mixture becomes syrupy. 6 To serve, spoon the couscous into a shallow serving bowl. Sprinkle the pine nuts over the top. Arrange the kebabs on the couscous and brush them generously with the sauce. Garnish with the cilantro leaves and serve.

CHEF'S NOTE: This is also a great recipe for thick rib pork chops. Grill them as directed in the Master Recipe for Grilled Pork Chops (page 105). If you want to include the apricots and onions, skewer and cook them separately.

Apricot Sauce

¼ cup reserved marinade

⅓ cup apricot jam

¼ cup homemade chicken stock or canned low-sodium chicken broth

½ cup pine nuts, toasted

Cilantro leaves, for garnish

Jacob's Pork Skewers with Pancetta-Wrapped Figs

Jacob Kenedy is a chef from London who spent a year as a guest chef at Boulevard, my wife's restaurant in San Francisco. Jacob loves figs and came up with this recipe for skewered pork and figs based on similar skewers he ate on one of his many visits to Italy. Jacob uses small fresh black Mission figs, but says you can use dried figs if you soak them first for 20 minutes in hot water. SERVES 4

Olive Oil–Rosemary Marinade

2 tablespoons extra-virgin olive oil

2 teaspoons chopped fresh rosemary

¼ teaspoon ground cinnamon

1 teaspoon kosher salt

½ teaspoon freshly ground black pepper

1 to 1¼ pounds pork tenderloin, cut into 1-inch cubes (about 16 cubes)

8 thin slices pancetta or good-quality bacon

16 small fresh black Mission figs, or dried figs soaked for 20 minutes in hot water and drained

8 small bamboo skewers, soaked in warm water for 30 minutes to 2 hours

1 For the marinade: Combine all of the marinade ingredients in a bowl. 2 Add the meat to the marinade and toss until each piece is well coated. Marinate for 2 hours at room temperature or up to 24 hours covered in the refrigerator. 3 Set up a gas or charcoal grill for a medium-hot fire. 4 To assemble the skewers: Cut the pieces of pancetta or bacon in half crosswise and wrap a piece around each fig. On each skewer, alternate 2 cubes of pork and 2 wrapped figs. (You will have 8 finished skewers, with 4 pieces on each.) 5 Grill the skewers over medium-hot coals until the bacon is crispy and the pork firm to the touch, about 8 to 10 minutes total. Turn the skewers frequently to prevent burning. Serve hot.

Spiedini

Spiedini are skewers of various kinds of meat that are popular throughout Italy. Depending on the region, they might be made with fresh pork belly, rabbit wrapped in pancetta, quail wrapped in grape leaves, various sausages, or pork cured in brine. Sometimes you'll find skewers with alternating chunks of rough country bread and meat. We prefer to grill bread and meats on separate skewers.

While not necessary, brining adds great flavor and makes the pork particularly juicy. We make our *spiedini* with meat cut from the Boston butt, which has a bit more fat; you could also use pork tenderloin, pork loin, or meat from the sirloin. SERVES 4

1½ pounds Boston butt, cut into 1½-inch cubes

2 cups brine (for Petit Salé of Pork on page 292 or another Flavor Brine of choice)

4 garlic cloves, thinly sliced

½ cup olive oil

Fresh sage leaves or bay leaves

16 (2-inch diameter) cremini or white mushroom caps

1 red onion, cut into 1½-inch squares

1 loaf French or Italian bread, crust removed and cut into 1½-inch cubes

1 Put the meat in a 1-gallon zip-lock plastic bag, plastic storage container, or bowl, and pour the brine over it. Seal the bag or cover the bowl and refrigerate for 2 hours. Drain and discard the brine and pat the meat dry. 2 Put the garlic in a microwaveable container and cover with the olive oil. Microwave on high for 1 to 2 minutes. Set the garlic-flavored oil aside. 3 Set up a gas or charcoal grill with a medium fire. 4 Thread the meat onto skewers, alternating the cubes with sage or fresh bay leaves. Thread the mushrooms and pieces of onion, alternating them, on separate skewers. Thread the bread onto still separate skewers. Brush all the skewers, especially the bread, generously with the garlic oil. 5 Grill the skewers until the pork is firm to the touch, the vegetables are soft and beginning to color, and the bread is golden and nicely toasted. Turn the skewers frequently to prevent burning. The bread will cook the fastest and will take less than 5 minutes to become golden brown all over. The meat and vegetables should take about 10 minutes to cook, but remember that grilling times and temperatures vary a great deal, so watch carefully and pay attention to the visual clues for doneness. 6 To serve, slide the bread from the skewers over the bottom of a platter. Remove the meat and the vegetables from the skewers and scatter over the bread. Let sit for 5 minutes before serving so that the bread can soak up some of the meat juices. If there is any garlic oil left, drizzle a little bit over all and serve.

CHEF'S NOTES: There are many variations of *spiedini* and these are some of my favorites: 🐖 Make meat skewers with 1 pound lean pork cut from the loin and ½ pound fresh pork belly. (Cut the pork belly into pieces ½ inch thick and 1½ inches long.) Brine both the lean and fatty meat together, then skewer, alternating the lean meat with the fat. 🐖 Cut pork tenderloin into medallions ½ inch thick. Place a small sage leaf on one of the cut surfaces of each medallion and wrap a thin slice of pancetta around the meat and the leaf. Skewer to secure the pancetta. 🐖 Poach 4 of your favorite sausages, such as mild or hot Italian, until fully cooked, about 10 minutes in 180° F water. Cut into 1-inch rounds and alternate on skewers with fresh (not brined) blade-end loin or sirloin. Add red, green, or yellow bell peppers to the mushroom/onion skewers above. Or omit the mushrooms and just make skewers of bell peppers and red onion. 🐖 Divide chicken or duck livers into individual lobes. Wrap each in pancetta or bacon. Alternate on skewers with 1-inch rounds of poached sausage (see above). Serve with skewers of red onion, bell peppers, and mushrooms. Before serving, drizzle with the best balsamic vinegar you can afford. In fact, you can drizzle balsamic vinegar over any of the *spiedini*. If you're feeling extra-generous, drizzle with truffle oil. 🐖 Do the same bacon or pancetta wrap on the livers as above, but instead of sausage use fresh pork belly, cut into ½-inch-thick by 1½-inch-long rectangles. Alternate with the wrapped livers and chunks of red onion. Brush radicchio wedges with oil, grill, and serve with the skewers. Or grill strips of sweet red bell peppers and eliminate the vegetable skewers altogether.

Tamarind-Marinated Pork Belly Skewers

 One of the most memorable evenings I spent while on a culinary tour of Vietnam, led by cookbook author Mai Pham and sponsored by the Culinary Institute of America, was a cooking class and meal at the home of Nguyen Doan Cam Van. Called the Julia Child of Vietnam because of her popular TV cooking shows, Cam Van is a shy, very gracious woman who welcomed us into her home and taught us how to prepare many Vietnamese dishes, including this tamarind-marinated pork belly. SERVES 6 TO 8 AS AN APPETIZER

Cam Van's Tamarind Marinade

1 tablespoon tamarind paste (see Chef's Notes)

2 teaspoons brown sugar

1 tablespoon Vietnamese fish sauce (*nuoc mam*), (see Chef's Notes)

2 teaspoons minced fresh ginger

1 tablespoon minced shallot or green onions

½ teaspoon Chinese five-spice powder

1 pound pork belly, skin removed and sliced into ¼-inch-thick slices (page 180)

1 Combine all of the marinade ingredients in a small bowl. 2 Add the sliced pork belly to the marinade and marinate for at least 30 minutes or up to 2 hours at room temperature. 3 Set up a gas or charcoal grill with a medium fire. 4 Remove the pork from the marinade, thread on skewers to keep the slices from curling, and grill over medium coals for 2 to 3 minutes per side or until nicely browned. Serve at once.

CHEF'S NOTES: Tamarind paste and Vietnamese fish sauce can be found in Asian markets (see Sources on page 318). Instead of pork belly, use thinly sliced Boston butt, boneless pork loin, pork tenderloin, or thinly sliced country-style spareribs. Use the pork belly meat for a Vietnamese-style sandwich made of the pork belly with pickled zucchini or cucumbers, chopped peanuts, and cilantro, all piled on soft French rolls and drizzled with *sriracha* hot sauce. To make pickled zucchini toss 2 cups shredded zucchini with 1 tablespoon kosher salt and let sit in a colander for 30 minutes. Rinse, drain, and squeeze dry. Stir together with 1 tablespoon each of rice vinegar, *sriracha*, soy, sesame oil, and a pinch of sugar.

How to Choose Ribs

Hands down, **spareribs** are my favorite ribs for barbecuing, grilling, and roasting. Spareribs are cut from the belly after the rest of the belly (fresh belly or bacon meat) is removed. A slab of spareribs should have at least 11 but could include all 14 ribs. Look for slabs that weigh at least 3 pounds, are well trimmed, and have plenty of lean meat. You should be able to see a nice layer of meat over the ribs; otherwise you'll be paying for a pile of bones. A good slab can have a 2-inch layer of meat at the larger end of the slab. Don't buy previously frozen slabs, which could be leftover from last year's barbecuing season, and avoid ribs with discolored fat and dry edges. Figure that a nice meaty slab of ribs will feed three, unless you're entertaining a patio full of serious rib-eaters like myself, then figure half a slab per person.

St. Louis–style spareribs have a more regular rectangular shape than ordinary spareribs and are made by cutting away the breast bones and cartilaginous part of the spareribs that have almost no meat. I really like St. Louis–style ribs because they are both trimmed down to the meat of the matter and cook more evenly. If you can't find St. Louis–style spareribs, then buy regular spareribs and trim away the breast bones yourself. Use the trimmed bones and cartilage to add body and flavor to soups and stews. Good meaty St. Louis–style ribs should weigh at least 2 pounds, but 2½ pound slabs are better if you can find them.

Back ribs are the rib bones cut from where the ribs join the spine. They're the pork chop rib bones that remain when the butcher cuts out a boneless pork loin. Sometimes these upper rib bones are called **baby back ribs,** but trust me, they come from a full-grown pig. Some meat cutters do such a good job cutting the loin meat from the ribs bones that no meat is left on the ribs except for a tiny bit between the bones. Considering how much these "baby" back ribs or just plain back ribs cost, I consider them overpriced. Try to find back ribs that have an inch or so of meat attached to the bones, otherwise don't bother. Back ribs are much leaner than spareribs and can dry out, but at the same time because they're so tender you can cook them quickly over direct heat on the grill. Back ribs are very common these days, especially in restaurants, where they're typically served in half-slab portions. It may seem like a lot of meat on the plate but looks are deceiving. So, if you do cook them at home, figure about one pound of back ribs per portion (slabs tend to weigh around 1½ pounds). If you can find 2-pound back rib slabs, so much the better. Because of their small size and quick cooking, back ribs make great hors d'oeuvres and they take well to many different marinades and dry rubs. Look for meaty ribs that have not been previously frozen and show no signs of discoloration or dry edges. If substituting back ribs for St. Louis–style ribs or regular spareribs, you'll need to provide 1½ times as many slabs for each sparerib or St. Louis slab.

Country-style ribs are actually blade-end loin chops that have been butterflied or cut into two pieces. One half contains a rib bone and the other half the blade bone. They have plenty of fat for slow cooking, but are tender enough to grill over direct heat. I like them because you get value for your money (more meat, less bone) and they have great flavor. Country-style ribs are also sold boneless and are ideal for stews as well as cut into cubes for kebabs. Technically, your meat purveyor should label country-style ribs from the blade end of the loin as **pork loin country-style ribs** to distinguish them from Boston butt, which is butterflied and cut into thick strips, which are also sold as country-style ribs. To be correct, these should be labeled as **pork shoulder country-style ribs.** In any event, they can be used interchangeably with blade-end country-style ribs. The shoulder variety does tend to be thicker, however, so adjust cooking times accordingly. Often **country-style ribs** are labeled simply **country ribs** as an alternative name.

    See Butcher's Chart of the Pig (endpapers).

Master Recipe: Oven-Roasted or Grill-Roasted Ribs

Whether you bake spareribs indoors in an oven (oven-roasting), or outdoors over indirect heat in a covered grill (grill-roasting), each is a great way to prepare them. Flavor the ribs with a marinade, which can be applied a day ahead, or dry rub, which can be applied right before cooking, and then cook them at moderate temperatures of 300° to 350° F. Once the ribs are cooked, they can be quickly grilled over direct heat, glazed, and placed under a broiler to be glazed or to produce a caramelized exterior. Ribs cooked at these temperatures will be juicy but only moderately tender because this higher temperature method of cooking ribs does not result in falling-off-the-bone meat. For that you need to slow-cook them (200° to 250° F) as in traditional barbecue (page 174), but baked ribs are still quite delicious and take only 1½ to 2 hours to cook versus 4 hours minimum for traditional barbecued ribs.

I prefer to use St. Louis–style ribs because they're easier to eat and often instead of glazing them with a sauce I serve a flavorful dipping sauce alongside.

FLAVOR STEP Combine dry rub, paste, or wet marinade ingredients. Coat the ribs with a dry rub or paste and put them in a large zip-lock plastic bag. Or immerse the ribs in a wet marinade as described in each recipe. If using a dry rub, you can bake the ribs immediately, but they will improve in flavor if allowed to sit at room temperature for up to 2 hours or refrigerated, covered, overnight (16 to 30 hours). For pastes and wet marinades, marinate the ribs for 16 to 30 hours in the refrigerator.

To Oven-Roast Ribs Preheat the oven to 350° F. Remove the ribs from the marinade and let the excess drip off. Save the marinade if it's being cooked into a dipping sauce (consult individual recipes) or use to baste. Put the ribs fat-side up, on a rack over a baking pan. Put in the oven and roast until the meat begins to pull away from the bones, about 1½ to 2 hours, basting every 20 minutes with the marinade. For paste or dry rub–coated ribs, do not remove the coating first, just bake on the rack.

If you want to brown and caramelize the surface of the ribs after they're baked, put them under a broiler about 3 to 4 inches from the heat until they begin to bubble and brown, about 2 to 3 minutes. Serve as is or with a dipping sauce (consult individual recipes). You may also brown the roasted ribs directly over a charcoal or gas grill.

Cooking Ribs for a Crowd

Some folks will tell you that the easiest way to cook a mess of ribs is to boil them first, until they're almost done, then throw them on the grill directly over the coals and slather with some sauce to finish them off. Hogwash! This is a terrible idea. Not only does boiling toughen the meat, it leaches out flavor and any marinade or dry rub just ends up in the cooking water. Boiling ribs just gives you flavorless, dry, and stringy meat.

To cook ribs successfully for a crowd, cook them first until they're just about done (see Oven-Roasted or Grill-Roasted Ribs—Master Recipe on page 145). You ought to be able to cook 4 or 6 slabs in your oven; you could even cook them in batches. Then let the ribs sit at room temperature for up to 2 hours. When your guests arrive, light the barbecue and quickly grill them over direct heat (about 5 to 6 minutes per side) to crisp and caramelize them. If you want to glaze or sauce the ribs, do that right before the final grilling step. Your ribs will be juicy and delicious and I guarantee your guests will think you slaved for hours over your barbecue.

To Grill-Roast Ribs build a fire on one side of a covered grill or if using a gas grill only light one burner. Put the meat opposite the fire so there is no fire directly underneath the meat. If you're grill-roasting more than 2 slabs, put them in a vertical rack specially designed for cooking several rib racks at one time. Cover the grill and try to maintain a temperature of 300° to 350° F. When the meat begins to pull away from the bone, the ribs are done. This may take anywhere from 1¼ to 2 hours, depending on the temperature maintained in the grill. If you like a smoky flavor, add some wood chips or chunks to the coals from time to time and if you want more of a grilled flavor or caramelized exterior, grill both sides of each slab briefly over a hot fire (you may need to add more coals) for 2 to 3 minutes per side after they're cooked. Serve the ribs as is or with a dipping sauce (consult individual recipes).

If you're using back ribs (1½-pound slabs) instead of St. Louis–style spareribs (see How to Choose Ribs on page 143), oven-roast or grill-roast them for less time, about 45 minutes to 1 hour. If you're using regular untrimmed spareribs, then cook them 15 minutes longer than St. Louis–style spareribs so the breast portion, which is tougher, can cook more.

Spareribs with Coffee-Molasses
Marinade

The coffee in this marinade accentuates the bitter and smoky flavors of molasses, which is particularly delicious with pork ribs. This recipe is a favorite for marinating ribs of any kind: beef prime ribs or short ribs, as well as bone-in rib pork chops. My absolute favorite is pork spareribs because of their high ratio of fat to meat. If that weren't enough, this marinade also makes a wonderful dipping sauce because it's not too salty. SERVES 6

1 Follow the Master Recipe instructions for either oven-roasting or grill-roasting on page 145. Make sure to save 1 cup of the used marinade. 2 Put the reserved 1 cup marinade in a small saucepan and bring to a boil over high heat. Reduce the heat and simmer for 2 to 3 minutes. Serve the reduced marinade as a dipping sauce for the ribs.

Marinade

1 cup strong coffee

1 cup coarsely chopped red onion

½ cup mild molasses

½ cup red wine vinegar

¼ cup Dijon mustard

1 tablespoon Worcestershire sauce

¼ cup soy sauce

1 tablespoon Tabasco, or other hot sauce

2 tablespoons chopped shallot or green onions

2 slabs (about 2½ pounds each) St. Louis–style spareribs (page 143), 2 slabs spareribs (about 3 pounds each), or 3 slabs back ribs (about 1½ pounds each)

Jerk-Marinated Ribs

The essence of Jamaican barbecue is a spicy and very aromatic paste called jerk. Jerk is a wet paste made from very hot, fresh Scotch bonnet or habañero chilies, lots of ground allspice, and minced green onions. Each "jerk" chef (not chefs who are jerks) individualizes his or her recipe with other herbs, spices, and flavorings. For my recipe, I've added a little nontraditional soy sauce, five-spice powder, and, of course, a jigger of rum. For the best results, and full-flavor development, generously smear the jerk paste over the meat, wrap it tightly in plastic, and let it sit overnight in the refrigerator. SERVES 6

Jerk Marinade

1 cup coarsely chopped red onions

4 scallions, coarsely chopped

2 Scotch bonnet or habañero chilies, seeded and chopped

3 garlic cloves, peeled

1 tablespoon ground allspice

1 teaspoon Chinese five-spice powder

2 tablespoons brown sugar

2 teaspoons freshly ground black pepper

2 teaspoons fresh thyme or 1 teaspoon dried

¼ cup freshly squeezed lime juice

2 tablespoons dark rum (optional)

⅓ cup soy sauce

¼ cup olive oil

½ teaspoon ground nutmeg

¼ teaspoon ground cinnamon

1 teaspoon ground fennel seeds

1 teaspoon kosher salt

2 slabs (about 2½ pounds each) St. Louis–style spareribs (page 143), 2 slabs spareribs (about 3 pounds each), or 3 slabs back ribs (about 1½ pounds each)

Combine all jerk marinade ingredients in a blender. Blend to form a wet paste. Follow the Master Recipe instructions for either oven-roasting or grill-roasting on page 145.

CHEF'S NOTE: Jerk is also excellent on rib or blade pork chops, country-style ribs, and pork shoulder steaks.

Hong Kong–Style Ribs

Since I love ribs and I love all manner of Chinese food, I often order the ribs you see hanging in the windows of Chinese take-out places, which typically have a sweet red glaze based on hoisin and honey. Several years ago I went to Hong Kong on a Chinese cooking tour and had a drier type of roasted spareribs. Instead of a sweet glaze, those ribs were coated with a spice rub based on five-spice powder. A huge pile came to the table with a slightly sweet and salty dipping sauce, and though I was never able to get the recipe I recently came across a Chinese-inspired dry rub by Steve Johnson of the Blue Room in Cambridge, Massachusetts. I've adapted his recipe and to my best recollection, these ribs taste pretty darn close to the ones I enjoyed in Hong Kong.

SERVES 6

1 Combine rub ingredients. Follow the Master Recipe instructions for either oven-roasting or grill-roasting on page 145.

2 To make the dipping sauce: In a small saucepan, combine all of the ingredients except the green onions, cilantro, and peanuts. Bring to a boil, reduce the heat to a simmer, and cook for 3 minutes. Remove from the heat. Stir in the green onions, cilantro, and peanuts and serve warm.

Hong Kong Spice Rub

1½ tablespoons paprika

2 tablespoons brown sugar

1 tablespoon ground fennel seeds

1 tablespoon Chinese five-spice powder

1 tablespoon kosher salt

2 teaspoons minced garlic

2 slabs (about 2½ pounds each) St. Louis–style spareribs (page 143), 2 slabs spareribs (about 3 pounds each), or 3 slabs back ribs (about 1½ pounds each)

Hoisin Dipping Sauce

1 teaspoon minced garlic

2 teaspoons minced fresh ginger

2 tablespoons soy sauce

2 tablespoons rice vinegar

1 tablespoon hoisin sauce

1 teaspoon brown bean paste

1 teaspoon Asian sesame oil

4 tablespoons water

2 tablespoons finely chopped green onion

3 tablespoons chopped cilantro

2 tablespoons chopped roasted peanuts

Franco's Rosticiana Ribs

Italians, especially those from Tuscany, love ribs—almost as much as Americans do. And since pigs in that area of the world tend to be bigger and are much more flavorful, cooks often simply roast the meat with a minimal amount of seasoning, perhaps just a little salt, pepper, fresh herbs, or spices. These spiced ribs come from our friend Franco Dunn, who serves them at his restaurant Santi in Geyserville, California. Franco either roasts the ribs in an oven, cooks them indirectly over a charcoal fire, or even spit roasts them. Though Franco's recipe differs from our Oven-Roasted Ribs (page 145), we decided to include his method here because it shows that good tasty ribs can be made with more than one technique. SERVES 6

Franco's Rosticiana Rib Rub

1½ tablespoons kosher salt

2 teaspoons freshly ground black pepper

1 teaspoon crushed red pepper flakes

1 tablespoon chopped fresh sage

1½ tablespoons fennel seeds

2 tablespoons chopped fresh rosemary

1 teaspoon paprika

2 tablespoons olive oil

2 cups water

1 teaspoon high-quality balsamic vinegar (optional, see Chef's Note)

2 slabs (about 2½ pounds each) St. Louis–style spareribs (page 143), 2 slabs spareribs (about 3 pounds each), or 3 slabs back ribs (about 1½ pounds each)

1 To make the rub: In a small bowl mix all of the seasoning ingredients together except the water and balsamic vinegar. 2 Generously pat the rub onto both sides of the ribs. Let sit at room temperature for 2 hours, or wrap the ribs in plastic wrap and refrigerate overnight (16 to 30 hours). 3 When you're ready to cook the ribs, preheat the oven to 300° F. 4 Put each slab of ribs, fat-side up, in a large (10 by 15-inch) baking dish. Add 1 cup water to each dish and cover with foil. Bake for 1½ hours. Remove the foil, increase the heat to 375° F, and continue to bake, uncovered, for 30 minutes or until the rib meat pulls away from the bone. Brush the ribs with the optional balsamic vinegar and bake 5 minutes more. (If not using the vinegar, remove from the oven now.) 5 Remove the ribs from the oven and let rest for 10 minutes. Cut between the ribs and serve.

CHEF'S NOTE: If using balsamic vinegar, it's important to use a fairly high-quality brand in this dish, not the supermarket kind that is harshly acidic. You don't have to have an expensive fifty-year-old balsamic, just one that has some age and is sweet and mellow. Aged balsamic vinegars are available in gourmet markets everywhere but read the labels to see if they've been aged at least ten years.

Blackberry-Glazed Back Ribs

If you're a fan, as I am, of dark, intense fruit glazes, then this blackberry glaze is for you. Instead of blackberries, you can use any summer berry, including blueberries or raspberries, though not strawberries. The glaze is also good with Grilled Pork Tenderloin (page 162), Grilled, Brined, and Fresh Herb–Coated Pork Chops (page 105), and baked ham. SERVES 6

1 To make the rub: Combine all of the rub ingredients in a small bowl. 2 Massage the rub into the ribs. Let sit at room temperature for 2 hours or wrap the ribs in plastic wrap and refrigerate overnight (16 to 30 hours). 3 To make the glaze: put the chicken stock, vinegar, cassis, grape juice, mustard, blackberry jam, and blackberries in a small saucepan. Bring to a boil over high heat, whisking occasionally. Reduce the heat slightly to maintain a simmer and cook until the liquid becomes syrupy. Stir in the cornstarch mixture and cook for a few seconds more until the sauce has thickened lightly. Season with salt and pepper and strain through a fine-mesh strainer. The glaze can be refrigerated for up to 2 weeks. Reheat before serving. 4 Set up a covered gas or charcoal grill for indirect heat. Remove the ribs from the refrigerator and place them on the grill so that there is no heat directly underneath them. Cover, and try to maintain a grill temperature of 250° to 300° F. After 1 hour, brush the ribs generously with the blackberry glaze. Grill for 15 minutes more. The ribs are done when the meat begins to pull away from the bone tips and is quite tender. 5 Serve the ribs with the remaining glaze passed separately.

Back Rib Rub

½ teaspoon dried sage

½ teaspoon dried thyme

1 teaspoon dry mustard

1 tablespoon kosher salt

2 teaspoons freshly ground black pepper

1 tablespoon paprika

2 teaspoons light brown sugar

½ teaspoon cayenne pepper

3 slabs baby back ribs (about 1½ pounds each)

Blackberry Glaze

1½ cups homemade chicken stock or canned low-sodium chicken broth

2 tablespoons red wine vinegar

½ cup *crème de cassis* or grape juice

1 tablespoon Dijon mustard

¼ cup blackberry jam

2 cups fresh or frozen blackberries

2 teaspoons cornstarch mixed with 2 tablespoons water

Kosher salt

Freshly ground black pepper

8
Roasts

About the Best Pork Cuts for Roasts

The most desirable attribute for a pork roast is tenderness, but because many of the tender cuts come from the loin or leg they're also lean. Care must be taken, therefore, not to overcook them. You want a final internal temperature of 145° to 155° F. If well-done pork is your preference (160° F and above), consider roasting fattier meat: Boston butt or blade-end pork loin roast.

My own favorite cut for roasting is a whole **fresh leg-of-pork**, also called **fresh ham**. This cut is packed with porky goodness and more depth of flavor than any loin roast, which is the most popular cut with consumers. The leg is fairly easy to carve and if you leave the skin on you will have all those crunchy, crispy cracklings to munch on (see Chinese method for crisp skin, page 179). Leg meat is juicier than loin meat and more forgiving; if it gets away from you and cooks to 155° to 160° F, it will still be adequately juicy. In order to decrease your risk of the meat drying out, you can soak it in any of the Flavor Brines (pages 29 to 32) for 3 days, which will also add flavor. Any leftover roast leg-of-pork will make the best pork sandwiches you've ever eaten, but too many leftovers can also be a problem; a whole leg-of-pork is big—damn big. Weighing in at close to 20 pounds, it may be just a bit much for a Wednesday night dinner for 4. Twenty pounds is more than some Thanksgiving turkeys weigh, so you'll probably want to reserve a whole pork leg for a special occasion. In many stores around the country, whole leg-of-pork is available only around the holidays and must be special-ordered at other times of the year. Here's another little bonus: Whole leg-of-pork is a bargain and costs less than half of the what you pay for a bone-in rib roast and even less than a smoked ham. Besides that, it's even more delicious.

An option if you're serving a smaller group is to purchase a half leg-of-pork, which is sold either as the **shank end leg-of-pork**, or **butt end leg-of-pork**. Each of these weighs 8 to 10 pounds and is ideal for 10 to 12 people. The shank end is easier to carve, but the butt end is a bit more tender and flavorful. If you get your butcher to remove the aitch bone (part of the hip-bone) from the butt end of the butt half (or a whole leg for that matter), it too is easily carved.

A few enlightened meat purveyors have realized that they can make good money and provide their customers excellent pork roasts by boning out the leg and turning it into boneless roasts. Each of these roasts weighs 4 to 6 pounds, which makes it ideal for feeding 4 to 8 people with some leftovers. The best of the boneless leg roasts is called **pork leg inside** or **top leg (inside) roast**. It's the pork equivalent of a top round beef roast, tender and quite flavorful. The **bottom leg (outside)** roast is a little leaner and a bit less flavorful, but still makes an excellent roast. It's equivalent to the bottom round roast in beef. Sometimes you can also find pairs of insides and outsides tied together face to face, which makes a perfect 8- to 12-pound roast. Some butchers will also bone out a single muscle from the outside and call it a **pork leg eye** roast and another small roast from above the shank (about 2 to 3 pounds) is known as the **pork leg knuckle**. It's a good roast for a small group, say, a family of 4. All of the above roasts should be tied to give them more uniform shape to cook evenly.

My next favorite cut for roasting is an **8-bone center-cut rib roast (center rib roast)**, bones attached and chine bone removed. This is the rib section of a center-cut pork loin (the other part of the center-cut loin, or center loin roast, is simply called loin). It weighs about 6 pounds and feeds 8 people, each of whom will receive a thick pork rib chop slice. It's the pork equivalent of a standing rib roast, the king of all beef roasts. I like this cut because there is a little fat near the bone, and though the meat is lean, it has good flavor. The juiciness of this roast is much improved, however, by first flavor-brining (pages 29 to 32) the meat. I also like a **bone-in blade-end loin pork roast,** which has more fat than the adjacent center loin rib roast, but because of the presence of the blade bone is more difficult to carve. The **boneless blade-end loin roast** alleviates the carving problem and has good flavor despite the absence of bones (I think bone-on meat always tastes better). This roast weighs about 3 to 4 pounds and is perfect for 4 to 6 people. If you like your pork well done, there is ample fat in this roast to still remain juicy. If you want to serve your guests a large and spectacular roast, get your butcher to sell you a pork loin with the blade end still attached to the rib section. This will give you an 11-rib roast, weighing 8 to 10 pounds, and if the butcher removes the chine bone and the blade bone and meat above it, you can easily carve this roast into 10 single chops. As a boneless roast, this would also be excellent for a group of 10.

Next on my list of favorite cuts for roasting is a boneless **Boston butt,** especially when I'm in the mood for well-done meat that's roasted long enough to have a beautifully browned exterior. This roast tastes best and is most tender cooked to about 160° F and can even go above 180° F or more and still be juicy if roasted in a slow oven. I make sure to have it tied or netted so that it cooks evenly and stays together during roasting. Usually boneless Boston butts weigh about 4 to 6 pounds and should be kind to your budget. If you can't find a boneless pork butt and it comes with the blade bone attached, this small flat bone is very easy to remove yourself and might be a place to begin developing your boning skills. Once the roast is boned out, make sure to tie it with several loops of string.

Pork tenderloin, the pork equivalent of the beef filet or beef tenderloin, is a very lean, tender muscle. It makes a good roast to serve 2 to 3 people. One tenderloin weighs 12 to 20 ounces and because it's so lean, care must be taken not to overcook it. I recommend flavor brining to insure a juicy and succulent result. You can easily turn a pork tenderloin into something special by butterflying and stuffing it (Spanish Pork Tenderloin Roulade on page 168), or you can tie two tenderloins together so the thin end of one is aligned with the thick end of the other, which gives you a nice cylindrical roast that's ideal for 4 to 6 people. The tenderloin's small size and quick cooking make it ideal for roasting in a covered barbecue. Don't let its higher cost scare you away: There's no waste, so 5 or 6 ounces of uncooked meat makes an adequate serving per person.

The **sirloin end of the pork loin** (that's the area around part of the hip and adjacent to the leg) makes a pretty good roast. Composed of several muscles, it's sold boneless, and weighs 2½ to 3½ pounds, making it ideal for 4 to 6 people. Sirloin is similar in taste to leg, but the meat is a bit leaner, so for the best results I recommend flavor-brining it for 16 o 24 hours before roasting.

My least favorite pork roast is probably the one you're most familiar with—the **boneless loin roast.** This is sold in pieces as small as 2 pounds to an entire pork loin (from blade end through sirloin end) and can weigh as much as 8 to 12 pounds. While it's true that I like the loin areas from the blade and rib areas because they usually have a little intramuscular fat, I do not like the section of the loin that includes the top loin (New York) and short loin (T-bone). This meat is very lean and has the least flavor. Unfortunately, once the whole loin is boned and trimmed down to its eye, it's very difficult to recognize the section of loin you're buying. My best advice when roasting a boneless loin is to flavor-brine it first so that your roast will have more flavor and juiciness. Occasionally you can purchase a double boneless pork loin in which the whole loin is cut in half and the two pieces are tied together. This doubles the diameter of the roast and insures that at least one of the two pieces is from the rib and shoulder area. I prefer these roast to a single loin roast even though it will take longer to cook.

There are a couple of specialty roasts that need mentioning. The **crown roast of pork** is made by tying two center-cut rib roasts (with their chine bones removed) back to back, and then cutting between each rib slightly so the roast can be shaped into a round "crown" with all the rib bones in the center and the meat facing out. This roast looks spectacular and will feed 16 people, with one chop per diner. Usually the center of the roast is filled with a stuffing. The problem is that by the time the stuffing is safely cooked to at least 150° F the surrounding meat is completely overcooked. A better approach is to cook the stuffing separately, then spoon it into the center of the crown roast just before serving. Cook a crown roast exactly as you would any of the recipes for bone-in pork loin rib roasts. The lack of skilled butchers means most of us would be hard-pressed to find one who can put together a crown roast. The option is to do it yourself, which though time-consuming, is not too difficult. For an equally stunning presentation, consider the **double crossed rib pork roast.** Two 8-bone rib roasts are "frenched," meaning that some of the meat is removed from around each rib bone to expose it, and then the roasts are cooked separately and presented on a platter back to back with the ribs interlaced. The roasts can be placed on a bed of stuffing or just presented on the platter as is.

A **fresh pork belly** can be transformed into a very special and unusual roast when stuffed (page 181). A pocket is cut the length of the belly and filled with a mixture of ground pork or sausage, leafy greens, and bread, then sewn closed (or left open). If the skin has been left on, it forms a wonderful crackling crust when the belly is roasted. For a special occasion, when you want to wow your guests with something truly delicious, consider roasting a pork belly, but keep in mind that a little of this rich (read fatty) meat goes a long way.

One of the most glorious roasts of all is a **boneless loin wrapped in skin-on pork belly.** For the recipe for this roast, see David's Porchetta on page 178. If you have a butcher who cuts up whole pigs, ask him to leave the boneless loin attached to the belly, then roll the loin up in the belly so that it surrounds the loin. You will need to trim the belly to a thickness of about ½ inch so that the fatty layer is not too thick and the belly rolls up easily. If you purchase the loin unattached to the belly, then buy a separate piece of belly the same length as the loin you wish to wrap. Shave the fat side of the belly to a thickness of ½ inch and wrap it around the loin so that it just encloses it. Tie in several places with twine to hold the roast together. With skin-on belly, you'll have some fabulous cracklings on the roast as a bonus. If you can't find skin-on belly, use skinless belly but you won't get any cracklings.

Apple and Cornbread–Stuffed Pork Loin with Roasted Apple Gravy

Not only are apples used to stuff this pork loin, but the loin is also baked on apples, which are then served alongside the pork. The "double butterfly" method used to open the pork creates a pinwheel pattern of stuffing in the sliced pork that makes an attractive presentation. Use firm and slightly tart apples such as Granny Smith or Pippin. While ham is optional in the stuffing, it does lend the dish a nice, smoky taste. SERVES 8

Apple and Cornbread Stuffing

1½ tablespoons butter

½ cup finely chopped smoked ham, crumbled cooked country sausage, such as Brown Sugar and Sage Breakfast Patty (page 259, optional), or diced smoked sausage

½ cup finely chopped onion

¼ cup finely chopped celery

Kosher salt

Freshly ground black pepper

¾ cup diced (¼ inch) peeled apple

½ teaspoon dried sage

1½ cups crumbled and dried homemade cornbread or dried cornbread stuffing mix

¼ cup apple juice, or more

1 egg, beaten lightly

1 boneless pork loin (4 pounds)

Kosher salt

Freshly ground black pepper

1 To make the stuffing: Heat the butter in a heavy medium skillet over medium-low heat and add the optional ham or sausage and cook 3 minutes. Add the onion, celery, and a pinch each of salt and pepper. Cover the pan and cook, stirring occasionally, until the vegetables are quite soft, about 10 minutes. Stir in the diced apple and cook 1 minute, stirring until well combined. Transfer the apple mixture to a good-sized bowl. Sprinkle with the sage and stir in the cornbread crumbs, apple juice, and egg. The mixture should be moist but not wet. Add more apple juice if the mixture seems dry. Taste for seasoning and set aside. 2 Preheat the oven to 450° F. 3 To double butterfly the pork loin: Lay the meat, fat side down, on a work surface and make a horizontal lengthwise cut two-thirds of the way into the depth of the loin and about 1 inch from the long edge nearest you, taking care not to cut all the way through. Flip the loin over so that the cut you just made is opposite you. Make another lengthwise cut, again 1 inch from the edge. Open up the two cuts so you have a large rectangle of meat whose diameter is roughly 3 times the thickness of the meat. Place

fat-side down and cover with a sheet of plastic wrap. Using the flat side of a cleaver or a meat pounder, gently flatten the meat to an even thickness. Remove the plastic wrap and spread the apple stuffing evenly over the meat, leaving a generous ¾-inch border. Roll up the meat jelly-roll style so that the stuffing is in a spiral pattern. Tie the roast at 2-inch intervals with butcher's twine. Combine 2 teaspoons salt, 1 teaspoon pepper, and the sage and sprinkle over the roast. 4 Lay the sliced apples on the bottom of a roasting pan just a bit larger than the roast and set the roast, fat-side up, on the apples. Put the roast in the oven and cook for 15 minutes. Turn the oven down to 325° F and roast for 45 minutes. Check the internal temperature of the roast with an instant-read thermometer: The roast is done when it reaches 140° to 145° F. If it is not ready, continue to roast, checking the temperature every 10 minutes. When the roast is done, transfer it to a cutting board, tent loosely with foil, and let rest for at least 10 minutes while you make the sauce. 5 With a slotted spoon, transfer the apples in the roasting pan to a bowl and keep warm. Pour off any fat from the roasting pan, leaving the meat juices on the bottom. Put the pan over medium-high heat, add the Calvados, and deglaze the pan allowing the alcohol to burn off, about 15 seconds. Transfer to a small saucepan and add the stock apple juice and cream. Increase the heat to high and bring the liquid to a boil. Simmer, stirring, until reduced by half. Taste for salt and pepper. Keep the sauce warm while you carve the pork roast. 6 Remove the twine from the roast and cut it into ½-inch-thick slices. (If you cut the slices too thin, they will fall apart.) Arrange the pork on a serving platter. Spoon the sliced apples around the meat and pour the sauce over all.

1 teaspoon dried sage

3 medium apples, peeled, halved, cored, and cut into ½-inch slices

¼ cup Calvados or apple brandy

1¼ cups Dark Pork Stock (page 87), homemade chicken stock, or canned low-sodium chicken broth

1 cup apple juice or cider

¼ cup heavy cream

Capezana's Roast Pork with Fresh Grape Juice

A few years ago, my wife and I were guest chefs at Capezana, a cooking school on a wine and olive oil estate in the Tuscan hills. Besides the excellent salami made by the Italian butchers and some of the sausages made by me, we ate wonderful simple meals prepared by the estate's resident chef. One of our favorites was a guinea hen roasted with the juice made from pureeing fresh grapes rather than the more traditional and predictable wine. In experimenting with this method, I found that it's a great technique for roasting pork loin as well. Try it yourself with red seedless grapes such as the Ruby Red variety. SERVES 6

Capezana Sage Rub

16 sage leaves

1 sprig fresh rosemary (4 inches), leaves removed and stems discarded

2 teaspoons kosher salt

1 teaspoon freshly ground black pepper

1 bone-in loin pork roast (6 bones), chine removed (about 4 pounds)

1 pound seedless red grapes (enough to make 2 cups grape juice)

1 cup finely chopped onions

½ cup finely chopped celery

½ cup finely chopped carrot

6 garlic cloves

2 tablespoons olive oil

2 teaspoons cornstarch mixed with 2 tablespoons of water (optional)

Fresh grapes and sage leaves, for garnish

1 To make the rub: Finely chop the sage and rosemary leaves and combine with the salt and pepper in a small bowl. 2 Cut some slashes in the fat side of the pork roast and rub the herb mixture into the slashes and all over the surface of the meat. 3 Puree the grapes in a blender. Set the juice aside. 4 Preheat the oven to 450° F. 5 Scatter the onions, celery, carrot, and garlic in a roasting pan, sprinkle with salt and pepper, and drizzle with the olive oil. Place the pork roast, fat-side up, on the vegetables. Put in the preheated oven for 15 minutes. Lower the temperature to 325° F. Pour 1 cup of the grape juice over the roast and roast, adding water if the juice completely evaporates. After 45 minutes, begin checking the internal temperature and remove the roast when it reaches 140° to 145° F on an instant-read thermometer, which may take a total time of 1 to 1¼ hours. Transfer the roast to a platter and cover loosely with foil for 15 minutes while you prepare the sauce. 6 Put the roasting pan over medium-high heat and add the remaining 1 cup grape juice. Bring to a boil, scraping up any browned bits from the bottom of the pan. Transfer the contents of the roasting pan

to a small saucepan, let stand a few minutes, and remove the fat from the surface. Reduce the pan juices over high heat until slightly syrupy. If you'd like a fresher grape taste, reduce the sauce less and thicken it with the cornstarch-water mixture by adding to the sauce and bringing it to a boil so it becomes syrupy. 7 To serve, separate the bones from the meat and cut into individual rib bones. Slice the meat into ½-inch slices and pour the sauce over them. Garnish the platter with some fresh grapes, sage leaves, and the separated rib bones.

Nancy's Fennel-Brined Roast Pork Loin

Flavor-brining pork loin is standard procedure at Boulevard restaurant. Over the years, my wife has come up with many brine variations, but she particularly likes this one with fresh fennel because it seems not only to enhance the juiciness of the pork but also brings out some of the subtle licorice undertones inherent in roasted pork. I like to use this brine for pork chops and tenderloins as well, especially if they're going on the grill. SERVES 6

1 To make the brine: In a large bowl combine the water, sugar, and salt. Stir until the salt and sugar are dissolved. In a small skillet toast the fennel seeds until fragrant, then crush them in a mortar and pestle or spice grinder. Add to the brine with the chopped fennel fronds and Pernod. 2 Put the pork roast in a large zip-lock plastic bag and add the brine. Seal and refrigerate for 48 hours. 3 Preheat the oven to 325° F. 4 Remove the pork from the brine, rinse, and pat dry with paper towels. Discard the brine. 5 In a medium-large skillet heat the olive oil over medium-high heat. Add the pork and brown on all sides, about 10 minutes. Mix together the pepper, fennel fronds, garlic, and rosemary. Pat onto the pork. Put the pork in a small roasting pan or baking dish (you could also use the skillet if it has an oven-proof handle) and roast in the oven until the internal temperature reaches 140° to 145° F on an instant-read thermometer. Begin checking after 45 minutes, but it may take up to 1¼ hours for rib-on roast. Remove the roast from the oven, cover loosely with foil, and let stand for 10 minutes before slicing. Carve into chops with the bones attached.

Fresh Fennel Brine

2 quarts water

½ cup sugar

½ cup kosher salt

2 tablespoons fennel seeds

1 cup chopped fennel fronds

¼ cup Pernod

1 (6-rib) pork loin (about 4 pounds) or a 3-pound boneless pork loin

2 teaspoons olive oil

1 teaspoon freshly ground black pepper

¼ cup chopped fennel fronds

2 teaspoons minced garlic

1 teaspoon chopped rosemary

Master Recipe: Grilled Pork Tenderloin

See Pork Tenderloin in Best Pork Cuts for Roasts on page 156.

For the best results, tenderloins should be flavored first. Any of the recipes in this book for Dry Rubs, Pastes, or Wet Marinades can be used, but the easiest way to insure flavor and juiciness with this ultra-lean cut is to flavor-brine it (pages 29 to 32). If you want to go a step further, after it's been brined, season the meat with a dry rub, omitting the salt from the recipe. I particularly like Franco's Rosticiana Rib Rub (page 150), or for the master recipe below, try an Asian dry rub, like the one used for the Hong Kong–Style Ribs (page 149).

Tenderloins can be grilled directly over the coals, or seared and then grill-roasted indirectly in a covered barbecue. For this particular recipe, I prefer the gentler method of grill-roasting because the sugar in the brine may burn in the time it takes the meat to cook directly over the coals. I've given instructions for both methods. SERVES 4 TO 6

Soy-Orange Brine

½ cup soy sauce

1 tablespoon finely chopped fresh ginger

2 (2-inch) strips orange zest

1¼ cups orange juice

2 tablespoons kosher salt

2 tablespoons brown sugar

½ teaspoon Chinese five-spice powder

1 cup ice cubes

2 pork tenderloins
(¾ to 1¼ pounds each)

½ recipe dry rub, such as Hong Kong Spice Rub (page 149), without the salt (optional)

1 To make the brine: Put the soy, ginger, and orange zest in a small saucepan and bring to a boil over high heat. Reduce the heat to maintain a simmer and cook 2 minutes. Remove from the heat and set aside to cool. (This step creates an infusion that intensifies the flavor of the ginger and orange zest.) 2 Pour the orange juice into a bowl and stir in the salt and brown sugar until completely dissolved. Add the five-spice powder and the soy infusion, including the ginger and orange zest. Stir in the ice cubes to cool the mixture to at least 45° F. 3 Put the tenderloins in a 1-gallon zip-lock plastic bag, pour in the brine, seal the bag, and refrigerate for 4 to 6 hours (on the longer side for larger tenderloins), turning the bag occasionally to redistribute the marinade. 4 Remove the tenderloins from the brine, pat dry with paper towels, and coat with the optional dry rub. At this point you can continue with the recipe or wrap the tenderloins well in plastic wrap and refrigerate them until you're ready to grill them or for up to 24 hours. 5 **To cook the tenderloins over direct heat:** Prepare a charcoal grill or gas grill and

add 2 cups soaked wood chunks or chips if desired. Put the meat directly above the hottest part of the grill. If any flaming occurs, cover the grill; if you're not using a covered grill, move the pork to a cooler area. Sear the meat for about 1½ minutes on each side. Move the meat to a cooler section, cover, and cook for 2 to 3 minutes more per side, or until the meat is firm to the touch and the internal temperature is 140° to 145° F. If you're using a gas grill, continue to cook the meat over direct heat for 2 to 3 minutes more per side, cover, and move the pork to a turned-off area of the grill if flaming occurs, then move back to the heated area. Note that the meat will take 7 to 9 minutes total time to cook, whether on a charcoal or gas grill. 6 Transfer the tenderloins to a platter and cover loosely with foil. Let rest 5 minutes before carving into ½-inch slices. 7 **To cook the tenderloins over indirect heat (grill-roast):** Prepare a charcoal grill or preheat both sides of a gas grill: If using charcoal, once the coals are burning, bank them on one side of the grate with a drip pan placed underneath. (You can sprinkle 2 cups of soaked hardwood chips over the coals at this point.) If you're using a gas grill, shut off the burners on one side. 8 Sear the tenderloins on all sides directly over the coals or the gas flame, about 3 to 4 minutes total. Then move them either over the drip pan in the charcoal grill or to the unheated part of the gas grill. Cover and roast for 10 to 15 minutes, or until the internal temperature is 140° to 145° F. 9 Transfer the tenderloins to a platter and cover loosely with foil. Let rest 5 minutes before carving into ½-inch slices.

CHEF'S NOTES: Follow the instructions in the Master Recipe above, but vary the flavors by using a different brine, marinade, or dry rub. If sugar or another sweetener is not an ingredient, then you can cook the tenderloins over direct heat. An even quicker method for grilling tenderloins is to butterfly them, or cut them in half lengthwise, then gently pound the meat to a ¼- to ½-inch thickness. These thinner pieces will brine in 2 hours. You can also marinate them at room temperature 1 to 2 hours, or marinate them in the refrigerator for 4 hours. Grill them directly over coals for 2 to 3 minutes per side, taking care that they don't overcook since they are so thin. For best results, I recommend that you use a Flavor Brine to ensure these lean, thin cuts don't become too dry.

Stovetop-Smoked Pork Tenderloin 🐖

We all know that pork makes a perfect candidate for smoke-cooking: Think of bacon or ham that has spent days in the smokehouse. Lately, however, I've discovered the joys of the stovetop smoker, a simple device that allows me to smoke small, lean cuts of meat, like pork tenderloin, quickly, with a minimum of fuss, regardless of the weather. The stovetop smoker is basically a rectangular box with a drip pan and rack for the food. Small wood chips or sawdust are spread in the bottom and then the smoker is heated on the stove, causing the wood to smolder and smoke. The food is added, the lid on the box is closed, and within minutes I have a smoky little piece of meat ready for serving or saving. I've found that while not necessary, brining the pork, as in this recipe, helps to add a little more flavor and complement the smoky taste. These tenderloins are flavor-brined for longer than I normally recommend because they should be a little saltier to stand up to the intense smoke of the stovetop smoker. SERVES 6

Maple Brine

¼ cup maple syrup

3 cups water

¼ cup kosher salt

1 cup ice cubes

2 pork tenderloins
(1 to 1¼ pounds each)

1 tablespoon peanut oil

1 In a bowl stir together the maple syrup, water, and salt until the salt dissolves. Stir in the ice cubes to cool the mixture to 45° F or below. 2 Put the tenderloins in a 1-gallon zip-lock plastic bag and pour in the brine. Seal the bag and refrigerate for 16 to 24 hours. Remove tenderloins from the brine and pat dry with paper towels. 3 In a large skillet, heat the oil over medium-high heat. Add the tenderloins and cook, turning to brown them on all sides, about 5 minutes. Remove from the heat. 4 Sprinkle ½ cup wood chips or sawdust on the bottom of a stovetop smoker. Place the smoker's drip pan on top of the wood chips and put the tenderloins on the drip pan rack. Heat the smoker over medium-high heat until the wood begins to smoke, then close the smoker lid. Reduce the heat to medium. After 15 minutes, remove the lid and check the internal temperature of the pork. The pork is done when the internal temperature is 140° to 145° F on an instant-read thermometer. If necessary, replace the lid and continue to cook until the desired temperature is reached, checking at 5-minute intervals. (You may need to add more chips or sawdust.) Remove the tenderloins to a platter and let rest 5 minutes before slicing and serving.

CHEF'S NOTES: While smoking with a stovetop smoker is a simple process, you need a good exhaust hood and it must be kept running throughout the smoking process. If you don't have a good exhaust hood, then put your stovetop smoker on a hotplate outdoors or on a hot gas or charcoal grill. 🐖 Use only chips or sawdust provided by the stovetop smoker manufacturer or purchase wood chips or sawdust that are meant to be used for smoking 🐖 Leftover smoked tenderloin is delicious cold in sandwiches (like a mild ham). Or slice, briefly pan-fry, and serve for breakfast.

Green Olive–Stuffed Pork Tenderloin 🐖

This simple recipe takes the somewhat bland pork tenderloin to new heights. The tart and earthy flavors of the olives enhance the sweet and subtle flavor of the pork. I drew inspiration for this dish from a stuffed duck breast recipe that my wife, Nancy Oakes, learned while attending a class in the Napa Valley taught by cookbook author Patricia Wells. Be sure to save any leftover pork for sandwiches. In fact, you may want to make this to use specifically in sandwiches. SERVES 4 WITH LEFTOVERS

1 Preheat the oven to 450° F. 2 Lay the tenderloins parallel to each other with the thin end of one next to the thick end of the other (so that you end up with a roast that is evenly thick from end to end). With your hand lightly press on the tenderloins to flatten them a bit. 3 Squeeze each olive between your thumb and forefinger to pop out the pit, then roughly chop the olives. Place a layer of olives over one of the tenderloins. Place the other tenderloin on top and tie the roast at 2-inch intervals with butcher's twine. 4 Sprinkle the tenderloins all over with the thyme, salt, and pepper. 5 Heat a heavy ovenproof skillet over medium-high heat and add the of olive oil.

2 pork tenderloins
(¾ to 1¼ pounds each)

⅔ cup olives, preferably French *picholine*, or other mild-brined green olives

2 teaspoons chopped fresh thyme

Kosher salt

Freshly ground black pepper

1 tablespoon olive oil

Place the tenderloins in the pan and brown on all sides for about 3 to 5 minutes. Put the pan into the oven and roast. After 15 minutes, begin checking the internal temperature with an instant-read thermometer, checking every 5 minutes, until the pork registers 140° to 145° F. When done, remove the tenderloins from the skillet to a platter, cover loosely with foil, and set aside to rest for 10 minutes. 6 Remove the twine from the roast, cut the tenderloins into 1-inch-thick slices, and serve.

Roasted Double Pork Tenderloin Stuffed with Prosciutto and Herbs with Mushroom Pan Sauce

🐷 A savory stuffing stretches both the meat to feed more people and adds flavor and interest that would not be present by just seasoning the meat on the outside. It's a kind of inside-outside approach to flavoring that I like very much. To enhance the roast even further, I make a quick pan sauce with mushrooms and dry vermouth, but you can forgo it if you're pressed for time. SERVES 6

2 pork tenderloins
(1 to 1¼ pounds each)

Prosciutto and Herb Stuffing

2 thin slices prosciutto

½ cup fresh bread crumbs

1 teaspoon chopped fresh thyme

1 teaspoon chopped fresh rosemary

Freshly ground black pepper

1 tablespoon olive oil

Kosher salt

Freshly ground black pepper

½ teaspoon chopped fresh thyme

½ teaspoon chopped fresh rosemary

2 tablespoons olive oil

1 Preheat the oven to 450° F. 2 Lay the tenderloins parallel to each other with the thin end of one next to the thick end of the other (so that you end up with a roast that is evenly thick from end to end). With your hand lightly press on the tenderloins to flatten them a bit. 3 To make the stuffing: Cut the prosciutto slices into strips as wide as the pork and lay the strips over one of the tenderloins. 4 In a bowl, combine the bread crumbs, thyme, rosemary, pepper, and olive oil; spread evenly over the prosciutto. Place the other tenderloin on top and tie the roast at 2-inch intervals with butcher's twine. 5 Sprinkle the roast all over with salt, pepper, thyme, and rosemary. 6 Heat a heavy ovenproof skillet (large enough to hold the double tenderloin) over medium-high heat and add the remaining tablespoon of olive oil. Place the roast in the pan and brown on all sides for

about 3 to 5 minutes. Transfer the pan to the oven and roast. After 15 minutes, begin checking the internal temperature of the roast every 5 minutes with an instant-read thermometer until the pork registers 140° to 145° F. When done, remove the roast from the skillet to a platter, cover loosely with foil, and set aside to rest for 10 minutes, while you make the sauce.

7 To make the pan sauce: Put the roasting skillet over medium-high heat, add the mushrooms, and sauté for 2 minutes or until they start to color. Add the garlic and sauté for another 30 seconds. Add the vermouth and chicken stock. Bring to a boil, scraping any browned bits from the bottom of the pan, and reduce until the liquid begins to thicken, about 10 minutes. Stir in the butter until melted, then season with salt and pepper. 8 To serve, remove the twine from the roast, cut it into ¾- to 1-inch-thick medallions, and arrange them on the platter. Pour the mushroom sauce over the slices and sprinkle with the parsley.

CHEF'S NOTE: To vary or add additional flavors to the stuffing, substitute sage and savory or sweet basil and marjoram. Instead of prosciutto, try this roast with thinly sliced Westphalian ham, dry coppa, or Italian salami.

Mushroom Pan Sauce

½ pound sliced mushrooms, domestic or wild, or a mixture (about 2 cups)

1 teaspoon minced garlic

¾ cup dry vermouth

1 cup chicken stock or canned low-sodium chicken broth

2 tablespoons butter

Kosher salt

Freshly ground black pepper

2 tablespoons chopped fresh parsley, for garnish

Spanish Pork Tenderloin Roulade

🐖 I first encountered piquillo peppers when dining at an *asador*—a restaurant specializing in roasted meats—outside Seville. This *asador* specialized in two things: whole roasted baby lamb and whole roasted baby pig, cooked in giant hearth ovens and served with side dishes of stewed white beans and plates of deep-red piquillo peppers. Catalonian Romesco sauce is typically served with fish and poultry; I think it really perks up pork. SERVES 6 TO 8

2 pork tenderloins
(1 to 1¼ pounds each)

Kale Stuffing

2 teaspoons olive oil

½ cup diced red onion

1 teaspoon minced garlic

1 pound kale, rinsed and drained, stems discarded and leaves cut in thin julienne strips

1 tablespoon sherry vinegar

2 teaspoons honey

½ cup water

4 slices Serrano ham or prosciutto

1 (8-ounce) jar piquillo peppers, drained (see Chef's Notes)

Kosher salt

Freshly ground black pepper

1 tablespoon olive oil

1 To butterfly the tenderloins: make a deep lengthwise cut down the center, being careful not to cut all the way through. Open the tenderloin up like a book. Place the opened tenderloin between two pieces of plastic wrap. Pound with a meat mallet until ¼ inch thick. Repeat with the other tenderloin. 2 To make the stuffing: Heat the olive oil in a large skillet over medium heat. Add the onion and cook until lightly golden, about 6 to 8 minutes. Add the garlic and cook 1 minute more. Add the kale, vinegar, honey, and water. Increase the heat to high and continue to cook, stirring constantly, until the kale is wilted, about 2 minutes. Drain and set aside. 3 Lay 2 slices of ham or prosciutto over each butterflied tenderloin. Top with half of the kale stuffing, leaving a ¼-inch border. Carefully open the peppers and lay a single layer over the kale. Roll up each tenderloin and tie at 2-inch intervals with butcher's twine. 4 Preheat the oven to 450° F. 5 Sprinkle the tenderloins all over with salt and pepper. 6 Heat a heavy ovenproof skillet over medium-high heat and add the olive oil. Place the tenderloins in the pan and brown on all sides for about 3 to 5 minutes. Transfer the pan to the oven and roast. After 15 minutes, begin checking the internal temperature with an instant-read thermometer, checking every 5 minutes until the pork registers 140° to 145° F. When done, remove the tenderloins from the skillet to a platter, cover loosely with foil, and set aside to rest for 10 minutes. Remove the twine from the tenderloins, cut them

into ½-inch-thick slices, and serve with Romesco sauce.

7 For the Romesco sauce: In a food processor fitted with the metal blade, grind the almonds until they form a thick paste. Add the bread crumbs, olive oil, peppers, and capers and process until smooth. Taste for salt and pepper. Transfer to a serving bowl.

CHEF'S NOTES: To toast the almonds, spread them on a baking sheet and roast in a 350° F oven for 10 to 15 minutes, stirring occasionally, until lightly browned and the nuts give off an aroma. ▰ Piquillo peppers, which come cooked and peeled in jars or cans, are found in the specialty section of some markets and delis, or can be purchased online (see Sources on page 318). If you can't find piquillos, substitute jarred or canned fire-roasted red bell peppers or whole pimentos.

Romesco Sauce

½ cup toasted almonds (see Chef's Notes)

½ cup fresh bread crumbs

3 tablespoons extra-virgin olive oil

8-ounce piquillo peppers or fire-roasted red bell peppers or pimentos (see Chef's Notes)

1 tablespoon capers, drained

Kosher salt

Freshly ground black pepper

Roast Leg of Pork (Fresh Ham) with Cumin and Fresh Herb Crust

This behemoth roast will awe your guests and won't break your holiday party budget. The best part is that a whole leg of pork, in addition to feeding 15 people, can also provide a weekend's worth of great sandwiches and some mighty fine leftovers for stews.

SERVES 15 WITH LEFTOVERS

Cumin and Fresh Herb Rub

2 tablespoons chopped fresh basil or 2 teaspoons dried

2 tablespoons chopped fresh thyme or 1 tablespoon dried

1 tablespoon chopped fresh rosemary

1 tablespoon chopped fresh sage or 1½ teaspoons dried

1 tablespoon cumin seeds

2 teaspoons ground coriander

2 tablespoons chopped garlic

3 tablespoons kosher salt

2 tablespoons coarsely ground fresh black pepper

2 tablespoons olive oil

1 (16- to 20-pound) whole leg of pork, aitchbone and leg bone removed, skin left on

3 tablespoons olive oil

1 To make the rub: Put all of the ingredients for the rub in the bowl of a food processor and process for 30 seconds. Set aside. 2 Preheat the oven to 450° F and put a rack in the lower third of the oven. 3 Using your hands, smear about a third of the herb rub into the pocket left by the removal of the bone. Using butcher's twine, tie the roast in 4 or 5 places. With the tip of a sharp knife puncture the skin all over to produce dozens of little holes (this will help the skin become crisp and crackly). Then make several long slashes about 2 inches apart and about ¼ inch deep over the surface of the skin. Brush the skin with the olive oil and rub the remaining herb mixture all over the surface of the skin and into the slashes. Put the roast, skin-side up, in a large roasting pan. 4 Roast the pork for 20 minutes. Turn the heat down to 325° F. Turn the roasting pan occasionally to brown the roast evenly. Continue to cook for 1½ hours more, then turn the roasting pan again. Roast another 2 hours and turn the pan again. Now, begin checking the internal temperature of the roast with an instant-read thermometer, checking every 15 minutes or so until the temperature reaches 140° to 145° F. 5 Remove and let rest at least 30 to 45 minutes before carving. The skin should be crisp and crackling. 6 To serve, remove the skin from the roast. Slice the roast and serve with pieces of the skin.

Slow-Roasted Picnic Shoulder (or 9-Hour Pork Roast)

🐖 I found several versions of slow-roasted pork shoulder in my research. Some recipes instruct to leave the pork in the oven for as long as 24 hours. The point is, by slow-roasting the picnic shoulder, a chewy cut full of gristle, it becomes amazingly tender and succulent. This can happen in as few as 9 hours, or as many as 16 hours. (Twenty-four hours is overkill in my opinion and you may wind up with a dried-out mess.) My guess is that this method originated in Italian villages, where pieces of pork were brought to the communal oven to cook slowly overnight in the heat that remained from the day's bread baking. SERVES 8

1 Preheat the oven to 450° F. 2 Using a very sharp knife or box-cutter, score the pork skin and fat with slashes about ½ inch wide that come just short of cutting into the meat. 3 To make the rub: In a food processor fitted with the metal blade, puree the garlic, salt, rosemary, coriander, ground fennel seeds, red pepper flakes with the olive oil to from a paste. 4 Massage the paste into the pork shoulder, making sure to cover all the surfaces and rubbing the paste into the slits. Put the pork on a rack in a roasting pan, brush with some of the lemon juice, and put in the oven. After 30 minutes, lower the temperature to 250° F. Roast until the meat is very tender and the skin is crisp, at least 8 hours and up to 16 hours; the meat should fall from the bone. Brush with lemon juice several times during roasting. You can also turn the shoulder a few times during roasting so that it cooks evenly. 5 To serve, give each person some of the skin and meat, from all parts of the roast.

1 whole skin-on pork picnic shoulder (about 6 to 8 pounds)

Garlic-Fennel Seed Rub

6 garlic cloves, chopped

1 teaspoon kosher salt

2 teaspoons chopped fresh rosemary

½ teaspoon ground coriander

¼ cup fennel seeds, ground in a spice grinder or crushed in a mortar and pestle

2 teaspoons crushed red pepper flakes

3 tablespoons olive oil

⅓ cup freshly squeezed lemon juice

Grill-Roasted Pork Shoulder Cuban Style

The Cubans are masters at slow-roasting pork. The pinnacle of their craft is *lechon,* a whole, spit-roasted baby pig. Not many of us have the wherewithal to roast a whole pig, even a small one. Instead, large chunks of pork such as whole legs, Boston butt, or even whole shoulders make a more than adequate substitute. Nowadays when you order *lechon* at a Cuban restaurant, you will more than likely be served roasted leg or even shoulder meat. No matter, it's the tangy marinade that makes this dish so delicious anyway. Some of the marinade is also used to make a sauce for the sliced meat. The meat, by the way, is best cooked well done, to the point where it's falling off the bone. SERVES 8

Cuban Marinade

¼ cup Triple Sec or Grand Marnier

½ cup freshly squeezed lime juice

½ cup freshly squeezed orange juice (sour oranges are preferred)

2 tablespoons brown sugar

1 tablespoon whole cumin seeds

2 tablespoons chopped fresh oregano or 2 teaspoons dried

1 tablespoon grated lime zest

2 tablespoons minced garlic

½ cup soy sauce

2 teaspoons freshly ground black pepper

3 tablespoons olive oil

1 bone-in or boneless Boston butt, 5 to 7 pounds

1 To make the marinade: combine all of the ingredients in a bowl. Set aside ⅓ cup and refrigerate. 2 Place the pork into a 2-gallon zip-lock plastic bag and pour in the marinade. Seal and refrigerate overnight or up to 2 days. Turn the bag from time to time to redistribute the marinade. 3 When ready to grill-roast, remove the pork from the marinade, shake off the excess, and discard the marinade. 4 Set up a charcoal grill with an equal amount of coals banked on opposite sides and a pan in the center to catch the juice. It takes a long time to cook the pork so make sure you have extra coals available to replenish the fire. 5 Place the roast over the drip pan. Cover the grill and adjust the vents to maintain a temperature within the grill of between 300° and 325° F. Add more charcoal as needed. Begin checking the roast after 2 hours. When the meat is fork-tender, the roast is ready to come off the grill. Transfer the pork to a cutting board and cover loosely with foil. Let rest at least 15 minutes or up to 30 minutes. 6 While the roast is cooking, make the sauce: Pour all the sauce ingredients into a saucepan except the optional cilantro and cornstarch. Bring to a boil, reduce the heat to maintain a simmer, and cook for 5 minutes. Adjust the acidity and sweetness to

your taste with additional lime juice and sugar. Stir in the cornstarch mixture and bring to a boil for 30 seconds to thicken slightly. Set aside. Right before you are ready to serve, rewarm the sauce for a moment and stir in the optional cilantro.

7 Carve the roast into ¼-inch-thick slices, arrange on a platter, and drizzle with a little of the sauce, serving the remaining sauce in a sauceboat at the table.

CHEF'S NOTES: Alternatively you can roast the Boston butt in a preheated 325° F oven. The cooking time and range for doneness are roughly the same. ‍🐖 For a special presentation, try to buy a whole pork shoulder (Boston butt and picnic all in one piece). Then double the marinade and sauce recipes and grill-roast the shoulder for 3 to 4 hours. This will serve 12 to 16 people.

Citrus Sauce

⅓ cup reserved Cuban marinade

¾ cup freshly squeezed orange juice

¼ cup freshly squeezed lime juice, or to taste

1 teaspoon sugar, or to taste

½ cup chopped cilantro (optional)

2 teaspoons cornstarch dissolved in 2 tablespoons water

Real Barbecued Pork

This is true Southern barbecue in which meat, usually pork, is slow-roasted with smoke-infused heat. The heat source can be charcoal, gas, or electricity; smoldering logs, chunks of hardwood, chips, or sawdust produce the smoke. The equipment for barbecue can be as simple as a covered kettle-type grill (I use a Weber), a custom-made smoker, an electric heated water-smoker, gas grill, or huge pit hauled by a semi-trailer truck. No matter the equipment, the principle is the same. Highly seasoned pork is cooked very slowly (200° to 250° F) with plenty of smoke until the meat is so tender that it's falling off the bone, or lacking a bone, comes apart with a gentle prod. Once cooked, the meat is wrapped in foil and allowed to rest for up to an hour, then served with sauce on the side.

Some "'cue" experts like to baste their meat during the slow cooking process with a "moppin'" sauce, usually a diluted barbecue sauce or a blend of vinegar and spices. My recipe doesn't require this step because I think the meat gets plenty of flavor from the spice rub, but if moppin' sauce is your thing by all means use one, and then when you're done barbecuing you can come and mop my kitchen floor (just kidding).

The recipe that follows is for Boston butt and was designed for my Weber kettle, but, if you own a water-smoker or other special barbecuing apparatus, consult your owners' manual for how to prepare your barbecue. If you own a gas-fired grill, your major problem may be getting it to provide a consistent source of low heat. In my experience, many gas grills just can't achieve or maintain a low temperature. So before you ruin a perfectly good chunk of meat, make sure your grill will maintain a low heat for a few hours. Also figure out if there's a way to provide smoke (many models come with smoke boxes). You may find that a purchase of a charcoal kettle grill for $100 or less may be the best solution if you want to do barbecue on a regular basis.

This recipe for barbecued Boston butt will give you the classic pulled pork, which can be slapped into buns or eaten as is with some sauce and coleslaw. It reheats well (see Chef's Notes) so you should consider making plenty of it. In fact, if you're going to go to the trouble, invite some friends to keep you company while you tend the grill and help you scarf up the rewards. SERVES 16 TO 20

---

1 Season the Boston butts on all sides with a generous coating of the spice rub and let sit at room temperature for 2 hours. For maximum flavor, wrap each butt in plastic wrap and refrigerate overnight. 2 Set up a covered barbecue grill for indirect grilling by banking 20 to 30 hot briquettes on one side of the grill. Put a drip pan on the other side underneath

the grill rack. Soak 16 hardwood chunks in warm water for at least 2 hours or up to several days and put 4 of these chunks on the coals. Put the pork butts over the drip pan, making sure that there is no fire directly underneath the meat. Cover the grill and if it does not have a built-in thermometer, drop the probe of an instant-read thermometer into a partially opened vent hole. It's very important that a temperature range between 200° and 250° F is maintained at all times. The closer the temperature stays to 200° F the more succulent the meat will be but the longer it will take to cook (up to 12 to 14 hours). At 225° to 250° F, it may be done in 6 to 8 hours. To control the heat of the grill, adjust the bottom and top vents: If it's too hot, partially close the vents and if it's too cold open them wider. From time to time you'll need to add additional coals (about 6 to 10 at a time) and additional wood chunks, 4 chunks at a time. The vents should always be at least partially open because if you close them completely, it may starve the coals of oxygen and they'll die out. Every once in a while you may have to turn the butts if the edges facing the coals are getting too dark.

2 Boston butts, preferably untrimmed (about 6 to 8 pounds each)

1 recipe Bruce's Spice Rub (recipe follows)

Vinegar Sauce

1½ cups cider vinegar

1 tablespoon kosher salt

1 tablespoon sugar

2 teaspoons freshly ground black pepper

2 teaspoons crushed red pepper flakes

Kosher salt

Freshly ground black pepper

Tabasco sauce

3 After approximately 6 hours, begin checking the meat. It's done when it becomes so soft and tender that you can remove a piece with tongs or a fork. When the meat is done (remember that it could take as many as 14 hours) gently lift the meat from the grill, using a large spatula or flat cookie sheet to keep it in one piece. Wrap each butt in heavy-duty foil, then wrap the foil bundle in several layers of newspaper and put them in a pan or on a baking sheet to trap the juices. Let the meat rest for at least 30 minutes or up to 1 hour. 4 Unwrap the pork and pull it apart with a fork or chop it and put it in a large bowl. 5 To make the sauce: Combine the vinegar, salt, sugar, pepper, and pepper flakes and pour about ½ cup over the meat. Toss, taste, and add more vinegar sauce if you'd like. Or simply add more salt, pepper, or Tabasco. When the meat is seasoned to your liking, serve it with coleslaw, baked beans, and soft hamburger buns for those who want to make sandwiches. Have some warm barbecue sauce (page 177) for the table for those who like to use it.

Bruce's Spice Rub for Pork BBQ 🐖 MAKES 1¼ CUPS

The key to this spice rub is to use the freshest dried herbs and spices you can get; not those impotent musty ones that have been sitting on your shelf for a year (or more).

Put all of the ingredients in a pint jar with a tight lid. Seal the jar and shake until the spices and herbs are well combined. Store out of direct light or heat for up to 2 months.

CHEF'S NOTES: Pulled or chopped pork can be wrapped in foil and reheated in a 325° F. oven for 15 minutes. Or you can rewarm the meat gently in the barbecue sauce in a pan on the stove. You can also reheat it, covered, in a microwave. 🐖 Barbecued spareribs are prepared the same way as Boston butts. Regular spareribs will probably require 4 hours of cooking before they're done, which is when the meat begins to pull away from the bone, exposing the rib tips and the ribs are loose enough to twist. At this point, remove the ribs from the barbecue, lay them on a sheet pan covered with foil and several layers of newspapers, and let them rest for at least 20 minutes and up to 40 minutes. Instead of the vinegar sauce, serve the ribs alongside one of the Two Barbecue Sauces (opposite). Figure on one 3-pound slab for 2 to 3 people.

2 tablespoons paprika, preferably Hungarian

2 tablespoons chili powder

2 teaspoons cayenne pepper

2 tablespoons garlic powder

2 tablespoons brown sugar

1 tablespoon ground cumin

1 tablespoon ground coriander

1 tablespoon Colman's dry mustard

2 teaspoons dry sage

2 teaspoons dried oregano

3 tablespoons freshly ground black pepper

⅓ cup kosher salt

Two Barbecue Sauces

Molasses Barbecue Sauce MAKES 3 CUPS

1 tablespoon vegetable oil

½ cup finely chopped onion

1 tablespoon minced garlic

1 cup cider vinegar

⅓ cup Worcestershire sauce

1 cup ketchup

3 tablespoons yellow mustard

2 teaspoons Tabasco

¼ cup unsulfured dark or blackstrap molasses

2 teaspoons lemon zest

Kosher salt

Freshly ground black pepper

Dr Pepper Barbecue Sauce MAKES 2½ CUPS

1 tablespoon vegetable oil

½ cup finely chopped onion

1 tablespoon minced garlic

½ cup cider vinegar

2 tablespoons Worcestershire sauce

1 cup ketchup

3 tablespoons yellow mustard

2 teaspoons Tabasco

½ cup Dr Pepper

1 tablespoon chili powder

1 teaspoon liquid smoke (optional)

Kosher salt

Freshly ground black pepper

To make either sauce: Heat the oil in a medium saucepan over medium heat, add the onion and garlic, and cook until soft, about 5 minutes. Stir in the remaining ingredients and bring the liquid to a boil. Lower the heat to maintain a simmer and cook, uncovered, stirring occasionally, until the sauce is thickened and almost syrupy, about 45 minutes. The sauce will keep, covered, in the refrigerator for up to 2 weeks.

David's Porchetta
(Belly-Wrapped Pork Loin) 🐖 In Northern Italy,

porchetta is usually made by boning an entire 60- to 100-pound pig. The cavity is filled with chunks of meat and/or sausage and sometimes organ meats. Then the pig is roasted slowly until the skin is crackling and crispy. It's often sold at farmers' markets by the kilo or sliced and stuffed into *panini. Porchetta* is a unique and delicious treat and makes for some great "pig-outs."

Peck's, the famous food emporium in Milan, produces one of the best *porchette*. My friend (and Italian cook) David Shalleck worked there and mastered the recipe, but few of us have access to a whole pig, let alone the skill to bone out an entire animal. Instead of a whole pig, David has adapted the recipe to a small but no-less-delicious presentation by wrapping a boneless pork loin in a fresh pork belly. In the animal the loin is attached to the belly. If you know a friendly butcher, you could ask him to sell you some of the boneless loin with the belly attached. Then you can trim the belly down to a thickness of ½ inch and roll the loin up in it, so it's enclosed in a layer of streaky fat with skin all around. In order to keep it rolled and compact you will need to tie it every 2 inches with butcher's twine.

If you can't find a loin piece with the belly attached, the next best thing is to purchase a boneless pork loin from the 8-rib center-cut section and get a separate piece of belly that is the same length as the loin and wide enough to wrap its circumference. Don't worry, though, if it's an inch or two short because you can put it, gap-side down, in the roasting pan. SERVES 12

---

1 For the seasoning blend: Stir all of the seasoning blend ingredients together in a small bowl. (This can be done up to 2 days ahead and refrigerated.) 2 Put the pork belly skin-side down on a work surface. Sprinkle with one third of the seasoning blend, pressing it on to make sure it adheres. Pat the pork loin with another third of the seasoning blend, and put the loin on the bottom third of the belly with the long sides parallel. Roll up the loin inside the belly, then tie the roast at 2-inch intervals with heavy butcher's twine. Rub the remaining seasoning blend over the exterior of the roast. You can either cook it at this point or refrigerate it overnight. You can also use the Chinese method for crispy skin and season the roast right before cooking (see Chef's Note). 3 Preheat the oven to 450° F. 4 Put the roast, seam-side down, on a rack in a roasting pan. Roast for 30 minutes, lower the temperature to 350° F, and continue to cook for 1¼ hours or until an instant-read thermometer registers

140° to 145° F. Rotate the pan in the oven once or twice during cooking so that the roast browns evenly. 5 Transfer the *porchetta* to a cutting board, tent loosely with foil, and let rest for 15 to 30 minutes. 6 To serve, remove the twine and carve the *porchetta* into ½-inch slices. You can serve the roast hot or at room temperature. Or reheat it the next day in a 350° F oven. Warm or cold, *porchetta* makes a great sandwich.

CHEF'S NOTE: The Chinese method for crisp skin: Dissolve 1 tablespoon baking soda and 1 tablespoon kosher salt in 2 cups water. Set aside. Using a stiff wire brush, beat up the skin on the belly to create small puncture holes and a rough texture. With a pastry brush, paint the baking soda mixture all over the skin. Put the roast on a rack in front of a fan to dry for 2 hours, or leave the roast uncovered in the refrigerator for 36 hours or until the skin is dry. Cook the *porchetta* in a 425° F oven for 30 minutes, then sprinkle with the seasoning blend. Return to the oven and lower the temperature to 350° F. When the *porchetta* is done, the skin should be blistered and crisp and look something like Rice Krispies. This method can be used with any skin-on pork roasts. See Franco and Tom's Award-Winning Stuffed Pork Belly on page 181 or Roast Leg-of-Pork (Fresh Ham) with Cumin and Fresh Herb Crust on page 170.

Porchetta Seasoning Blend

1 tablespoon finely chopped lemon zest

1 tablespoon chopped fresh rosemary

1 tablespoon chopped fresh sage

1 tablespoon minced garlic

2 tablespoons fennel seeds, toasted and lightly crushed

6 bay leaves, toasted and ground

2 tablespoons kosher salt

1 tablespoon freshly ground black pepper

1 (4 to 5 pound) skin-on pork belly, fat trimmed ½ inch thick and cut to the same length as the loin

1 (6-pound) boneless pork loin, preferably from the center-cut rib section

Pork Belly

Pork belly, which has so enamored chefs across the country, is the fresh pork belly, before it's been smoked for bacon or cured for pancetta. It's versatile, is incredibly succulent, and most important, popular: Diners (including yours truly) are ordering and loving it. Pork belly is usually served in small portions, most frequently on the appetizer/first course side of the menu, and it lends flavor, texture, and richness to other dishes. Occasionally you'll see chefs use small cubes of pork belly as they would another fatty morsel—*foie gras*—in sauces and stuffings, to enrich side dishes, or as a tasty garnish. What you generally don't see is a big, thick slab of pork belly plunked on a plate next to some mashed potatoes. It's best in small bites that serve to elevate a dish in richness and complexity.

Even as fresh pork belly gains in popularity, it's still difficult to find in your average supermarket. You can ask the meat manager to special order it but that may entail having to buy the entire belly, which could be as much as 12 pounds or more. Chinese markets sell pork belly, as do many Hispanic markets, and sometimes German and Eastern European markets sell it as well. But if you don't live near any ethnic stores, you can order it from an Internet source. An excellent mail-order source for high-quality and exceptional pork is Niman Ranch (www.nimanranch.com), which carries both skin-on and skinless pork bellies that average 6 to 7 pounds.

Should you be able to buy pork belly, look for the leanest one you can find (even the very leanest have a good amount of fat for braising and other slow-cooking methods). Get one that's well trimmed into a nice rectangle, and leave the skin on for braising and roasting (if you like the taste and texture of skin), or ask to have the skin removed. If you're going to use the belly to make your own bacon or pancetta, have the skin removed, which makes it easier to slice and fry. And please don't ignore pork belly simply cured in brine, as in the recipe for Petit Salé of Pork (page 292): cured belly is a great addition to soups or stews (especially Choucroute Garni on page 242), or Pot-au-Feu (page 213).

Franco and Tom's Award-Winning Stuffed Pork Belly

When the National Pork Producers' Council invited professional chefs to send their best pork recipes for its contest called Taste of Elegance, they never imagined that a recipe made with fresh pork belly would ever be submitted, much less win a $2,000 runner-up prize—usually the contest is won by recipes featuring the more popular tenderloin or loin cuts. While pork belly is not a roast for dieters, it is certainly worth making for special occasions. And if you do try it, you'll easily see how it won such high honors.

Franco Dunn and Tom Oden are Italian-American chefs, co-owners of Santi, a restaurant in the north Sonoma wine area of Geyserville, California. SERVES 6 TO 8 WITH LEFTOVERS

1 To make the stuffing: First prepare the chard by stripping the leaves from the stems. Cut the stems crosswise into ½-inch pieces and the leaves into 1-inch strips; set aside. 2 Heat the olive oil in a large skillet over medium heat, add the onions, and cook until soft and translucent, about 5 minutes. Add the chard stems and cook until softened, about 3 minutes. Stir in the chard leaves, garlic, and red pepper flakes, and cook and toss until the chard is wilted and any liquid that's been released by the chard has evaporated, about 4 minutes. Put the chard mixture in a medium mixing bowl, and let cool. Add the ground pork and egg. Squeeze the bread crumbs to remove any remaining milk, then add to the chard-pork mixture. Drain the currants and add them to the bowl along with the toasted pine nuts, rosemary, nutmeg, 2 teaspoons kosher salt, and 1 teaspoon freshly ground black pepper. Stir until the stuffing mixture is well

Stuffing

12 to 14 ounces Swiss chard, cleaned

1 tablespoon olive oil

1½ cups diced onions

1 large garlic clove, finely chopped

¼ teaspoon crushed red pepper flakes

1 pound ground pork or mild Italian sausage, removed from casings

1 large egg, beaten lightly

1 cup fresh bread crumbs soaked in ½ cup milk

2 tablespoons currants or raisins soaked in hot water until soft, about 15 minutes

3 tablespoons pine nuts toasted in a 350° F oven for 10 minutes until golden

1 teaspoon fresh chopped rosemary

Pinch grated nutmeg

Kosher salt

Freshly ground black pepper

½ skin-on pork belly (about 5 pounds)

combined. 3 Prepare the pork belly for stuffing by cutting a pocket in the meat: Place belly, skin side up, on work surface. Starting on one long side of the belly, with your knife parallel to the cutting board, insert the knife about ½ inch down from the skin, and 1 inch from side of the belly. Cut to the other side. Be careful not to cut through, stopping about 1 inch from the other side. You have now transformed the belly into a hollow tube. Using a very sharp knife or box cutter, score the skin in diagonal lines in both directions, about ¾ inch apart and cutting no more than about ¼ inch deep, being careful not to cut too deeply into the fat. 4 Preheat the oven to 350° F. 5 Firmly pack the stuffing into the pocket, leaving the pocket open. Don't worry if some of the stuffing falls out of the opening. Put the stuffed pork belly, skin-side up, on a rack in a roasting pan, sprinkle generously with salt and freshly ground black pepper, and place in the oven for approximately 2½ hours or until the meat is tender when pierced with a fork (or cut a sliver and taste it). When the pork is done, if the skin is not golden and crackling crisp, increase the heat to 450° and continue to roast for another 20 minutes. Remove the pork belly from the oven, tent with foil, and let rest for 20 minutes or up to 45 minutes before cutting into ¾-inch slices. Consider serving the pork belly alongside mashed potatoes or soft polenta.

CHEF'S NOTES: Leftover pork belly can be sliced and then served at room temperature or reheated for 15 minutes in a 350° F oven. You may also treat the skin using the Chinese method for crisp skin (page 179).

9
Ham

About Ham

"Ham" is a very confusing word indeed. On my first attempt to search the Internet for information on ham I simply typed in "ham." The over 3 million responses I got included: ham—amateur radio operators; ham—overdone actors; ham—various species and/or cuts of meat called "ham"; and ham—a leg of pork.

It is ham—a leg of pork—that we culinarians are most interested in. In butcher terminology, the fresh uncured or unsmoked chunk of meat that is derived from the hind leg of a pig is known as a fresh ham. This 20-pound behemoth makes a superb roast of pork. Technically, when the fresh leg of pork is infused with salt it is referred to as a cured ham. Many other cuts that are infused with salt, such as pork shoulder, front leg, even turkey meat, are also called "hams." I concentrate on ham made from a whole or part of the pig's back leg that is cured in salt, then smoked, aged, or cooked.

There are two ways in which salt is introduced into the meat: either in dry form, by simply being rubbed onto the meat as for country-style hams, prosciutto, and serrano hams, or in wet form called a brine, by dissolving the salt in water and immersing the meat in the salt solution. In both methods, salt penetrates the center of the meat slowly by a process of diffusion. Two to three weeks are needed for complete penetration. To speed things up, nowadays the salt/water solution is forced into the meat by numerous needles that pump the brine in under pressure. This reduces the curing time to only a day or two. But to my taste the result is an ill-considered compromise, producing ham with a soft, spongy texture and flabby taste. When you taste ham produced in the traditional time-intensive way, you too will detect the difference.

Once a ham is cured, smoking is not mandatory, although most American hams are smoked. Some of the most appreciated hams of Europe, such as Prosciutto di Parma from Italy, Serrano ham from Spain, and Bayonne ham from France, are not smoked. These dry-cured hams are simply salted, air-dried, and aged for as long as 2 years. Most are eaten raw, in thin slices.

The smoking of hams with various hard woods is essential for the numerous country hams produced mainly in the southern United States (see Sources on page 318). Each wood—be it hickory, maple, applewood, or pecan—contributes a special flavor to give the ham unique taste.

Great Hams of the World

Prosciutto Cured with salt only; air-dried and aged for at least 10 months and up to 2 years; sliced very thin and eaten raw; the best varieties come from Italy. Those from the Parma region of Italy are called Prosciutto di Parma.

Serrano ham From Spain; cured with salt only; air-dried and aged; like prosciutto, Serrano is sliced thinly and eaten raw; also used to flavor other dishes like pastas, snacks, and soups; the best are aged for 2 years.

Iberico ham Dry-cured Spanish ham from the black-footed Iberico semiwild pig; somewhat fatty and quite expensive; always eaten raw and sliced thin; the most sought-after Iberico hams come from the region of Jabugo, where the pigs gorge on acorns.

Bayonne Another dry-cured ham from the area of Bayonne in southwest France; usually sliced thin and eaten raw; sometimes used in cooked dishes as a flavoring.

Westphalian From Germany; cured with juniper and heavily smoked, often with juniper; usually eaten cold, sliced thin.

Country-style ham Dry-cured, then smoked with various woods and aged for 6 to 18 months; quite salty and in need of soaking (page 195) and long cooking in water before baking; different areas of the U.S. South produce different varieties (see Sources); some producers sell country hams that are soaked and fully cooked at the factory.

Jambon de Paris (Paris style) Mildly cured and either unsmoked or lightly smoked; sold cooked; great in sandwiches, such as *croque monsieur*.

York ham (page 290) A mild English ham similar to jambon de Paris; cured in a salt-water brine, either left unsmoked or lightly smoked, then poached and sometimes glazed and baked; when cold ideal for sandwiches.

Common Types of Wet-Cured American Hams

Deli hams (also called sandwich hams, tavern hams, or buffet hams) Boneless pieces of leg meat reshaped to form oval or large cylindrical "hams." They are sold whole or in pieces in the meat departments of most supermarkets; they are also sold sliced in delicatessens. Although they can be reheated by steaming in a foil-covered roasting pan with a little water on the bottom, the taste and texture tend to be on the rubbery side, qualities that are not improved by heating. They're best eaten cold in sandwiches.

Fully cooked supermarket hams May or may not have a bone, but will have the natural shape of the pork leg or ham and will include some external fat and sometimes the skin. These hams are available whole—10 to 20 pounds—and can also be found in halves, either the butt end or shank end. Most of these hams contain added water and all contain phosphates. The vast majority will be labeled "fully cooked" or "ready-to-eat."

Traditional partially cooked ham These old-fashioned hams can be mail-ordered from small smokehouses in the Southeast, New England, and other parts of the country (see Sources on page 318). Expect to pay more for these hams as they contain less water. They should be cooked to 145° to 150° F so that the final internal temperature of the meat after resting is 150° to 155° F.

Spiral-cut hams These have gained in popularity over the last few years, especially for entertaining and for buffets. Thin slices are cut around the bone by a special spiral-cutting machine. While very convenient to serve, these hams usually come with a very sweet, commercial glaze. Even the simplest homemade glaze of brown sugar and mustard, I think, tastes better and because spiral-cut hams are presliced they have a tendency to dry out when reheated. Give me a good bone-in ham, my own glaze, and a sharp knife, and I'm a happy eater.

Country ham comes from the plantation tradition where certain pigs fattened on peanuts, other nuts, acorns, or corn were processed in the fall and then the hams were hung in the smokehouse to absorb smoke from small smoldering fires. This process called "cold smoking" (smoking without cooking) is still practiced today by small ham producers scattered throughout the South. In olden days, plantations developed a local following built on the taste and quality of their hams. The most famous name in country hams is Smithfield, produced in the town of Smithfield, Virginia. But other great country hams are produced in other areas of

Virginia, North Carolina, Kentucky, Tennessee, and Missouri as well as other states (see Sources). Because country ham is saltier than modern supermarket ham, it is best to use it not as a center-of-the-plate item, but in appetizers and side dishes. Small amounts can be used to embellish green beans, peas, pasta, pies, and potato dishes, while the savory flavors of country ham are ideally paired with cooked oysters, scallops and shirred eggs.

Unlike country ham, the mass-produced hams sold today are more likely to be bathed in a vaporized cloud of atomized liquid smoke. Instead of spending weeks in smokehouses, modern hams spend only a few hours in smokehouses where temperature and humidity is tightly controlled. Once the hams have been flavored by the smoke, these smokehouses become giant ovens that fully cook hams to an internal temperature of 148° F. The results are mild ham with a juicy but soft, spongy/rubbery texture. Not an artisanal product of which to be proud.

MODERN HAM In the old days (15 to 20 years ago), hams were sold "partially cooked" to an internal temperature of 137° F. They required baking by the consumer to an internal temperature of at least 148° F, but more likely to 160° F, to be ready to eat. Usually these hams did not contain any added water and if they did they were required to be labeled with the unmarketable name "imitation ham." Today most hams sold are fully cooked and contain water and phosphates, which are pumped into the meat. The more water they contain, the cheaper the price, the spongier the texture.

These hams may or may not contain a bone. The ones that have the natural shape of a pork leg are best for roasting, while most of the reshaped ones are best used cold as deli meat. Hams suitable for baking are available whole at sizes of 10 to 20 pounds. Half hams, sold as shank or butt halves, are also available. The best of today's hams are simply labeled "ham" and contain no added water and must have at least 20.5 percent of their weight from protein (the rest is the natural water normally contained in pork tissue). Hams labeled "ham with natural juices" (a somewhat misleading term) contains added water and must have at least 18.5 percent protein by weight. Cheaper hams labeled "water added" contain even more water but must have at least 17 percent protein by weight. The cheapest and least appealing of modern hams are labeled "ham and water product" and will contain as much water as the manufacturer cares to pump into it. The percentage of added water is printed on the label and may be in excess of 30 percent.

While I recognize that modern-style processed ham dominates the market, it is worth searching out either an old-fashioned country ham (see Sources) or consider making ham. (See York-Style Ham, page 290).

Ham Cuts, Serving Portions, and Storage

A whole ham, a 10- to 20-pound cured hind leg of pork with the bone intact, is the most flavorful and least wasteful cut. It will serve 20 people, probably with leftovers—perhaps for several lifetimes! A short, plump shape with a stubby rather than elongated shank is the best choice. For smaller groups, you can buy a cut section of the whole ham: either the rounded part called the butt (the upper thigh of the animal) or the lower shank end. The butt half is somewhat more meaty, but more difficult to carve because of the aitchbone. A 6- to 8-pound shank will serve 10 to 12 people, and a 6- to 8-pound butt will serve 12 or more. From the flat-cut end of either butt or shank, several slices of individual ham steaks can be cut off and cooked separately.

Ham is also available boneless—whole, in halves, and in chunks of various sizes. These are not as flavorful as bone-in hams when baked, but they're easier to carve. Small chunks or re-formed hams are best not baked at all (see Deli hams in Common Types of Wet-Cured American Hams).

Allow 8 to 12 ounces per serving for a bone-in ham, 6 to 8 ounces for a boneless ham. Ham is best served warm or cool; it's never as good chilled from the refrigerator. If a rainbow iridescence appears on sliced ham, it's merely due to light refraction on the film caused by the phosphates injected into the ham to help retain moisture after cooking; it doesn't indicate spoilage.

Non—Hind Leg Hams

Smoked Boston butt (also called cottage ham, daisy ham, or smoked Boston shoulder) From the upper shoulder, or Boston butt; great simmered, or sliced and fried.

Picnic ham Made like rear-leg ham, but from the front leg and part of the shoulder. While somewhat fatty, great for cutting up and using in soups, sauerkraut dishes, beans, and other casseroles. Their bargain price is also appealing. I do not, however, recommend using a picnic ham for an attractive sliced ham presentation because it's composed of many muscles and tends to fall apart when sliced.

Tasso Highly seasoned chunks of pork shoulder; heavily smoked, it's used mostly chopped up to flavor such Cajun classics as gumbo, red beans, and jambalaya.

The rule is that all ham must be kept refrigerated—with two notable exceptions: small, unopened canned hams, not labeled perishable, and country hams, or Smithfield hams, which can be kept indefinitely in a cool, dry, dark place. For the best results, uncanned whole hams should not be stored in the original package in the refrigerator for more than 10 days before cooking. Smaller portions should not be kept longer than 3 to 5 days. Sliced ham is best used within 2 days. Freezing any ham is not recommended because of the rapid deterioration of texture and flavor; canned ham is especially vulnerable because of its high water content. Once it's been baked, you can keep ham lightly covered for an additional 7 to 10 days in the refrigerator.

Buried Treasure—A Ham Bone

No, I'm not talking about a treat for Fido. When you cook a whole bone-in ham and have run out of ideas for the leftovers, it's time to consider the ham bone. Even better yet, leave a little meat on the bone and you have all you need to make a great ham stock for such family favorites as Split Pea Soup Van Leeuwenhoekhuis (page 94), or any bean soup. And if you still have a pound or two left over, dice it up and add to the above dishes 5 minutes or so before serving for a little extra flavor.

Master Recipe: Baked Glazed Ham 🐖 While a

sweet glaze makes for a glorious presentation, it only flavors the outside of each ham slice.
I also like to serve an accompanying sauce that guests can add to their ham to suit their own
tastes. Here are recipes for two glazes and two sauces.

Read About Ham (page 186). A WHOLE HAM SERVES 15 TO 20 AND A HALF
HAM 8 TO 10.

---

1 (16- to 20-pound) whole bone-in or boneless ham, or half ham, or 8-pound homemade ham (page 290)

1 recipe Ham Glaze (page 192), or ½ recipe for half ham or boneless homemade ham

1 recipe Ham Sauce (page 194) or ½ recipe for half ham or boneless homemade ham

1 Preheat the oven to 325° F. Trim away any skin and trim external fat to a thickness of about ¼ to ½ inch. Lay ham fat-side up in a sturdy roasting pan. Place a rack low enough in the oven so that the ham does not touch the roof of the oven while baking. Place the ham in the oven. 2 You'll need to roast a whole ham for about 2½ to 3 hours, or approximately 10 minutes per pound. Since today's ham is sold already fully cooked, the purpose of baking it is threefold: to warm it through, to concentrate some of the flavors, and to improve the texture. At 2½ hours, begin monitoring the internal temperature with an instant-read thermometer. If not yet at 130° F, continue to check the ham every 15 minutes. When the temperature reaches 130° F, it is time to apply the glaze. If you don't want to glaze the ham, continue to bake it until it reaches 135° to 140° F. Remove the ham, transfer it to a carving board, and let it rest for 20 to 30 minutes before carving. Tent loosely with foil, if desired. That way the ham can complete its cooking (final temperature will be 5 to 10 degrees more) and the juices can be gently reabsorbed into the meat and not end up on the carving board. While the ham rests is an excellent time to put the finishing touches on the rest of the meal or to finish the sauce you may wish to serve with the ham.

Baking a Ham in a Covered Barbecue

Read about Indirect Grilling (page 47).

Baking a ham in a covered barbecue over indirect heat (grill-roasting) is a wonderful way to enhance the flavor of a store-bought ham with smoky nuances. You can increase the smoky flavor even more by adding soaked hardwood chunks or chips (see Sources on page 318).

Whether you use a gas or a charcoal grill, the technique for cooking the ham is the same. The ham is cooked with indirect heat. If using a covered charcoal grill such as a Weber kettle, bank hot coals to opposite sides. About 20 to 30 coals in each pile are enough since you want a moderate heat of between 300° to 350°F for cooking. For a covered gas grill, light the right and left sections, leaving the middle section unlit. Maintain a temperature within the grill of 300° to 350° F.

Place the ham in a roasting pan and add 2 to 3 cups water or about ½ inch water in the bottom of the pan. Place the pan in center of the grill rack so that there is no fire underneath it. Cover the grill and grill indirectly until the center registers an internal temperature of 130° F.

From time to time you may need to add more water to the roasting pan to maintain a level of ½ inch and more coals to the fire. Begin checking the internal temperature of the ham after 2 hours and continue monitoring it every 15 minutes until it reaches 130° F. Since controlling the exact heat of a grill is less precise than an oven, I cannot give you more exact timing information, but it could take anywhere from 2 hours to more than 4 hours to cook your ham.

If you like a little more smoky taste to your ham, add soaked hardwood chips or hardwood chunks to the coals from time to time; if using a gas grill, add chips to the smoking box if one is provided.

Instead of trying to glaze the ham in the grill, which involves increasing the temperature (difficult to do with a charcoal fire but easy with a gas grill), transfer the ham to a preheated indoor oven and follow the instructions for glazing on page 192. If using a gas grill, increase the gas setting to provide a temperature of 425° F inside the grill box and apply the glaze as instructed on page 192). Let the ham rest, carve, and serve your grill-roasted ham as you would the oven version. Whether to serve it with a sauce (page 194) is up to you, but it sure makes for some mighty fine eating.

Glazes, and other flavorings, provide a sweet finish to a ham as well as an appetizing appearance. A coating of melted and caramelized sugar, the simplest glaze, is made by generously sprinkling the surface of the ham with white or brown sugar or even powdered sugar. Amounts are not critical as long as the surface is pretty well covered. The sugar melts and caramelizes by a brief bake of the ham in a hot oven (425° F) for 15 to 20 minutes. Here are a couple of glaze recipes that embellish the sweet theme.

Brown Sugar, Mustard, and Pineapple Glaze
Instead of chopped pineapple you can substitute other cooked or dried fruit such as dried cherries, apricots, prunes, or raisins, briefly soaked in hot water and drained. Or try canned mandarin oranges, canned sour cherries, or peaches.

2 to 3 cups water, chicken stock, or apple cider

½ cup Dijon mustard

1 cup finely chopped canned pineapple or other fruit

1 cup packed light or dark brown sugar

1 cup gingersnaps or dried bread pulsed in a food processor to form crumbs

1 Once the ham reaches an internal temperature of 130° F, remove it from the oven. Turn up the oven to 425° F. 2 Pour the water, stock, or apple cider into the bottom of the roasting pan to a ½-inch depth. The liquid will catch the melting glaze and prevent it from burning on the bottom of the pan as well as provide the base for a delicious sauce. 3 Score the surface of the ham in a crisscross diamond pattern. Brush the mustard over the entire top of the ham. In a small bowl, combine the pineapple and sugar and using a large spoon spread a generous layer over the top surface of the ham, pressing it down with the back of the spoon. Return the ham to the oven. After 10 minutes, the sugar should begin to melt. Sprinkle the gingersnap crumbs over the ham (the crumbs give the surface a crust). Press the crumbs on with your hands to help them adhere and form a thick layer. Bake another 5 to 10 minutes or until the surface has browned a bit and become crusty. Remove the ham, let it rest, and carve as per instructions in the main recipe.

Basic Fruit Glaze   This glaze uses marmalade, jam, or preserves as its base. Orange, lemon, or tangerine marmalade, apricot, peach, plum, cherry, or currant jam, or various berry preserves are all options. The choice is up to you and your own preference. The bread crumbs are your call, too.

1 Pour the liquid into the roasting pan and score the ham as directed in Brown Sugar, Mustard, and Pineapple Glaze. 2 Mix the marmalade, jam, or preserves with the cloves and brown sugar. Spoon the glaze generously over the ham. Apply the crumbs, if desired, pressing them on with your hands to help them adhere. Bake as directed above.

2 to 3 cups water, chicken stock, or apple cider

1½ cups of your favorite marmalade, jam, or preserves

½ teaspoon ground cloves

½ cup packed light brown sugar

1 cup dry bread crumbs or gingersnaps (optional)

Fruit-Flavored Sauce

Use the same choice of marmalade, jam, or preserves for the sauce as you did for the glaze.

Chicken stock

½ cup same marmalade, jam, or preserves used to glaze the ham

2 tablespoons cider vinegar, or more

Kosher salt

Freshly ground black pepper

2 teaspoons cornstarch dissolved in 2 tablespoons water

Once you remove the ham from the oven (or barbecue) place it on a cutting board. Scrape up any baked-on bits stuck to the bottom of the pan into the pan juices. Pour this liquid into a 4-cup glass measuring cup. Remove and discard any fat on the surface and add enough chicken stock to bring the volume up to 2 cups. Strain these juices into a saucepan and stir in the marmalade, jam, or preserves and the vinegar. Bring to a boil, taste for salt and pepper, and add more vinegar to taste. Stir the cornstarch solution and pour it into the pan. Boil, stirring, until the sauce just thickens. You may strain out the bits of fruit or peel from the sauce, if you wish, but I prefer to leave them. Serve in a gravy boat and let guests serve themselves.

Sweet Molasses Mustard Sauce

This sauce is less sweet than the fruit-flavored one above. It's ideal with Brown Sugar, Mustard, and Pineapple Glazed–Ham.

Chicken stock

1 tablespoon blackstrap or dark unsulfured molasses

1 tablespoon dark brown sugar

¼ cup Dijon mustard

Kosher salt

Freshly ground black pepper

2 teaspoons cornstarch dissolved in 2 tablespoons water

Prepare this sauce according to the directions for Fruit-Flavored Sauce. Once you strain the juices into the saucepan, stir in the molasses, brown sugar, and mustard and bring to a boil. Taste for salt and pepper and thicken with the cornstarch mixture as directed. Serve in a gravy boat.

Baked Country Ham 🐖

Unless you live in the South, country ham is rarely found in supermarkets and must be ordered by mail from a regional smokehouse or fancy food catalogue. Country ham is found throughout the South and each area has its own style. I list a number of my favorites in Sources on page 318.

All country hams are quite salty. They may be aged for a few months to more than a year. Both the salt level and how long the ham has been aged will affect how long you will need to soak and cook it. Unfortunately, it's difficult for me to generalize. I recommend taking a conservative approach by trying to extract as much salt as possible from the ham; even then the ham will be salty. Some country ham producers will sell you fully cooked hams that have been soaked and boiled at the smokehouse. This is a good way to begin if you're a novice or wish to send the ham to a Northerner as a gift.

Country ham is an acquired taste; it is not for the timid. The hams are always salty, even after being soaked and parboiled. And since they're aged, they take on some of the characteristics of other aged foods, such as cheese. Some have a whitish blue-green mold on the outside. It's perfectly harmless—just scrub it off before soaking the ham. Real ham lovers think nothing beats the aged flavors of a country ham, which intensify in your mouth, like a well-aged Parmesan. SERVES 16 TO 20

---

1 (12-to 16-pound) country ham

2 cups packed light or dark brown sugar or granulated sugar

1 Wash the ham under cold water, scrubbing the skin with a stiff brush to remove any black pepper coating and mold. 2 Put the ham in a very large pot or tub or in a clean sink big enough so that it can be completely submerged. Cover the ham with cold water and soak for 48 hours, changing the water 6 to 8 times to extract as much salt as possible. Drain and scrub the ham again to remove any remaining mold or pepper. Rinse the ham thoroughly. 3 Put the ham in a very large pot and cover it completely with cold water. Bring to a boil and discard the water. Refill the pot with water to cover the ham, bring the liquid to a boil, and again discard the water. Do this one more time. Finally, cover the ham again with cold water, bring it to a boil, and reduce the heat to barely a simmer. Take care not to let the water actually boil; it should read about 180° F on your instant-read thermometer. Poach the ham at a slow simmer, uncovered, for 4 hours. 4 Slice off a bit of ham and taste it. It should be firm but tender and palatable, and it will probably still be quite salty. You may need to cook it for 1 to 2 more hours, depending on its salt level and how long it was aged. Taste it from time to time to

judge its progress. 5 Once done, you can let the ham cool in its poaching liquid, then remove it, and wrap it loosely in foil. Refrigerate it to bake and glaze the next day. Or, you can bake and glaze it immediately after it's cool. Discard the liquid. 6 Preheat the oven to 350° F. 7 Put the ham on a platter or clean work surface and carefully remove all the skin and any dark or discolored areas of the meat. Trim the fat, leaving a ⅛- to ¼-inch layer, then score the fat in a crisscross diamond pattern across the top. Put the ham, fat-side up, in a foil-lined roasting pan and cook for 30 minutes. Or, if you are cooking the ham directly from the refrigerator, cook it for 1 hour. 8 Increase the heat to 425° F. Spread a generous layer of the brown or granulated sugar over the ham and bake it for 20 to 30 minutes, or until the surface is glazed and browned. 9 Place the ham on a cutting board or platter and let it rest, covered loosely with foil, for 20 to 45 minutes. Cut into thin slices. Serve warm or at room temperature. Leftover ham can be served cold or rewarmed. Thick slices of cooked country ham can be fried and served with steamed greens. The ham can also be used as a flavoring in any recipes calling for bacon or pancetta or use in Pam's Ham and Apple Breakfast Pie (page 61).

CHEF'S NOTES: You may also glaze country ham (see Ham Glazes on page 192) and serve glazed country ham with a sauce (see Ham Sauces on page 194) as well. Another way to glaze a country ham is to sprinkle the surface with a generous layer of confectioners' sugar.

Ham in Tangy Chablis and Mushroom Sauce

It was afternoon and I had just completed a grueling 18-hour plane ride to Paris. My goal was to visit the vineyards of Burgundy with a food and wine-loving pal. We rented a car and headed east but as the dinner hour approached, we had only made it as far as the Chablis area. We pulled off the road into a small village and headed for the restaurant that had the most cars parked outside. While I've long forgotten the name of the village or the restaurant, the meal has stayed fresh in my mind. First came a freshly caught pink trout stuffed with bread crumbs and chunks of smoky bacon, all blanketed with a light cream sauce. Next was one of the most remarkable ham dishes I've ever eaten—thick slices of mildly cured, perfectly juicy ham covered with a sauce of tangy crème fraîche, earthy mushrooms, and early spring peas. Maybe it was the combination of travel fatigue and sleep deprivation, but to this day, I still think that meal was one of the best I've ever eaten in France.

You can certainly use this sauce to pour over reheated leftover baked ham or freshly cooked ham steaks, but the best way to do it justice is to make it with a homemade ham like the York-Style Ham (page 290), which is poached with herbs and vegetables in a court-bouillon of lager or white wine. The poaching liquid can be used to make the sauce. SERVES 6

1 Heat the butter in a large skillet over medium-high heat until it sizzles. Add the shallot and mushrooms, sprinkle with salt and pepper, and cook, stirring frequently, until the mushrooms have exuded their liquid and begin to brown, about 5 to 6 minutes. Set aside. 2 Pour the wine into a medium nonreactive saucepan, bring to a boil over high heat, and reduce to ½ cup. Add the stock and reduce to 1 cup. Add the crème fraîche, and the reserved mushrooms with any accumulated juices and reduce the sauce until it begins to thicken. Stir in the cognac and peas. Cover and cook 3 minutes more. Season to taste with salt and pepper. Keep the sauce warm off the heat. 3 If you've cooked your own ham, slice it, arrange it on a platter, spoon the sauce over it, and serve. If you're using leftover ham slices, put them in a pan, add ½ cup water or stock, cover, and gently rewarm for 3 to 5 minutes. You can also warm the ham in a microwave, again with a little liquid and in a covered container, making sure not to overcook it. Pour off the liquid, arrange the warm slices on a platter, and nap with the sauce. 4 If you use a ham steak, brown it in butter for 3 minutes per side, then cook for 10 minutes at a simmer in stock. Remove the steak and cover in sauce.

2 tablespoons butter

3 tablespoons finely chopped shallot

1 pound mushrooms, thinly sliced

Kosher salt

Freshly ground black pepper

2 cups dry white wine, preferably Chablis

2 cups ham stock (if you've cooked your own ham) or homemade chicken stock

1 cup crème fraîche

2 tablespoons cognac

1 cup fresh sweet peas

2 pounds sliced ham or a 2-pound ham steak

10
Pot Roasts and Other Braises

About Pork Braises

Braising is defined as cooking pieces of meat like roasts, shanks, or bellies in a small amount of liquid in a sealed pot. This can be done on top of the stove or in an oven. The best cut for a pork pot roast is the **Boston butt** (also referred to as pork shoulder butt); it has great flavor, ample fat, and enough connective tissue to give it succulent meat even when cooked to the point of falling apart. Boston butt takes well to many flavors and is the roast of choice for Chinese and Mexican cooks who use strong flavors. A bone-in Boston butt has only a small bone so there is little waste. You can purchase a whole bone-in Boston butt that weighs about 5 to 7 pounds, or a boneless Boston butt that weighs about 4½ to 6½ pounds, and some stores even sell half Boston butts, weighing 2½ to 3½ pounds. Figure on about 8 to 12 ounces of raw meat per serving for most recipes, just the right amount to serve 8 people. Since a boneless Boston butt is composed of several muscles, it's a good idea to tie it or ask your butcher to put it into netting to keep it from falling apart, especially if you are cooking it until fork-tender. Look for a roast that has had the external fat trimmed to no more than ¼ inch thick.

Next to the Boston butt is the arm (front leg) portion of the shoulder known as the **picnic shoulder,** also called **picnic shoulder arm roast.** This roast is usually sold with the bone-in and skin on around the shank portion. It has a good deal of waste from the bone, tendons, and pockets of internal fat, but it is usually inexpensive. A whole picnic shoulder weighs 6 to 8 pounds and some stores sell smaller picnics that have had a couple of arm steaks removed. These may weigh about 4 pounds. If you have a friendly and skilled butcher, you may be able to get him to remove the shank from the picnic, remove the leg bone, and tie it into a cylindrically shaped roast. This would make carving a breeze. Picnic shoulders, when pot-roasted long and slow to well past 170° F, will be tender and very flavorful. Because there is so much waste on a 6- to 8-pound bone-in picnic shoulder, figure that it will feed about 6 people with a little left over if you're lucky.

Heading south towards the ham (ass end) of the pig from the Boston butt is the **blade end of the loin.** The flat T-shaped blade bone extends into this section at the shoulder end and some rib bone is also present. (This is the pork equivalent of a 7-bone blade beef chuck.) As you move to the ham end of the blade roast, the blade bone has tapered off and only rib bones remain. The blade area is composed of several muscles with pockets of fat interspersed between the muscles. This makes the blade roast an ideal candidate for pot-roasting. Purchase a whole blade roast, which should weigh about 4 pounds, or you can purchase a boneless blade roast at about 3 pounds. This should supply enough meat to feed 6 people. Since the roast is composed of many muscle groups, it tends to fall apart as it cooks, so tie it in several loops to hold it together.

Warning: Some so-called butchers who don't know any better may try to sell you **center-cut loin** or **sirloin** as meat suitable for pot-roasting. You will not be happy because the result will be dry and stringy meat. You can use the cuts for braising however, if you pay special attention to prevent the meat from cooking beyond an internal temperature of 145° F.

On the other hand, if you are doing business with a truly skilled butcher who knows how to bone out a fresh ham and sell it as individual roasts, by all means purchase what is called the **knuckle** from the area of the leg around the knee. This is a good cut for pot-roasting since it has ample connective tissue and some fat. Even better, after you ask this butcher to marry you (because his skill with pork makes him a prince), ask him to place two boned knuckles boned side to boned side and tie or net them into a perfect 4 to 6 pound pot roast. Other boneless leg roasts—pork leg-inside roasts, and pork leg-outside roasts—are too lean for pot-roasting but are ideal for dry-heat roasting (page 155).

Casserole-Roasted Pork on a Bed of Cabbage and Sauerkraut

Back when I was a scientist I spent an autumn in Amsterdam as a guest of the Dutch National Cancer Lab. I was housed in one of those narrow little houses for which Amsterdam is known. The house was so narrow that my room was scarcely wider than the single iron bed that occupied most of the space. The kitchen wasn't much larger and the stove had only had two working burners and no oven. Since there was no other common room, the kitchen was where my fellow scientists and I gathered each night. Elected as chef, I had to come up with substantial meals that could be cooked using the limited facilities to feed my colleagues. This pork and cabbage recipe was one of several sauerkraut dishes with which I experimented. In Holland, sauerkraut is sold fresh in bulk and sometimes I could find heads of cabbage pickled whole. While it's hard to get freshly made sauerkraut these days, buy the best brand you can find, preferably *not* canned. SERVES 8

Dutch Pork Rub

1 teaspoon dried sage

1 tablespoon chopped fresh rosemary or thyme or 1 teaspoon dried thyme (not dried rosemary, which I abhor)

1 tablespoon Hungarian paprika

2 teaspoons kosher salt

1 teaspoon freshly ground black pepper

1 (4-to 6-pound) boneless Boston butt, tied or netted

¼ pound slab bacon or salt pork, diced

1½ pounds green head cabbage, thinly sliced

2 medium onions, thinly sliced

1 To make the Dutch rub: Combine the herbs, paprika, salt, and pepper in a small bowl. 2 Rub the seasonings all over the pork. Cover and let stand at room temperature for 1 hour, or wrap in plastic wrap and store overnight in the refrigerator. 3 Preheat the oven to 350° F. 4 In a large casserole or Dutch oven, cook the bacon or salt pork over medium heat until lightly browned, about 7 minutes. Transfer the meat with a slotted spoon (leaving the fat in the pot) to a plate and set aside. Add the pork roast to the pot and brown on all sides in the fat remaining in the pot, about 5 to 7 minutes. Transfer the roast to the plate with the bacon. Discard all but 2 tablespoons of the fat in the pot. Add the cabbage, onions, and carrot, cover, and cook until the vegetables begin to soften, stirring occasionally, about 10 minutes. Stir in the sauerkraut and all the remaining ingredients. Scrape up any

browned bits that have stuck to the bottom of the pot. Put the roast, fat-side up, and bacon back in the pot, on top of the sauerkraut/cabbage mixture. Reduce the heat to a simmer, cover, and cook for about 1½ hours. Check the pot once or twice during cooking for liquid and add more if necessary. Check the meat with an instant-read thermometer; it should be tender and registers 160° to 170° F. Spoon the cabbage mixture and any juices into a shallow bowl or serving platter. Remove the string or netting on the roast, carve it into ½-inch slices, and arrange over the cabbage. Serve immediately.

CHEF'S NOTE: This dish would also be good made with Petit Salé of Pork (page 292), smoked Boston butt (page 188), smoked picnic ham, or a whole smoked pork rib roast. The cooking time will be shorter for the smoked rib roast, about 30 minutes less.

1 carrot, cut in half lengthwise and thinly sliced

1 pound good-quality sauerkraut, drained

½ teaspoon caraway seeds

2 tablespoons Hungarian paprika

2 teaspoons chopped fresh rosemary or thyme

½ teaspoon dry sage

2 bay leaves

1 tablespoon tomato paste

1 teaspoon coarsely ground black pepper

1 cup dark lager, such as dark Dutch or German beer

Alex's Pierna (Banana Leaf–Wrapped Pork)

Throughout the Yucatan Peninsula, pork, wrapped in large banana leaves, is cooked in a rock-lined pit. Our version of that preparation comes from Alex Padilla, one of the senior cooks at Boulevard. Though he's only thirty-three years old, Alex has been working with my wife, Nancy, for seventeen years. This recipe is how pork barbecue is prepared in Alex's native Honduras, where the dish is called *pierna,* but it is very similar to *cochinita pibil* from Mayan Mexico. In Honduras, Alex would use starfruit (also called *carambola*) to make the spice paste, but we substituted kiwis; tomatoes are another choice. SERVES 6 TO 8

2 kiwis, peeled, or 4 medium tomatoes, peeled, seeded, and chopped

¼ cup freshly squeezed lime juice

½ cup orange juice

½ cup roughly chopped red onion

1 tablespoon cumin seeds, toasted

½ bunch cilantro

2 teaspoons dried oregano

3 tablespoons achiote paste or paprika

6 garlic cloves

3 tablespoons olive oil

4 teaspoons kosher salt

2 teaspoons freshly ground black pepper

6 pounds boneless Boston butt, cut into 2 equal pieces

2 (24-inch-long) banana leaves, defrosted if frozen (see Sources on page 318)

Citrus-Marinated Red Onions (recipe follows)

1 Put all of the ingredients except the pork and banana leaves in a blender. Blend until the mixture forms a paste. 2 Spread the paste over all sides of the pork, then put the pork in a zip-lock plastic bag, seal, and refrigerate overnight. 3 Preheat the oven to 375° F. 4 Cut off any long, hard sides of the unfolded banana leaves. Run them, one at a time, over a high flame or hot electric burner until they're softened and shiny. Put the banana leaves in a shallow 9- by 13-inch baking dish and top with pork and any juices from the marinade. Pull the leaves up and tuck in the sides to enclose the pork. Transfer the pork to the oven and bake for 4 hours or until the meat is falling apart. 5 Remove the pork from the banana leaves, and pour off the liquid into a serving dish. (If the liquid is very watery, reduce it just to concentrate the flavors; it doesn't need to be thickened.) Break the pork apart into chunks or shred it and combine with the cooking liquid. Serve with the Citrus-Marinated Red Onions and lots of warm tortillas and rice.

Citrus-Marinated Red Onions

Toss all of the ingredients together in a medium bowl and let marinate at room temperature for 3 hours. To store, cover the bowl and refrigerate for up to 4 days.

CHEF'S NOTE: Banana leaves are sold in Mexican or Asian specialty stores or see Sources (page 318). If you can't find them, use aluminum foil.

4 cups sliced red onions, ¼ inch thick

1½ teaspoons kosher salt

½ teaspoon freshly ground black pepper

½ cup freshly squeezed lime juice

½ cup orange juice

¼ cup chopped cilantro (optional) or 1 teaspoon dried Mexican oregano

Boston Butt Braised in Milk

For many years I taught at a cooking school in San Francisco owned by Loni Kuhn. We became very close friends and I often ate at her home. On one particular occasion she served pork braised in milk. I loved the luscious pork surrounded by clumps of caramelized sauce. Loni learned to make this dish from Italian food expert *extraordinaire*, Marcella Hazan, who often taught at Loni's school. A Boston butt is fattier than the traditional loin used for this recipe, and when braised yields very juicy and tender meat. Serve the pork with brown rice, barley, or spelt. SERVES 4 TO 6

---

1 (3-pound) boneless Boston butt, rolled and tied or netted

Kosher salt

Freshly ground black pepper

1 teaspoon chopped fresh sage

1 teaspoon chopped fresh thyme

1 to 2 tablespoons olive oil

1 tablespoon chopped garlic

4 fresh sage leaves

1 sprig thyme

1 quart whole milk

2 bay leaves

2 tablespoons freshly squeezed lemon juice

Zest from 1 lemon

1 Trim away and discard most of the visible fat from the roast and tie at 2-inch intervals with butcher's twine. In a small bowl combine the 1 teaspoon each of salt and pepper, the sage and thyme and rub all over the meat. You may continue with the recipe at this point or cover the roast with plastic wrap and refrigerate overnight. 2 Preheat the oven to 325° F. 3 Heat 1 tablespoon oil in a heavy casserole (with a lid) or Dutch oven over medium heat. Add the roast and brown it on all sides, about 7 to 10 minutes total. Transfer the roast to a plate and set aside. 4 Pour off and discard all but 1 tablespoon of fat in the pot. Add the garlic, sage leaves, and thyme sprig, and cook over low heat, stirring, for 30 seconds. Add the milk, bay leaves, and lemon juice and zest and bring to a boil, scraping any browned bits from the bottom of the pot. Return the meat to the pot, cover, and braise in the oven for 1 hour and 15 minutes. Remove the cover and continue to braise another 45 minutes or until the meat is fork-tender and the sauce has reduced and formed dark curds. If the sauce has not reduced by the time the pork is tender, transfer the pork to a warm platter and cover with foil. Place the pot on a burner and reduce the liquid, stirring frequently so it does not burn. (The finished sauce will have a nut-brown color with dark curds.) With tongs, remove and discard the thyme sprig, bay leaves, and lemon zest. Taste for salt and pepper. 5 Slice meat into ½-inch-thick slices, arrange on a platter, and spoon the sauce over them. If the sauce is too thick or if it has cooled and congealed, stir in a little water to loosen and thin it.

Italian Porcini and Pork Pot Roast 🐖

While this recipe easily will feed 8, you may wish to serve it to a smaller group so that you will be blessed with some coveted leftovers to use in a great pasta sauce or for Italian-style sandwiches (see Chef's Notes). SERVES 6 WITH LEFTOVERS

1 In a small bowl, combine the fennel seeds, rosemary, salt, and pepper and sprinkle all over the pork roast. Set aside while the mushrooms soak. 2 Put the mushrooms in a 2-cup glass measuring cup and pour the boiling water over them. Soak for at least 1 hour, then drain. Strain the soaking liquid into a bowl and reserve 1 cup. Chop the mushrooms. 3 Preheat the oven to 325° F. 4 Heat the oil in a large casserole (with a lid) or Dutch oven over medium-high heat. Add the pork roast and brown it on all sides, about 7 minutes. Transfer the roast to a plate and pour off and discard all but 2 tablespoons of the fat in the pot. Add the garlic and onions to the pot; reduce the heat to medium, cover, and cook, stirring occasionally, until the vegetables soften, about 5 minutes. 5 Add the 1 cup reserved mushroom soaking liquid, wine, and optional grappa, and scrape up any browned bits from the bottom of the pot. Stir in the tomatoes, stock, and basil and bring the liquid to a boil. Add the chopped mushrooms and return the pork roast, fat-side up, to the pot. Cover the pot with foil, then put the pot lid on top of the foil to seal tightly. Put the pot in the middle of the oven and cook for 1½ hours. Check the meat with an instant-read thermometer; the meat should be tender and register 160° to 165° F. Transfer the roast to a platter and cover loosely with foil. Let rest for 15 minutes before serving. (The final temperature should be 165° to 170° F.) 6 While the meat is resting, skim off and discard any surface fat from

2 teaspoons fennel seeds, crushed

2 teaspoons chopped fresh rosemary

2 teaspoons kosher salt

1 teaspoon freshly ground black pepper

1 (4-to 6-pound) boneless pork shoulder roast (Boston butt), tied or netted

1 ounce dried porcini

1½ cups boiling water

2 tablespoons olive oil

2 tablespoons chopped garlic

1½ cups diced onions

2 cups dry white wine

¼ cup grappa (optional)

1 cup canned diced tomatoes in puree

1 cup Dark Pork Stock (page 87), homemade chicken stock, or canned low-sodium chicken broth

2 tablespoons chopped fresh basil

the juices in the pot. Put the pot over high heat and reduce the liquid until it becomes syrupy. Remove the string or netting on the roast and carve it into ½-inch-thick slices. Place the slices on creamy polenta. Spoon the juices over all and serve immediately.

CHEF'S NOTES: Plan to have leftover meat and sauce to make Italian-style sandwiches. For 4 sandwiches, rewarm 1 to 1½ pounds thinly sliced pork in its juices. Sauté some sliced onions until golden. Pile the meat and onions into sandwich rolls and garnish with some roasted red bell pepper strips and sliced cherry peppers. Dip the sandwiches into the sauce. (If you don't have enough sauce or it's too thick, add a little pork or chicken stock.) 🐖 To make a pasta sauce, simply chop or cube the leftover pork and rewarm it in the sauce. Add a cup or so of canned or fresh diced tomatoes, if you prefer your sauce a little more on the "tomatoey" side. I like to serve the sauce over sturdy pasta like penne or *orecchiette*.

Braised Stuffed Pork Loin Wrapped in Cabbage Leaves 🐖 Back in the late 1970s,

an accomplished home cook named Ann Yonkers started a popular cooking school called the American Table, which she ran from her home in Washington, D.C. I met Ann in the late 1980s and we became fast friends, enjoying many a good meal together with her husband and my wife. Ann is passionate about the foods of the French and Italian countryside, and this prune-stuffed pork loin wrapped in cabbage that she shared with me is a good example of the simple rustic flavors she loves. Use a roast that is no more than 8 inches long because large unwieldy roasts are more difficult to wrap in the cabbage. The cabbage leaves help to preserve moisture as well as provide a balance to the sweetness of the fruit stuffing. SERVES 6

Prune Stuffing

2½ cups dried pitted prunes

1 cup dry white wine or vermouth

¼ cup kirsch

⅔ cup pecans, toasted and roughly chopped into large pieces

¼ cup fresh bread crumbs

1 To make the stuffing: Put the dried prunes in a medium bowl and pour in the wine and vermouth, adding as much as is necessary to cover the fruit. Let soak for 1 hour to soften. Pour off the soaking liquid and reserve. Chop the prunes coarsely by hand or in a food processor. Return the prunes to the bowl and stir in the pecans and bread crumbs. Set aside.

2 To prepare the pork loin: With a long thin-bladed knife, cut a 1-inch slit in the center of the loin. It may be necessary, depending on the length of your knife blade, to cut into the pork from both ends. Using your fingers, a sharpening steel, or the handle of a wooden spoon, work the hole to enlarge it to 1½ inches in width. Stuff the pork loin with the prune stuffing. Season the roast generously with the salt, pepper, and fresh herb.

3 Bring a large pot of salted water to a boil. Spread out near your workspace some clean kitchen towels. Core the cabbage and place the head in the boiling water. With tongs, remove the outer leaves as they loosen and place the blanched leaves on the towels to drain. Continue to blanch and remove leaves until you have about 8 or 10. (You can save the remainder of the cabbage to use in another dish.) Shave off and discard the cabbage ribs. 4 To wrap the pork loin: Lay the some of the larger blanched cabbage leaves on the work surface, overlapping them and arranging them in the shape of a rectangle. Place the pork loin in the center of the rectangle and pull up the cabbage to enclose it. Use the remaining cabbage leaves to cover the top of the loin. Tie the roast at 2-inch intervals with butcher's twine. 5 Preheat the oven to 375° F. 6 In a casserole just large enough to hold the pork loin snugly,

1 boneless pork loin (2½ to 3 pounds, no more than 8 inches long)

Kosher salt

Freshly ground black pepper

1½ tablespoons chopped fresh thyme or rosemary

1 large head (1 to 1½ pounds) Savoy or green cabbage

2 tablespoons olive oil

¼ cup finely diced smoked ham

½ cup chopped carrots

½ cup chopped celery

¼ cup diced shallots

2 bay leaves

1 sprig fresh thyme

Soaking liquid from the prunes

½ cup homemade chicken stock or canned low-sodium chicken broth

2 tablespoons heavy cream

heat the olive oil over medium-high heat. Add the ham, carrots, celery, and shallots and cook, covered, stirring once or twice, until the vegetables are soft and golden, about 10 minutes. Add bay leaves and thyme sprig and pour in the prune soaking liquid and stock. Put the pork in the casserole, cover, and braise the loin for 45 minutes or until it reaches an internal temperature of 140° to 145° F on an instant-read thermometer. Remove the pork to a platter and let rest for 10 minutes. 7 While the pork is resting, make the sauce: Remove bay leaves and thyme sprig and discard the fat from the surface of the pan juices, then put the casserole over medium-high heat. Stir in the cream and cook until the sauce is reduced and thickened slightly. Taste and adjust the seasonings with salt and pepper. Slice the loin into ½-inch-thick pieces, arrange on a deep rimmed platter, and serve immediately, with the sauce poured around the meat.

Carnitas

 Every time I visit my favorite Mexican market in Oakland, I can't resist buying a pound or so of pork *carnitas* for the ride home. These beautifully browned and succulent pork nuggets (*carnitas* in Spanish means "little meats") are made by slowly cooking large chunks of pork in a copper vat filled with hot lard. Usually the meat is seasoned with nothing more than salt, then cut up or shredded and eaten either wrapped in tortillas as tacos or burritos, or used as a filling for a Mexican sandwich called a *torta* (see Chef's Notes). I also like to eat the meat as is, shredded, or chopped and topped with fresh tomato salsa, some Citrus-Marinated Red Onions (page 205), and a scoop of guacamole. MAKES ABOUT 4 CUPS

Carnitas Spice Rub

2 teaspoons ground cumin

1 teaspoon ground coriander seed

2 teaspoons kosher salt

2 teaspoons pasilla chili powder (or any pure ground chili, such as ancho or New Mexico)

3 pounds boneless Boston butt, cut into 1½-to 2-inch pieces, trimmed of visible fat

¼ cup olive oil

½ cup red wine vinegar

1 tablespoon honey

½ cup chicken stock or canned chicken broth

1 large onion, diced

1 To make the rub: In a medium bowl, combine all of the rub ingredients. 2 Add the pork to the rub and toss well to coat. Cover the bowl with plastic wrap and refrigerate overnight, or up to 48 hours. 3 In a large, deep covered skillet or casserole, heat the olive oil over medium-high heat. Working in small batches to prevent overcrowding the pan, cook the pork until browned on all sides, about 10 minutes. Transfer the pork with a slotted spoon as it's cooked to a plate and continue cooking the remaining pieces. When all the pork is browned, set the pot aside, leaving the fat and juices in it. (Do not drain.) 4 In a small bowl or measuring cup, stir the vinegar with the honey until the honey dissolves. Stir in the chicken stock and add the mixture to the pot, scraping up any browned bits on the bottom. Add the onion and bring the liquid to a boil over high heat. Lower the heat to maintain a simmer, return the pork to the pot, cover, and cook, stirring occasionally, until the pork is fork-tender, 1 to 1¼ hours.

5 Remove the cover and increase the heat slightly to maintain a lively simmer. Continue to cook until the liquid has evaporated and the fat from the pork is bubbling, about 30 minutes. As soon as the pork begins to brown, stir regularly to prevent burning. The pork is done when it has become golden to dark brown and is nicely crisped. Remove the pot from the heat and set aside to cool slightly. Transfer the pork with a slotted spoon to a rimmed baking sheet lined with paper towels. 6 At this point, the cooled pork can be shredded by hand, chopped with a knife, or left as is, with a mixture of large and small pieces.

CHEF'S NOTES: For a simple but classic variation on this recipe, put the uncooked pork in a large casserole or Dutch oven with water to cover by ½ inch. Add the juice of 1 freshly squeezed orange, 2 bay leaves, 1 cup diced onion, and 2 teaspoons kosher salt. Bring the liquid to the boil, cover, and lower the heat to maintain a simmer. After 1 hour, uncover, increase the heat to medium-high, and cook until the liquid is evaporated and the meat begins to brown in its own rendered fat, about 45 minutes. Stir to prevent scorching. When cool, shred the meat by hand and sprinkle with a little salt before eating. Use *carnitas* to stuff warm tortillas. To make *tortas,* spread shredded meat on soft Mexican rolls called *bollios,* slather with guacamole and mayonnaise, and top with shredded cabbage and thinly sliced tomatoes. If you can't find *bollios,* use French rolls instead. To rewarm *carnitas,* wrap in foil and heat in a 350° F oven for 15 minutes.

Black Bean–Infused Foil-Wrapped Pork Shanks

Wrapping pork in foil before roasting it is a great way to cook the meat slowly and produce a concentrated sauce at the same time. Pork shanks are my favorite cut for this method of braising, but I also find it works well with Boston butt, picnic shoulder, or blade-end loin roasts. These cuts will take less time to cook, so begin checking them after about 1½ hours. SERVES 6 TO 8

8 dried shiitake mushrooms

Fermented Black Bean and Cilantro Paste

1 tablespoon chopped fresh ginger

2 garlic cloves

½ cup chopped cilantro

1½ tablespoons fermented black beans rinsed in cold water and drained

1 teaspoon brown bean paste

1 teaspoon peanut oil

1 teaspoon sugar

2 teaspoons Chinese black vinegar or balsamic vinegar, or more to taste

2 large pork shanks (about 4 pounds total), or 2 (2-pound) chunks of Boston butt, or 2 (2-pound) blade-end pork loin roasts (see Chef's Note)

¼ cup Shaoxing wine or dry sherry

½ cup reserved mushroom soaking liquid

½ cup homemade chicken stock or canned low-sodium chicken broth

½ cup thinly sliced green onions

1 teaspoon soy sauce, or more to taste

Sugar to taste

1 Cover the dried mushrooms with 1½ cups boiling water and let soak at least 45 minutes or up to several hours. Drain the mushrooms and reserve the soaking liquid. Cut off the mushroom stems and discard, then thinly slice the mushrooms and set aside. 2 For the paste: Put the ginger, garlic, cilantro, black beans, brown bean paste, oil, sugar, and the 2 teaspoons black vinegar in a food processor or blender and process until the mixture forms a smooth paste. 3 Preheat the oven to 325° F. 4 Cut 6 to 8 deep, equally spaced gashes in the meaty part and along the length of each pork shank. Fill the gashes with the bean and cilantro paste and rub any remaining paste over the rest of each shank. 5 Put the Shaoxing wine, the ½ cup reserved mushroom soaking liquid, and chicken stock in a small saucepan and reduce the liquid over high heat to 4 tablespoons. Add the 1 teaspoon soy sauce and set aside. 6 Measure 2 (18-inch) squares of heavy-duty aluminum foil. Place half of the green onions and half of the sliced shiitake mushrooms into the center of each sheet. Spoon half of the reduced wine/mushroom soaking liquid over the vegetables. Place 1 pork shank on top of each vegetable mound

with the bone vertical. Loosely pull the foil around the shank, taking care not to let any of the liquid spill out. Pull the foil tightly up around the shank to seal in the liquid. If your shanks have some naked bone, you may leave the bone exposed. 7 Lay the foil-wrapped shanks vertically in a small deep casserole or high-sided 10-inch skillet with an ovenproof handle. Roast for 2 to 3 hours or until the meat is almost falling from the bone. Remove from the oven. Carefully remove the foil over a bowl so as to not lose any of the braising juices. Pour the juices into a saucepan, degrease, and add sugar, vinegar, or soy sauce to taste. 8 Lay the shanks in a serving bowl, pour the sauce over them, and serve with rice.

CHEF'S NOTE: For Boston butt or blade-end pork loin, omit the slashing step and rub each piece all over with the paste. Enclose the pork cut completely in foil to seal and roast for 2 hours or until quite tender.

Pot-au-Feu (Boiled Dinner with Petit Salé Pork)

Pot-au-feu is a French boiled dinner. Instead of corned beef, the star of this meal-in-one is homemade Petit Salé, but you could also make this dinner with a fresh Boston butt, smoked picnic ham, or a homemade smoked Boston butt. This recipe will provide plenty of leftovers that can be reheated for a second night's dinner, or chopped for an incredible hash. SERVES 8 WITH LEFTOVERS

1 Put the meat in a large soup pot or Dutch oven and cover with water. Bring to a boil over high heat, lower the heat to maintain a simmer, and skim off and discard any foam from the surface. Add the bay leaves, onion, peppercorns, garlic, green part of leeks, celery, carrot, and thyme. Cover and simmer until the meat is tender. This can take as short as 1½ hours (for Boston butt or ham) and as long as 2½ to 3 hours (for bellies and picnics). If you're cooking several different cuts in the same pot, remove each as it becomes tender and set it aside until all the meat is cooked. When all the meat has been removed, strain the stock and discard the solids. Degrease the stock and refrigerate it and the meat separately overnight.

5 pounds Petit Salé of Pork (page 292)—smoked picnic ham, smoked Boston butt, Boston butt, pork belly— or any combination thereof

2 bay leaves

1 medium onion, halved

10 whole black peppercorns

6 garlic cloves, unpeeled

3 leeks, green part only, washed and roughly chopped, with the white part reserved

3 celery ribs

1 carrot, coarsely chopped

2 sprigs fresh thyme or 1 teaspoon dried

2 cups peeled baby carrots

Reserved white part of 3 leeks, washed and thinly sliced

2 parsnips, cut into 2- by 2½-inch pieces

3 turnips, cut into 2- by 2½-inch pieces

1 small head (¾ to 1 pound) Savoy or green cabbage, quartered

12 small red potatoes

Condiments

Bottled horseradish sauce

Prepared mustard

Mostarda di frutta (Italian bottled mustard-infused fruit conserve)

2 Return the stock to the pot. Add the carrots, white part of leek, parsnips, turnips, cabbage, and potatoes. Bring the liquid to the boil, lower the heat to maintain a simmer, and cook until the potatoes are tender, about 20 minutes. Return the meat to the pot until heated through, about 5 minutes. 3 With a slotted spoon, transfer the vegetables to a warm platter. Slice or break apart the meat and arrange it on the platter with the vegetables. Serve with any or all of the suggested condiments. You may serve the stock as a separate course or save to use as a stock to make a hearty bean or vegetable soup.

Chinese Braised Pork Belly with Braised Cabbage 🐷 Read about pork belly on page 180.

In this Chinese braising method, pork belly is cooked in what is known as a master sauce. This highly flavored soy-based broth is used over and over again, becoming richer and richer with each use. (More soy, sugar, or other flavoring can be added if the sauce gets too watery.) As long as you bring the master sauce to the boil every 8 to 10 days, it can be kept indefinitely in the refrigerator. Besides pork belly, other foods that benefit from a simmering bath in master sauce are pork ribs, shanks, pork shoulder, picnic shoulder, loin, and pork chops. This recipe came from Andrew Hash, one of the talented cooks at Boulevard. SERVES 6 WITH LEFTOVERS

---

1 For the master sauce: Combine all the sauce ingredients in a large casserole or Dutch oven and bring to a boil over high heat. Add the pork belly, skin-side down, to the sauce. Reduce the heat to a bare simmer, cover, and cook, turning the belly over from time to time, for approximately 3 hours, or until the pork is tender when pierced with a fork. Remove the pan from the heat and let the pork belly cool to room temperature in the sauce. Strain the sauce into a jar and store in the refrigerator to use again and again. Refrigerate the belly separately or continue with the recipe.

Master Sauce

2 cups homemade chicken stock or canned low-sodium chicken broth

1 cup Chinese soy sauce

½ cup Chinese rice wine or dry sherry

2-inch piece fresh ginger, thinly sliced

2 tablespoons fermented Chinese black beans

2 whole star anise

4-inch piece Asian cassia bark or cinnamon stick

8 scallions, cut crosswise into 2-inch pieces

10 garlic cloves

2 tablespoons hoisin sauce

1 tablespoon brown sugar

1 tablespoon Szechwan or black peppercorns

6 dried Chinese mushrooms

3 cups water

½ skin-on pork belly (about 5 pounds)

2 For the cabbage: In a large high-sided skillet or Dutch oven, heat the oil over medium heat. Add the cabbage, black beans, and garlic and stir. Cover and cook, stirring the mixture from time to time until the cabbage is wilted. Add 1 cup of the master sauce and cook, uncovered, for 5 minutes until the cabbage is soft (napa cabbage takes less time, while green head cabbage may take more). 3 Cut the pork belly into ⅜-inch-thick slices (figure on one or two slices per serving) and arrange them over the cabbage in the skillet. Cover and cook 2 to 3 minutes or until the meat is warmed through. Carefully transfer to a serving platter and garnish with the green onions. Save any leftover unsliced pork belly for other recipes.

Braised Cabbage

2 tablespoons peanut oil

6 cups thinly shredded cabbage, napa, Savoy, or green head

1 tablespoon fermented Chinese black beans

3 garlic cloves, peeled and thinly sliced

Braising liquid from the pork belly

3 green onions, thinly sliced, for garnish

CHEF'S NOTES: Fresh pork shanks are also great braised in master sauce. Cook them as you would belly for about 2½ to 3 hours or until quite tender. Serve them with Hoisin Dipping Sauce (see Hong Kong–Style Ribs on page 149). To braise lean cuts such as pork loin in master sauce, add them in the beginning with all of the master sauce ingredients. When the liquid comes to a boil, cover the pot and turn off the heat. Let the meat sit in the sauce until the liquid cools to room temperature. Slice the meat and serve as is or rewarm the slices in a little of the sauce. Use this same method for back ribs, but once they're cooked and cooled in the liquid grill them quickly over coals to crisp the exterior. Not only is Chinese Braised Pork Belly good served over cabbage, once it's cooked and refrigerated, it can also be cut into cubes or rectangles that can either be rewarmed and used to complement seafood or vegetables, or deep-fried to be used in the same way, or served as an hors d'oeuvre, alone or in a sauce. I must warn you, however—deep-fried pork belly is so good you will be prone to overindulge (how can you resist something that is crunchy on the outside and soft, porky, and sweet on the inside?). To deep-fry braised belly, cut it into ½-inch by 2-inch rectangles and fry in small batches in a 2-quart saucepan filled halfway with peanut oil heated to 340° F. Cook until brown and crisp, about 5 minutes. You can also cut the braised belly into rectangles and skewer and grill it.

11

Stews, Baked Pastas, and Casseroles

About Pork Stews

Cuts suitable for pork stews have all the same requirements as cuts suitable for pot roasts. Since the meat is slowly cooked in a liquid to well-done, it must have ample fat and connective tissue. **Boston butt, picnic shoulder, blade-end pork loin roasts** are all ideal for stews. In most cases you'll want to purchase a boneless or bone-in version of any of these roasts, and then cut it into cubes no smaller than 2 inches (unless the recipe instructs you otherwise). You can do it yourself or have a friendly butcher do it for you. As you work through the cut of pork, you'll want to trim away and discard most of the external fat and any tough gristle. Figure on about 6 to 8 ounces of raw meat per serving.

Unless you buy your pork from a reputable butcher you can trust, never buy pork labeled "stew meat." You really can't be sure from where the meat was cut; if it's center-cut loin or sirloin, it will end up dry and stringy in your stew.

One of the best and easiest-to-find pork cuts, which is ideal for stews, is labeled as **"boneless country-style spareribs"** (**country spareribs** or just **country ribs**). They're really nothing more than the blade-end pork loin, cut into chops, boned, and butterflied. Do make sure that these chunks are cut thick enough so that you can cut them into 2-inch cubes. If you can't find boneless country ribs, then buy the ones with the bone on and after you cube the meat, throw the bones into the stew as well; they add great body to the sauce.

Sometimes enterprising meat managers who know how popular country-style ribs are will also cut up Boston butt into thick strips and sell them labeled **pork shoulder country spareribs** or **pork butt country spareribs**. These are great for stews and will save you time cutting them into cubes. If you like sucking on bones as I certainly do, then you can also use **back ribs** or **spareribs** for stews.

If you do use ribs, ask the meat clerk to cut the slabs lengthwise into 3 or 4 strips, then cut between the bones so you'll have short, manageable pieces for your stew. If you're a fan of fattier and very succulent meat, then use fresh pork belly to make your stew. Pork shanks, cut osso buco–style, or crosswise, are great in stews as well.

Some stews, especially ones made with beans or sauerkraut, are best made with smoked cuts of pork. **Smoked ham hocks, smoked picnic hams,** or **smoked neck bones** are ideal in these types of stews. Unsmoked neck bones can also be used for stews and are very budget friendly. Which brings me to my favorite cut of pork for stews—**cheeks.** Because the cheek muscles do so much work (chewing, after all), they're tough and loaded with collagen and interspersed with a fair amount of fat (chubby cheeks). When they're cooked with long, slow moist-heat, the collagen softens and gelatinizes and the ample marbling also bathes the lean meat in fat. The result is the most satiny smooth, silken stew you'll ever eat. So search out some cheeks, they're worth the effort and they're a great bargain to boot.

Poaching and Steaming

All the shoulder and belly cuts are suitable for poaching and steaming. Fresh pork belly or whole pork cheeks are particularly good, because each has a great deal of tough meat and connective tissue, which becomes soft and delicious when cooked over time (at least 2 to 3 hours).

SPECIAL CUTS FOR MOIST-HEAT COOKING Over the centuries various cultures have embraced the head-to-tail aspects of pork cookery and their cuisines reflect the popularity of those cuts with a great number of recipes using **pig's heads, feet,** and **tails.** Most of these cuts consist of skin, gristle, bone, and fat with little or no meat, and they all are cooked covered in liquid for a very long time, at least 4 hours or more, until everything is just about falling off the bone. They're usually cooled and then everything is removed from the bones (some folks eat pig's feet on the bone), chopped, and packed in a mold with some of the gelatin-rich cooking liquid. Once the molds have been refrigerated and the liquid is jelled, they can be sliced and served with a splash of vinegar, chopped onions, and pickles. If you enjoy savory jellied dishes, try the recipes on pages 284 to 287. They're easy and inexpensive to make.

Pork and Hominy Stew 🐖 Serve this old-fashioned Southern

stew with cornbread, or with pancakes made from cooked grits, cheddar cheese, and green onions, or over rice, or just with plain boiled grits alongside. SERVES 4

1½ teaspoons kosher salt

1 tablespoon chili powder, plus 2 teaspoons

½ teaspoon freshly ground black pepper

2½ pounds boneless Boston butt, cut into 2½-inch chunks, or 2½ pounds boneless country-style spareribs, cut into 2-inch pieces

¼ cup chopped bacon

1 cup diced tasso or smoky ham

2 cups thinly sliced onions

½ cup chopped carrot

2 tablespoons chopped garlic

2 mild green chilies (Anaheim or poblano), seeded and cut into ¼-by 2-inch slices

1 cup beer

1 cup chicken stock

1 cup canned tomatoes, seeded and chopped

1 teaspoon dried marjoram

1 (16-ounce) can whole white or yellow hominy, drained

Kosher salt

Freshly ground black pepper

Tabasco sauce

Chopped cilantro, for garnish

1 Combine the salt, the 1 tablespoon chili powder, and pepper and rub generously over the chunks of pork, making sure to use all of the spice rub. 2 Put the bacon in a Dutch oven and heat over medium heat. Cook until the bacon is lightly browned and crisp and the fat has rendered. Remove the bacon with a slotted spoon to drain on paper towels. Reserve until serving time. 3 Increase the heat under the pot to medium-high, add the pork, and brown it on all sides in the bacon fat, about 5 to 10 minutes. Remove to a bowl and set aside. 4 Reduce the heat to medium. Add the tasso, onions, carrot, and garlic to the pot, cover, and cook for 5 minutes, stirring and scraping up any browned bits from the bottom. Add the chilies and cook, stirring, for 1 minute. Stir in the beer, chicken stock, tomatoes, marjoram, and remaining 2 teaspoons chili powder. Bring to a boil and add the reserved browned pork and hominy. Reduce the heat to a simmer. Cover and cook for 1¼ to 1½ hours or until the pork is tender when pierced with a fork. 5 Remove the pork and other solids with a slotted spoon to a platter or plate and reserve. If the sauce is watery, bring to a boil and reduce until slightly thickened. Degrease if necessary. Taste for salt and pepper and add Tabasco if you like it zippy. Return the pork to the sauce to warm through. Serve the stew in shallow bowls and garnish with a sprinkling of the reserved bacon and some cilantro.

Pork Stew à la Provençale 🐖

The pig is a very important animal in Provence. Not only is it used in many *charcuterie* specialties like *pâté de campagne, rillettes, caillettes,* and *fromage de tête* (headcheese), but sandwiches made with *jambon cuit* and *jambon cru* are found in every café. In addition to all the preserved pork products, fresh pork is grilled, roasted, braised, and stewed. This simple stew combines pork with the heady and aromatic ingredients for which Provence is known. It's a wonderful one-pot meal that will bring the culinary essence of Provence into your very own kitchen. Serve with soft polenta. As with most stews, it tastes better if made the day before. SERVES 4 TO 6

2½ pounds boneless Boston butt or boneless country-style spareribs, cut into 2-inch pieces

Kosher salt

Freshly ground black pepper

2 tablespoons olive oil

4 cups thinly sliced onions

20 garlic cloves, peeled

2 anchovy fillets, minced

2 teaspoons fennel seeds, crushed

1 teaspoon chopped fresh thyme

2 teaspoons chopped fresh tarragon or 1 teaspoon dried

6 ripe tomatoes, chopped, or 1½ cups canned tomatoes, drained and chopped

¼ cup pitted and chopped green olives

1 tablespoon grated lemon zest

1 tablespoon drained capers, lightly chopped

1 cup homemade chicken stock or canned low-sodium chicken broth

1 cup dry white wine

½ cup black Niçoise olives, pitted

1 Sprinkle the pork generously with salt and pepper. Heat the olive oil in a large casserole or Dutch oven over high heat. Add the meat in 2 or 3 batches, being careful not to crowd the pan, and cook until the pieces are browned on all sides, about 7 to 10 minutes. Remove the meat as it's done and set aside in a bowl.

2 Lower the heat under the pot to medium and add the onions. Cover the pot and cook until the onions soften, about 10 minutes. Remove the cover and cook, stirring occasionally, until golden, about 5 minutes more. Add the garlic and cook for 2 minutes. Stir in the anchovies, fennel seeds, thyme, and tarragon and cook for 1 minute. Add the tomatoes, green olives, lemon zest, capers, stock, and wine. Return the meat to the pot and raise the heat to high. Bring the mixture to a boil, then lower the heat to maintain a simmer. Cover and cook until the meat is fork-tender, 1 to 1½ hours. Skim and degrease the sauce. If sauce is too watery, strain the solids and reduce until just syrupy. Return the solids to the pot. Add the Niçoise olives and adjust the seasonings with salt and pepper to taste. Serve as is or over soft polenta.

Pork Mole Verde (Pumpkin Seed and Green Chili Pork Stew)

Moles are at the heart of Mexican cooking. There are red *moles,* yellow *moles,* black *moles,* and green *moles,* and even a *mole mancha mantel,* which means tablecloth stainer. The black *mole* from Pueblo is famous and includes exotic ingredients like chocolate, roasted nuts, and assorted dried chilies. Oaxaca is the land of "seven *moles*" and includes a version of *mole negro* (black *mole*) and *mole verde* (green *mole*). Green *moles* are made throughout Mexico and usually contain toasted pumpkin seed (*pepitas*) and are sometimes referred to as *pipián verde;* some recipes get their green color and herby taste from romaine lettuce leaves or chard, while others, such as the *mole verde* from Oaxaca, use a local large-leaf herb, *hoja santa,* to flavor and color their *moles.* My recipe uses a last-minutes dollop of cilantro and green onion puree to give the *mole* a burst of herbaceous flavor. *Mole verde* can also be made with chicken instead of pork.

SERVES 8 TO 10

Poached Pork

6 cups homemade chicken stock or canned low-sodium chicken broth

1½ cups coarsely chopped onions

4 garlic cloves, chopped

1 teaspoon cumin seeds

1 teaspoon kosher salt

2 teaspoons fresh marjoram or oregano or 1 teaspoon dried

5 pounds boneless Boston butt or country-style spareribs, cut into 2-inch pieces

1 To poach the pork: In a large casserole or Dutch oven, bring the chicken stock to a boil with the onions, garlic, cumin seed, salt, and marjoram. Add the pork. Reduce the heat to maintain a simmer, and cook the pork, skimming occasionally, until tender, 1¼ to 1½ hours. Remove the pork with a slotted spoon to a bowl and set aside. Strain the poaching liquid through a fine-mesh sieve into a bowl and set aside to cool slightly. Reserve 3½ cups for the sauce. 2 To make the *mole:* In a food processor or blender, puree the 1¼ cups toasted pumpkin seeds. Add 1 cup of the pork poaching liquid, the ½ teaspoon salt, onions, tomatillos, allspice, jalapeños, garlic, cumin, marjoram, cilantro stems, and poblanos. Process to form a slightly lumpy paste.

3 Heat the lard in a large, deep skillet or Dutch oven over medium heat and add the pumpkin seed paste. Cook, stirring frequently, until the mixture becomes quite thick, about 10 to 15 minutes. Stir in 2 more cups of the reserved pork poaching liquid and simmer, uncovered, until the sauce has reduced and thickened. Add the cooked pork to the mole and reheat it in the sauce until hot, about 5 minutes. Taste for salt and pepper.

4 In the blender, puree the reserved cilantro leaves with the green onion tops, ½ more cup of the reserved poaching liquid, lime juice, and ½ teaspoon salt. Set aside until serving time.

5 To serve, ladle the *mole verde* into shallow soup bowls, stir in 2 heaping tablespoons of the cilantro puree, and top with a sprinkling of the remaining toasted pumpkin seeds.

Mole Verde

1¼ cups hulled pumpkin seeds (*pepitas*), toasted, plus additional for garnish

3½ cups broth from poaching the pork

Kosher salt

1½ cups coarsely chopped onions

12 tomatillos (about 1 pound), coarsely chopped

¼ teaspoon ground allspice

3 jalapeño peppers, stemmed, seeded, and ribbed

3 garlic cloves

1 teaspoon ground cumin

1 teaspoon fresh marjoram or oregano or ½ teaspoon dried

Stems from 1 bunch cilantro, leaves reserved

4 poblano chilies, fire-roasted, peeled, seeded, and chopped

3 tablespoons lard or olive oil

Freshly ground black pepper

6 green onions, green part only, cut into 1-inch pieces

¼ cup freshly squeezed lime juice or more to taste

Filipino Pork Adobo

Throughout the Spanish-speaking world, *adobo* refers to preparations of meat, fish, or fowl that are marinated in a mixture of vinegar and chilies of all degrees of heat, from mild Spanish paprika to fire-packed habaneros. In the Philippines, the name is the same but the flavorings are different; only vinegar is the common ingredient among the adobos of Mexico, Spain, and other Latin nations. I like this recipe because it is very simple, yet the flavor is rich and complex. If time allows, a day or two in the refrigerator, which gives the flavors a chance to get acquainted, improves this dish. Don't be afraid to add a touch more heat at the table with a little Asian hot chili oil or Tabasco. SERVES 4

2 pounds boneless Boston butt, cut into 3-inch chunks

½ cup rice or white vinegar, or more to taste

¾ cup light soy sauce

¼ cup Asian fish sauce (see Chef's Notes, page 97)

2 cups homemade chicken stock or canned low-sodium chicken broth or water

2 teaspoons brown sugar, or more to taste

2 teaspoons freshly ground black pepper

4 bay leaves

5 tablespoons chopped garlic

2 onions, thinly sliced

1 teaspoon Asian hot chili oil, or more to taste (optional)

Put the pork and all of the remaining ingredients in a casserole or large saucepan and bring to a simmer over medium heat. Cook, uncovered, until the pork is tender, about 1¼ hours. Skim and discard the fat from the surface. Taste the broth and add more vinegar, sugar, or chili oil to balance the flavors to your liking. Serve the adobo over jasmine rice.

Burmese Curried Pork

I got this recipe from my friend Henry Joe Peterson, whom I met through a shared love of barbecue. His wife's family, though Chinese, hails from Rangoon, Burma. Burmese cooking is strongly influenced by its Chinese, Indian, Thai, and Vietnamese neighbors. To quote Henry, "Unlike Indian curries, Burmese curries have distinct tangy qualities that are derived from the use of tamarind." His recipe strikes the balance between tangy, salty, and spicy, which I find really pleasing. I added the coconut milk to further defuse the heat, but you can leave it out. SERVES 6 (WITH LOTS OF RICE)

1 In a medium bowl, toss the pork with the curry powder, salt, and ½ tablespoon of the paprika. Set aside at room temperature for 30 minutes. 2 Heat the olive oil in a large casserole or Dutch oven over medium heat. Add the onion and cook until it softens and begins to brown, 8 to 10 minutes. Add the garlic and cook for 2 minutes. Add the red curry paste, remaining paprika, and red pepper flakes and cook for 30 seconds. Stir in the chilies and ginger, then add the pork, stirring to coat it well with the oil and spices. Lower the heat to medium-low, add 1 cup water, and cook, stirring occasionally, for 30 minutes to 1 hour. 3 When the oil has rendered from the meat, add the tomatoes, fish sauce, optional mango pickle, tamarind juice or paste, and half of the chopped cilantro. Cover and simmer for 10 minutes or until the tomatoes have released their juices and begun to break down. 4 Taste for seasonings. The curry should be fairly tart, spicy, and salty. Add more fish sauce, chilies,

2 pounds boneless Boston butt or boneless country-style ribs, cut into 1½-inch pieces

1 tablespoon curry powder

½ teaspoon kosher salt

1½ tablespoons paprika

2 tablespoons peanut oil

1 medium onion, diced

6 to 8 garlic cloves, minced

1 tablespoon red curry paste (see Chef's Notes)

2 teaspoons crushed red pepper flakes

2 serrano chilies, thinly sliced, or more to taste

1 (1-inch) piece fresh ginger, minced

3 ripe tomatoes, diced

2 tablespoons Asian fish sauce

1 tablespoon hot Indian mango pickle (see Chef's Notes), optional

½ cup tamarind juice (see Chef's Notes) or 1 tablespoon tamarind paste, or more to taste

Leaves of 1 bunch cilantro, chopped

⅔ cup canned coconut milk (optional)

6 cups steamed jasmine rice as an accompaniment

and tamarind as needed. It should also be a deep red, rather than yellow or brown, so add paprika to heighten the red color as necessary. Cook at a low simmer until the pork is tender, about 20 or 30 minutes more. Skim and discard any fat from the surface of the sauce.

5 Right before serving, stir in the optional coconut milk and taste for salt. Serve the curry over hot jasmine rice and garnish with the remaining cilantro.

CHEF'S NOTES: To make tamarind juice, you can buy a brick of tamarind pulp at Asian markets. It's a deep red, solid brick of sticky pulp with seeds. Cut off a 1-inch square wad and put it in a bowl. Pour about 1 cup boiling water over it and let steep for about 15 minutes. Strain out the seed, mashing the pulp and seeds with the back of a spoon and scraping the seed-free pulp from the bottom of the strainer. Add this to the rest of the juice you've collected. What you'll have is roughly 1 cup of a tangy brown liquid that is pucker-producing. You can also find jars of tamarind paste in Asian markets that work as well. 🐖 You can also find hot Indian mango pickle in oil in Asian or Indian markets. This is a spicy, salty Indian relish that really packs a wallop. Make sure to remove any hard pieces before serving it.

Hungarian Goulash (Pörkölt) 🐖 Bring on the

crowds! This is a stew best served for casual, winter entertaining. It's soul-satisfying and easy to make for a winter party, say Super Bowl, and like all good stews, should be made in advance, allowing the cook to simply reheat it before serving. I like to make a double recipe and freeze some for impromptu gatherings. SERVES 8

2 tablespoons lard, bacon fat, or olive oil

4 ounces bacon or smoky ham, diced

3 pounds boneless Boston butt or boneless country-style spareribs, cut into 2-inch pieces

Kosher salt

Freshly ground black pepper

All-purpose flour

1 In a large casserole or Dutch oven, heat the fat or oil over medium heat and add the bacon or ham. Cook until lightly browned, about 5 minutes. Transfer with a slotted spoon to paper towels to drain. 2 Season the pork with salt and pepper and toss with flour to coat lightly. Increase the heat to medium-high under the pot and add the meat. Cook until the meat is browned on all sides, in two batches if necessary. Remove with a slotted spoon and

set aside with the bacon. **3** Lower the heat to medium, add the onions to the pot, and cook, stirring frequently, until lightly colored, about 10 minutes. Add the garlic and cook 1 minute. Add the mild and hot paprikas, stir to combine, and cook for 2 minutes. Add the red bell peppers, carrots, caraway seeds, bay leaves, marjoram, and 1 teaspoon black pepper and stir to combine. Add the white wine or beer, stock, tomato puree or paste, and sauerkraut, scraping up any browned bits from the bottom of the pot. Increase the heat to high, return the meat and reserved bacon or ham to the pot, and bring to a boil. Lower the heat to maintain a simmer and simmer, uncovered, until the meat is tender, 1¼ to 1½ hours. **4** Remove the solids with a slotted spoon, and set aside. Skim and discard the fat from the surface, then reduce the liquid over high heat until thickened slightly. Return the meat and vegetables to the pot. Taste for salt and pepper. Remove the stew from the heat and stir in the optional sour cream. **5** Serve the goulash over spaëtzle, buttered egg noodles, or with steamed new potatoes. Garnish with the chopped parsley or dill.

3 cups thinly sliced onions

6 garlic cloves, finely chopped

⅓ cup mild Hungarian paprika

1 teaspoon hot Hungarian paprika

3 red bell peppers, cut in ½-inch dice

1 cup finely diced carrots

1 teaspoon caraway seeds

2 bay leaves

1 teaspoon dried marjoram

1 cup dry white wine or dark beer

2 cups Dark Pork Stock (page 87), homemade chicken stock, or canned low-sodium chicken broth

¼ cup tomato puree or 2 tablespoons tomato paste

1 pound sauerkraut, rinsed and drained

1 cup sour cream (optional)

Chopped Italian flat-leaf parsley or fresh dill, for garnish

Braised Pork Cheeks with Pappardelle and Radicchio

I first came across pasta with radicchio in Friuli, the northeastern region of Italy that borders Austria and the former Yugoslavia, now called Croatia. This area has a hearty cooking style influenced by its Slavic neighbors. Some versions of this combination had only radicchio and bit of *guanciale* (cured pork cheeks) and sauce, while others added pork and/or sausages. Even without the pork cheeks the sauce recipe is quite flavorful and makes a great topping for pasta. The orange juice in the recipe adds a subtle fruitiness that complements both the pork and the tomatoes, but if it's too weird or untraditional for you then omit it and replace it with white wine or water.

SERVES 4 WITH LOTS OF LEFTOVER SAUCE (SEE CHEF'S NOTES)

---

3 tablespoons olive oil

1 pound pork cheeks (see Chef's Notes) or 1 pound boneless country-style spareribs, cut into 1-inch cubes

Kosher salt

Freshly ground black pepper

¼ cup diced pancetta

¼ cup diced dry coppa or prosciutto

1 cup chopped onions

¼ cup chopped celery

¼ cup chopped carrot

2 tablespoons chopped garlic

2 cups fruity wine, such as Sauvignon Blanc or Friuli Tokai

1 cup orange juice

1 Preheat the oven to 325° F. 2 Heat the olive oil in a large casserole or Dutch oven over medium-high heat. Sprinkle the pork with salt and pepper. Put the pork cheeks in the pot and cook until browned on all sides, about 6 minutes. Transfer the cheeks to a plate and set aside. 3 Add the pancetta to the pot and cook until it begins to color. Pour off all but 2 tablespoons of the fat and save to use for cooking the radicchio. Add the coppa, onions, celery, carrot, and garlic. Lower the heat to medium, cover, and cook, stirring occasionally, until the vegetables have softened, about 10 minutes. Add the reserved cheeks, wine, orange juice, stock, tomatoes, and sage leaves. Increase the heat to high and bring the liquid to the boil, scraping up any browned bits from the bottom of the pan. Cover the pan and transfer to the oven. Bake until the cheeks are very tender, 1½ to 2 hours, or longer. Transfer the pork to a plate and set aside. At this point, you can continue with the recipe or cool the pork and sauce separately and refrigerate them for

up to 2 days. Rewarm before serving. About 20 minutes before you're ready to serve the dish, bring a large pot of water to a boil to cook the pasta. 4 Skim off and discard the fat on the surface of the sauce. Reduce the liquid in the pot over high heat until syrupy. In a large skillet, heat 2 tablespoons of the reserved pancetta fat over medium-high heat. Add the radicchio and cook, stirring frequently, until wilted, about 4 minutes. Add ¼ cup of the sauce and cook 1 minute or until the radicchio is tender. Season to taste with salt and pepper and set aside. 5 Shred or chop the pork cheeks into ½-inch pieces. (Reheat the meat first if it's been refrigerated.) This step is not necessary if you have used country ribs. 6 Put the pappardelle in the boiling water and cook until just tender. Drain. In a large heated bowl, toss the pasta, pork, radicchio, and enough of the braising sauce to moisten the noodles sufficiently. Sprinkle with the cheese and serve.

1 cup Dark Pork Stock (page 87), homemade chicken stock, or canned low-sodium chicken broth

1 cup canned diced Italian tomatoes

6 whole sage leaves

2 cups sliced radicchio

1 pound fresh pappardelle, or other wide egg noodle

Freshly grated Parmesan cheese, for garnish

CHEF'S NOTES: Save any extra sauce to serve over pasta—it's especially good with ravioli—or cook up a sausage or two, slice, and add it to the leftover sauce. 🐖 Pork cheeks, because they have lots of collagen, become quite tender and silky when cooked with slow, moist heat. If you can't find pork cheeks, then boneless country-style ribs or Boston butt are good substitutes. You may need to decrease the cooking time to 1 to 1½ hours because they become tender more quickly. 🐖 Instead of radicchio, you can use Savoy cabbage or kale.

Baked Rigatoni with Pork Rib Ragù

This recipe was adapted from an original family recipe from chef Tom Oden, who along with chef Franco Dunn, owns Santi, an ever-popular, authentically Italian restaurant in Geyserville at the north end of the Sonoma wine country. The best strategy is to make the *ragù* a day ahead, which not only lets the flavors mellow but makes it easy to remove the fat. SERVES 8

¼ pound diced pancetta

2 pounds boneless country-style spareribs, cut into 2-inch chunks

Kosher salt

Freshly ground black pepper

2 cups finely chopped onions

½ cup chopped carrot

½ cup chopped celery

2 tablespoons chopped garlic

2 bay leaves

4 sprigs thyme

2 cups dry red wine

2 cups chopped canned Italian-style tomatoes

1½ pounds rigatoni, penne, or other tubular pasta

1 cup whole milk ricotta

½ pound mozzarella, shredded

½ cup freshly grated Parmesan cheese ·

1 Heat a large casserole or Dutch oven over medium heat, add the pancetta, and cook until lightly browned. Transfer the pancetta with a slotted spoon to paper towels and set aside, leaving the fat in the pan. 2 Lightly season the ribs with salt and pepper and add to the pan. Turn up the heat to medium-high and brown until the meat begins to color on all sides, stirring from time to time. Remove the ribs and set aside. 3 Add the vegetables, cover, and reduce the heat to medium. Stir and cook until the vegetables are soft, about 10 minutes. Add the bay leaves and thyme sprigs and pour in the wine. Scrape up any browned bits from the bottom of the pan and bring to a boil. Continue to boil until the wine is reduced by half. Add the reserved pancetta and ribs. Add the tomatoes, reduce the heat to maintain a simmer, and cover. Cook until the meat is easily shredded, 1½ to 2 hours. Stir from time to time and add water if the liquid evaporates. The sauce should be slightly thick but not watery. When the meat is cooked, strain the liquid into one container; spoon the solids into another. Pull the meat into small pieces or shred. Cover both and refrigerate. The next day, scrape away and discard

the congealed fat from the surface of the liquids. Combine the sauce and solids in a pot and heat, covered, over low heat, stirring occasionally. 4 Preheat the oven to 400° F. 5 While sauce is warming, cook the pasta until al dente or slightly firmer than al dente, about 10 to 11 minutes (the pasta will further soften as it bakes). Drain. 6 In a large bowl, combine the pasta, ricotta, and sauce. Spoon the mixture into a 9- by 13-inch shallow baking dish. Strew the mozzarella over the top, then sprinkle Parmesan over all. Bake for 20 to 30 minutes or until the cheese is golden and the pasta is hot and bubbling.

CHEF'S NOTE: Tom's family recipe calls for using regular pork spareribs, cooked until the meat is falling off the bone, then shredded. The sauce made this way has a more intense flavor from the bones but is decidedly more fatty. If you use spareribs, increase the amount to about 3 to 4 pounds and separate the slabs into individual ribs before cooking.

My Best Bolognese

🐖 I've been experimenting with this sauce for years and just when I think I've perfected the recipe, I improve it. This is my most recent and least "tinkered with" version. To my taste, it has the right proportion of tomato to meat, with a hint of earthiness from the porcinis. I've tried it using pork only, but find that pork's inherent sweetness needs the balance of the meatier flavor of beef. The recipe makes about 3 quarts, but leftover Bolognese sauce freezes beautifully, and it's wonderful to have on hand to sauce gnocchi, ravioli, or pasta for a quick and comforting family meal. MAKES ABOUT 3 QUARTS

1 ounce dried porcini

1½ cups boiling water

½ pound pancetta, cut into ½-inch pieces (preferably homemade)

3 tablespoons olive oil

2 carrots, peeled and cut into 1-inch pieces

3 celery ribs, cut into 1-inch pieces

2 medium yellow onions, cut into 1-inch pieces

2 pounds ground pork

1 pound ground beef chuck

Kosher salt

Freshly ground black pepper

1½ cups dry white wine or vermouth

1½ cups whole milk

1 can (6 ounces) tomato paste

1 cup canned chicken broth or homemade chicken stock

1 can (28 ounces) crushed tomatoes (see Chef's Note)

1 Put the porcini in a small bowl, add boiling water to cover (about 1½ cups), and let stand until softened, at least 45 minutes or up to several hours. Drain the porcini over a bowl and reserve the soaking water. Strain the soaking water through a coffee filter or piece of cheesecloth into a cup and reserve. Finely chop the porcini and set aside. 2 Put the pancetta in a food processor and pulse until finely chopped. Heat the olive oil in a large saucepan over medium heat, add the pancetta, and cook, stirring occasionally, until the pieces begin to separate. While the pancetta is cooking, put the carrots, celery, and onions in the food processor and pulse in one- to two-second intervals until finely chopped. Add the vegetables to the pan and cook, stirring, until the onions have become translucent, about 5 minutes. Increase the heat to medium-high and cook until the mixture just begins to color, about 7 to 10 minutes more. 3 Add the pork and beef and cook, breaking the meat up with a spatula or fork as it cooks. Add a generous pinch of salt and pepper, and cook over medium-high heat until the meat begins to lose its raw color but is not completely gray, about 5 minutes. Add the wine, increase the heat to

high, and cook, stirring occasionally, until the wine is completely evaporated. Add the milk and cook, stirring often, over high heat until it is completely evaporated. 4 Add the tomato paste, chicken broth, reserved porcini soaking water, and the crushed tomatoes to the saucepan. Stir to combine well, bring to a boil, then reduce the heat so that the sauce bubbles slowly. Cook, uncovered, stirring occasionally to prevent the sauce from burning or sticking on the bottom, for 2 hours, until the sauce is quite thick and most of the liquid has evaporated. Taste for salt and pepper. If the sauce is too dry, add more broth.

CHEF'S NOTE: Look for San Marzano tomatoes, a variety of Roma tomatoes grown in volcanic soil in the San Marzano region of Italy. They're incredibly sweet and, to my taste, are the best canned tomatoes in the world.

Nancy's Meatball Lasagna

I know I don't need to tell you that lasagna is a great dish for feeding a small army because it can be made in stages, assembled a day ahead, and baked right before serving. Some of you may question the meatballs in the lasagna, but trust me that the idea is part of Neapolitan lasagna tradition and it makes this lasagna something special. This is a family recipe from my wife, Nancy Oakes. **SERVES 12**

Meat Sauce

1 tablespoon olive oil

¼ pound finely chopped pancetta

2 cups finely chopped onions

½ cup finely chopped carrots

½ cup finely chopped celery

1 pound mild Italian sausage, homemade (page 256) or store bought, casings removed

2 tablespoons minced garlic

¼ cup chopped parsley

½ cup dry white wine

2 cups Dark Pork Stock (page 87), homemade chicken stock, or canned low-sodium chicken broth

3 cups canned diced Italian tomatoes, drained

Pinch ground nutmeg

2 teaspoons chopped fresh oregano

2 fresh sage leaves, minced

Kosher salt

Freshly ground black pepper

1 To make the sauce: Heat the oil in a large saucepan over medium heat, add the pancetta, onions, carrots, and celery, and cook until the vegetables begin to turn color, about 7 to 10 minutes. Stir in the sausage and garlic and cook 2 minutes, breaking up the sausage with a spatula or fork. Add the parsley, wine, stock, and tomatoes and bring the liquid to the boil. Lower the heat to maintain a simmer, stir in the nutmeg, and cook for 30 minutes. Add the oregano and sage and taste for salt and pepper. The sauce can be made ahead up to this point. Cover and refrigerate for up to 4 days. 2 For the meatballs: Combine the sausage, sun-dried tomatoes, bread crumbs, eggs, and Parmesan in a large bowl and knead and squeeze until well mixed. Using a spring-release ice cream scoop, your hands, or a spoon, shape the mixture into 1-inch meatballs. Dredge the meatballs lightly in flour and set aside. 3 Heat 1 tablespoon olive oil in a large skillet over medium-high heat. Add the meatballs in batches (adding more oil as needed), and cook until browned on all sides, about 5 to 7 minutes. Remove the cooked meatballs to a plate and let cool. (You should have about 36 meatballs.) You can use the meatballs immediately or cover and refrigerate them for up to 1 day before you assemble the lasagna. 4 To make the béchamel sauce: Bring the milk to just below the simmer in a

saucepan over medium heat, set aside. In another medium saucepan, heat the butter over low heat until it foams. Add the flour, increase the heat to medium, and cook the mixture, whisking, for 2 minutes. Remove the pan from the heat and whisk in the warm milk until the mixture is smooth. Return the pan to the heat and cook over medium heat, stirring continuously until the béchamel thickens, about 2 minutes. Season with the salt and pepper to taste. The béchamel may be used immediately or you can put plastic wrap on the surface, allow it to cool, and refrigerate it for up to 1 day before assembling the lasagna. Warm gently over low heat before using. 5 Preheat the oven to 350° F. 6 To assemble the lasagna: Lightly oil a large baking dish (13 by 9 by 3 inches). Have ready and warmed to room temperature (if they've been refrigerated), the sauce and meatballs. Heat the béchamel until warm, adding more milk or cream if it's too thick. (You want it to be like thickened heavy cream.) Spread a little of the tomato sauce in the baking dish and cover with pasta sheets. Spread one third of the tomato sauce over the pasta, top with one fourth of the béchamel, and cover it with 12 meatballs, evenly spaced. Put another layer of pasta sheets over the meatballs, top with another third of the tomato sauce, and one fourth of the béchamel. Add 12 meatballs, more sauce, and more béchamel. Repeat once more, so that you have 3 layers of pasta, sauce, béchamel, and meatballs. Top the dish with pasta sheets (don't worry if the layers of pasta and sauce are higher than the sides of the baking dish). Spread the pasta with the remaining béchamel and, if you have any, tomato sauce. Sprinkle with the cheese. Cover with foil loosely. Place the baking dish on a baking sheet (to catch any sauce that bubbles over) and bake

Meatballs

1¼ pounds Boulevard's Pork and Mushroom Sausage (page 262), Italian-Style Sausage with Rosemary and Grappa (page 260), or good-quality store-bought Italian sausage, casings removed

¼ cup chopped sun-dried tomatoes

1 cup soft bread crumbs

2 eggs, lightly beaten

¼ cup freshly grated Parmesan cheese

All-purpose flour

2 to 4 tablespoons olive oil

Béchamel Sauce (Makes about 1⅔ cups)

2 cups milk

4 tablespoons butter

3 tablespoons all-purpose flour

½ teaspoon salt

Freshly ground black pepper

9 ounces (about 16) dried "no-boil" lasagna pasta sheets (3½ by 6½ inches)

1 cup freshly grated Parmesan cheese

for 45 minutes or until the pasta is tender and the lasagna is bubbling. Remove the foil and bake until the cheese is golden, about 5 more minutes. (If the pasta is tender but the top hasn't colored, increase the oven temperature to 450° F and bake a few minutes longer.) Let the lasagna rest for 15 to 20 minutes before serving.

CHEF'S NOTES: Fresh pasta sheets, either homemade or store-bought, are sublime and make this a very authentic dish. You'll need to substitute about 1 pound fresh pasta for the dried and the sheets will need to be boiled until just short of tender, drained, and dried on clean kitchen towels. Because the meatballs provide an adequate meaty punch to the lasagna, a simple marinara sauce such as Lisa's No-Fuss Tomato Sauce (page 277) can be used instead. If you're pressed for time, omit the meatballs. The meat sauce is still good without them. Instead of lasagna, you can turn this dish into baked rigatoni. Simply toss cooked rigatoni with some of the meat sauce and then layer as directed for the lasagna. The baking time will be the same.

Tourtière (Quebec Pork Pie)
Because Quebec is a cold place for a long part of the year, the locals have developed quite a few recipes for rib-sticking fare. My good friend and talented cook Jeff Bergman first ate *tourtière* while visiting his wife's family in Quebec and thought the pie tasty but a bit stodgy. Back at home in Seattle, he began experimenting with the pie and the result is this delicious version with an aromatic pork filling enclosed in a light flaky crust made with lard and a bit of butter. SERVES 6

¼ pound bacon, thickly sliced and coarsely chopped

2 pounds coarsely ground lean pork

1 cup Dark Pork Stock (page 87), homemade chicken stock, or canned low-sodium chicken broth

1 cup chopped celery

½ cup chopped celery leaves

2 large onions, chopped

2 garlic cloves, minced

1 Heat a large skillet over medium heat, add the bacon, and cook until it has just begun to release its fat, about 7 minutes. Add the pork and stir to break up the clumps of meat. Add the stock, celery, celery leaves, onions, garlic, parsley, savory, bay leaf, thyme, cinnamon, cloves, salt, and pepper. Cook over medium-low heat for 30 minutes, stirring occasionally, to prevent the meat from sticking. After 30 minutes, the mixture should be fairly dry; drain off the fat. Taste and adjust the seasonings—

the filling should be fairly lively with flavor. Transfer the mixture to a bowl and set aside to cool completely. Remove the bay leaf. When cool, add the eggs and stir to combine thoroughly. Refrigerate the mixture until you're ready to fill the pie. 2 To make the pie: on a well-floured work surface, roll one of the disks of dough into a round 11 to 12 inches in diameter and ⅛ inch thick. Transfer the dough to a 9-inch pie plate and press into the corners, leaving a slight overhang around the edge of the plate. Roll out the remaining disk of dough into a 12-inch round ⅛ inch thick. Fill the pie plate with the pork mixture, mounding it in the center. Top with the second dough round over the filling and press the edges together with the bottom crust, then crimp to seal. Brush the top with the egg wash and cut several evenly spaced slits in the top. Refrigerate the pie for 20 minutes to set the crust. 3 Preheat the oven to 400° F. 4 Bake the pie for 45 to 55 minutes or until the pastry is an even golden brown and crisp. Set aside to cool on a rack for 10 to 15 minutes. 5 Serve the *tourtière* warm or at room temperature with cornichons or fruit chutney.

½ cup finely chopped flat-leaf parsley

1 tablespoon chopped fresh savory or 1 teaspoon dried

1 bay leaf

1 teaspoon minced fresh thyme or ½ teaspoon dried

⅛ teaspoon ground cinnamon

⅛ teaspoon ground cloves

2 teaspoons kosher salt

½ teaspoon freshly ground black pepper

2 eggs, lightly beaten

1 recipe Jeff's Lard Piecrust (recipe follows), chilled

1 egg yolk, whisked with 1 tablespoon cream

CHEF'S NOTE: Baking the pie on a pizza stone will give it an exceptionally crisp crust, both on the bottom and sides.

Jeff's Lard Piecrust 🐖 MAKES 1 (9-INCH) DOUBLE-CRUST PIE

2½ cups all-purpose flour

1 teaspoon kosher salt

¾ cup homemade or freshly Rendered Lard (page 313), cut into small pieces and frozen

4 tablespoons butter, cut into small pieces, combined with the lard, and frozen

½ cup ice water

1 tablespoon sugar (for sweet pies only; omit if making Tourtière [page 236] or other savory pie)

In a large bowl, combine the flour and salt and stir well. Remove the lard and butter combination from the freezer and add to the flour mixture, tossing with a fork to coat the lard and butter with flour. With a pastry blender, cut the fat into the flour until it resembles coarse meal. Working quickly, drizzle 6 tablespoons of the ice water over the flour mixture, tossing with the fork (do not use your hands or the fat will soften) until the dough forms a shaggy mass. Add the remaining 2 tablespoons ice water if the dough seems too dry, 1 tablespoon at a time. Once the water has been added, gather the dough very quickly into a ball that just holds together. Avoid kneading or squeezing the dough; it should be moist but not sticky. Divide the dough in half, shape into 2 disks, and wrap each well in plastic wrap. Refrigerate for at least 30 minutes or up to 1 day.

Spanish Arroz con Puerco y Chorizo (Pork and Chorizo Paella) 🐖 This recipe is an all-pork

version of the Spanish classic, paella, which gets its name from the flat pan used to make the dish. Some of the best paellas I've ever eaten were in a little town outside Valencia. Once two of us were served a pan about 18 inches in diameter that was filled with a tasty mixture of tiny pork riblets, chorizo, and squid. At home, I've been making paellas ever since and my favorites, besides this all-pork version, combine rabbit and chorizo and chicken thighs, chorizo, and seafood. Use Spanish-style chorizo, which is air-dried and has a different flavor than Mexican-style. SERVES 8

1 Preheat the oven to 350° F. **2** To make the rub: Combine all of the ingredients for the rub. **3** Massage the rub generously over all sides of the ribs. **4** Heat the olive oil in a large ovenproof sauté pan (with a lid) over medium-high heat. Add the ribs and brown well on all sides, about 7 to 10 minutes. Transfer to a plate and set aside. Pour off and discard all but 2 tablespoons of the fat. Lower the heat to medium and add the chorizo, ham, onions, and garlic and cook until the vegetables have softened, about 5 minutes. Add the rice, stir until well coated, and cook for 2 minutes or until the rice begins to turn translucent. Stir in the paprika and black pepper and cook for 1 minute. Add the chicken stock and saffron. Increase the heat to high and bring the liquid to a boil, scraping up any browned bits from the bottom of the pan. Return the ribs to the pan, cover, and put in the middle of the oven. Bake for 35 minutes, then scatter the piquillos, olives, and peas on top of the rice. Bake until the rice is tender and all the liquid has been absorbed, about 10 to 20 minutes longer. **5** To serve, stir the rice a little to incorporate the peppers, olives, and peas and serve at once.

CHEF'S NOTE: If you can't find Spanish-style chorizo, then substitute Portuguese chorizo or *linguiça*, or Cajun *andouille*.

Paella Rub

4 teaspoons Spanish paprika

2 teaspoons freshly ground black pepper

1 tablespoon minced garlic

1 tablespoon kosher salt

1 teaspoon ground coriander

4 pounds boneless country ribs

2 tablespoons olive oil

8 ounces Spanish chorizo, sliced into ¼-inch rounds (see headnote)

4 ounces Serrano ham, prosciutto, or smoked ham, diced

4 cups chopped onions

4 tablespoons chopped garlic

3 cups Carnaroli or Arborio rice

2 tablespoons paprika, preferably Spanish or mild Hungarian

½ teaspoon freshly ground black pepper

6 cups homemade chicken stock, canned low-sodium chicken broth, or water

¼ teaspoon powdered saffron

½ cup piquillo peppers, pimentos, or fire-roasted red bell peppers, thinly sliced

½ cup pitted green olives

1 cup frozen green peas

Portuguese Clams or Mussels with Sausage 🐖

The Portuguese, who know a thing or two about cooking seafood, long ago discovered that clams and spicy sausage are a great culinary combination. In Portugal they've even invented a special copper vessel with a domed hinged lid, called a *cataplana,* that is used just for cooking what has become this almost national dish.

Usually Portuguese chorizo or *linguiça* is used, but other full-flavored sausages such as Cajun-style *andouille* also work well with the shellfish. Feel free to improvise with this dish, but don't leave out the sausage. SERVES 4

---

2 tablespoons olive oil

1 pound Portuguese chorizo or *linguiça,* or Cajun *andouille,* cut into ½-inch-thick rounds

2 cups finely chopped red onions

2 tablespoons chopped garlic

2 cups chopped peeled and seeded ripe tomatoes, or 2 cups canned diced tomatoes

2 teaspoons fresh chopped thyme

1 bay leaf

1 cup dry white wine

½ cup homemade chicken stock, canned low-sodium chicken broth, or bottled clam juice

¼ cup chopped Italian flat-leaf parsley

4 dozen medium hard-shell clams such as cherrystone or little necks, or medium mussels, cleaned and rinsed

Kosher salt

Freshly ground black pepper

8 tablespoons butter cut into ½ inch pieces (optional)

1 Heat the olive oil in a large casserole (with a lid) or soup pot over medium heat. Add the sausage and cook, stirring, for 2 to 3 minutes. Add the onions and garlic and cook until the onions are soft, about 5 minutes. Add the tomatoes and any juices, thyme, bay leaf, wine, and stock. Bring the liquid to a boil over high heat, then lower the heat to maintain a simmer and cook for 10 minutes. Stir in the parsley and add the clams or mussels. Bring the liquid to a moderate boil, cover the pot, and steam until the shellfish have opened. Mussels will take 4 to 8 minutes; the clams 10 to 12 minutes. 2 Using a slotted spoon, divide the shellfish among 4 large soup bowls. Taste the sauce for salt and pepper. If you want a sauce with richer flavor and more body, stir in the optional butter until incorporated. Ladle the sauce over the shellfish in each bowl and serve with crusty bread.

CHEF'S NOTES: You can also use this sauce for cooking shrimp. Large shrimp need about 3 to 5 minutes to cook. Or turn the dish into a shellfish stew by combining 3 or 4 different kinds of seafood. Make sure you add the longest cooking shellfish first, then follow with the shortest cooking. Instead of sausage, you can use marinated pork to flavor the dish. Marinate 1½ pounds diced blade roast, cut into ¾-inch cubes, in 1 teaspoon salt, 1 teaspoon freshly ground black pepper, 2 tablespoons red wine vinegar, 1 tablespoon Spanish paprika, and 2 teaspoons minced garlic overnight in the refrigerator. Then follow the recipe, cooking the pork (instead of the sausage) as the first step. Save any marinade to add with the wine and stock.

Choucroute Garni (Sauerkraut with Smoked Meats and Sausages)

The first time I ate this world-class peasant dish, I was traveling with a friend in Europe and he coerced me to visit his relatives in Alsace. We were there four days and it rained four days, so our main form of entertainment was eating and sleeping. The big meal was served midday and thank God for that, because all I could do afterward was nap. One day we sat down to a table spread with two of the largest platters I'd ever seen with sauerkraut and piles of smoked meat and sausages. I was seated next to Grandpa whose notion of hospitality was to make sure my wineglass and plate never went empty. I didn't know enough French to politely refuse.

Make sure to have an assortment of grainy and smooth mustards and some crusty rye bread. You can make the choucroute on top of the stove or in the oven. Oh, and don't forget the Gewürztraminer or German beer. SERVES 8 TO 10 WITH LEFTOVERS

2 tablespoons bacon drippings, lard, or olive oil

2 onions, thinly sliced

2 medium carrots, coarsely chopped

4 garlic cloves, chopped

3 pounds good deli sauerkraut, preferably not canned, briefly rinsed and drained

1 cup fruity wine, such as Alsatian Riesling

1 cup Dark Pork Stock (page 87), beef stock, homemade chicken stock, or canned low-sodium chicken broth

4 bay leaves

4 sprigs thyme or 1 teaspoon dried

10 juniper berries

20 coriander seeds

20 whole black peppercorns

1 Preheat the oven to 325° F. 2 Heat the bacon drippings in a large casserole or Dutch oven over medium-high heat. Add the onions, carrots, and garlic and cook, stirring frequently, until the vegetables are soft and beginning to color, about 10 minutes. Add the sauerkraut, wine, stock, bay leaves, thyme, juniper berries, coriander seeds, and peppercorns. Stir to combine and bring to a boil. Add the ham hock (or smoked Boston butt or Petit Salé) and the slab bacon (or alternatives, if using). Make sure the meats are buried in the sauerkraut. Cover and bake for 1 hour. 3 Remove the casserole from the oven, add the pork chops (or alternatives, if using) and bury them in the sauerkraut. Return the pot to the oven and bake for 30 minutes. Then turn the ingredients over well and add the sausages. Again, turn the mixture over so that the meats are covered as much as

possible with the sauerkraut. Bake for 20 minutes, at this point, check the smoked chops or loin to see if the meat is fork-tender. If not, bake 10 minutes more. 4 To serve the choucroute, transfer the contents of the casserole to a large platter or shallow bowl. If you used slab bacon, smoked Boston butt, smoked pork loin, or other large cuts of meat, slice them and arrange with the sausages on top of the sauerkraut. Let your guests help themselves by supplying them with a sharp knife for cutting off chunks of the sausages and a large spoon to scoop up the kraut. Then pass the mustard, please.

2 to 3 pounds ham hocks or 2 to 3 pounds smoked Boston butt (page 188), or 2 to 3 pounds Petit Salé of Pork (page 292)

1 pound slab bacon, fresh pork belly, or pancetta

6 bone-in smoked pork chops (about 3 pounds), or 3 pounds ham, 3 pounds Smoked Pork Loin (page 300), or 3 pounds Canadian bacon

3 pounds assorted sausages (see Chef's Notes)

Assorted mustards, for serving

CHEF'S NOTES: Basically you can make choucroute garni with any assortment of smoked meats, cured meats, and sausages you desire. Some of my favorite smoked meats are homemade Molasses-Cured Pork Shoulder Bacon (page 299), and Petit Salé (page 292), which can be substituted for ham hocks in the recipe (you'll need about 2 to 3 pounds). Instead of smoked pork chops, you can substitute 6 thick slices of ham, a 3-pound chunk of homemade Smoked Boneless Pork Loin (page 300), or a 3-pound piece of Canadian bacon. If you don't want to use slab bacon, you can leave it out or substitute fresh pork belly or an equivalent chunk of homemade pancetta. For the sausage assortment, you'll need about 3 pounds. I like to combine mild white sausage such as bockwurst, Toulouse Sausage (page 261), weisswurst, or fresh bratwurst with smoked sausage such as frankfurters, knockwurst, andouille, kielbasa, smoked bratwurst, cervelats, or Smoked French Country Sausage (page 266). The choice is yours, but no matter what you use, the method is the same and the enjoyment equal. Make sure to have and assortment of grainy and smooth mustards and some crusty rye bread. You can make the choucroute on top of the stove or in the oven.

Part Four: Preserving Pork

12

Strategy for Preserving Pork at Home

In this chapter you'll learn the ancient art of preserving pork, a tradition that has produced some of the pork butchers' finest works—bacon, ham, pâté, sausage, and various other cured pork products. It is a tradition that no doubt precedes recorded history and probably parallels the domestication of the pig. Before refrigeration, which didn't come about until the late nineteenth and early twentieth centuries, most meat needed to be preserved, and preservation meant that some of the water in the meat needed to be replaced with salt. Unlike other red meats, pork could withstand this treatment without becoming so hard and dry that it became inedible (pork jerky?). Not all pork preservation methods, though, require high levels of salt. Some methods preserved lighter salted cooked pork by reducing the meat's exposure to air. Pâtés, *confit*s, and *rillette*s preserve slowly cooked pork by covering it with a layer of fat that is virtually airtight.

Farmers and butchers have practiced the art of preserving pork because the results are both necessary in order to have meat available all year round and delicious. The process is simple, but care must be taken to provide meat that is properly treated and safe to eat.

Many of the traditions of sausage-making and pork preservation developed as far back as Romans times are still practiced in Italy today. *Salumi* (the Italian word for sausage, salami, ham, and other preserved meats) is a fine art with many regional specialties. Unlike their Roman ancestors, Italians today no longer need to import ham from Gaul, and their *prosciutto di Parma* is world famous. The keepers of the *salumi* craft are called *salumaii*, and today some still practice their art in small specialty shops (*salumerie*). But most of the famous products, such as Parma ham, *culatello,* and mortadella, are now made in factories. In the United States, almost all *salumi* is mass-produced, and many of the products no longer reflect the care and flavor of their artisanal roots. However, a growing number of chefs in this country, who demand the best-tasting products and are always seeking the best-quality ingredients, have taught themselves to make pancetta, salami, and prosciutto, and the tradition of housemade pâtés and fresh sausage has become even more widespread. I've written this chapter not only for chefs who are looking for new preserved pork recipes and techniques, but also for those serious home cooks who have the time and desire, as well as the equipment and space, to make *salumi* and *charcuterie* in their own kitchens. Some of you do not live in a geographical area that is suitable for aging some of the pork products (too humid in New Orleans, too warm in Los Angeles), and may lack proper space, but don't be discouraged. Except for the dried salami, pancetta, *lardo* (cured back fat), and *lonza* (air-dried pork loin), you can make just about every recipe in this chapter, including brine-cured ham, smoked bacon, fresh sausages, pâté, and *rillettes*.

Strategy for Preserving Pork at Home

Perhaps the question you're asking at this point is, "Why do I want to preserve pork when I can get anything I want at the supermarket?" My answer is simply that what you make will be satisfying and delicious, and there aren't many stores that will offer you anything that can compare to the sausages, pâtés, and hams you can make right in your own kitchen.

Is my use of the word "preserved" confusing you? While the traditions of sausage-making, pâté-making and ham-curing grew out of a need to preserve pork before refrigeration, refrigeration changed the methods of preservation and the amount of time that some pork products needed to be stored. A lightly salted ham, a fresh sausage, or smoked bacon can now be kept long enough to have ample time for you to enjoy it—not just a few hours but days for fresh sausage and weeks for smoked bacon, but not years as it used to be before refrigeration. What I haven't mentioned is that preserved pork products created through necessity to prevent spoilage **taste really good**. While we no longer need to preserve our pork to see us through the winter, the emphasis today is on making preserved pork items that really taste good.

Curing and Smoking

Curing The word means preserving, by removing and replacing some of the water in pork with salt. Depending on how much water is removed, spoilage bacteria cannot grow. Usually this is accomplished one of two ways: by dry-curing, coating the meat in salt, or by brine-curing, soaking the meat in a solution of salt and water (and often sugar, sodium nitrites, and spices in addition to the water). If enough water is removed, the pork becomes bacteriologically stable and organisms can no longer grow. This is why country ham and dry salami do not go bad at room temperature.

Dry-Curing I've not provided recipes for this time-honored technique because it's very difficult to control the saltiness of the final product and it takes considerable practice and skill to get it right. Such traditional pork products as country ham, box-cured bacon, prosciutto, and Serrano ham are made by dry-curing. I prefer to use wet-curing, i.e., brining, in which meat is soaked in a solution of water and salt because it's easier to control the saltiness of the finished product.

Brining This method is synonymous with pickling (as in pickled tongue) and corning (as in corned beef). Often brines contain sodium nitrite (see Insta-cure No. 1 on page 14), which retards the growth of botulism (remember those Roman sausages, page 6) and other spoilage organisms, and preserves the pink color that we associate with smoked or cured pork. Usually sodium nitrite is sold blended with salt and tinted a faint pink. Recipes for and practitioners of pork-curing and sausage-making call this salt blend "curing salts" to distinguish it from regular salt (sodium chloride). For the home curer or smoker of pork, curing salts are only necessary if the curing or smoking process requires that the meat be subjected to higher than refrigerator temperatures for more than an hour or two. You *must*, therefore, use "curing salts" when cold-smoking or air-drying and aging cured pork.

Brining Time and Brine Strength (Saltiness) Except for items such as pancetta, salami, *lardo*, and *lonza* that are air-dried and aged, it's not the purpose of my recipes in this chapter to preserve the pork for an extended period of time. I assume that the Petit Salé of pork, ham, and bacon you make will be stored in the refrigerator and consumed in 7 to 10 days. Or you will freeze it. For that reason, the saltiness of the brine and the length of time the meat soaks in the brine are less than would be specified in commercial products that require longer shelf lives and taste saltier than anything you will produce at home. In addition, the methods of brining, as instructed in this book, are very different from the commercial process. In commercial operations, a measured amount of brine is actually pumped directly into the meat by banks of multiple injection needles. My methods hark back to the "old days." They rely on passive diffusion of salt from the brine solution to the meat. This process is much slower than direct injection, but to my taste results in a greater depth of flavor. This passive diffusion method of curing works well for small pieces of meat like loin, belly, or butterflied shoulder, which have an average diameter of 4 inches or less at the thickest point. This method does not work for large pieces, such as whole bone-in legs or whole Boston butts. When curing by passive diffusion, you're in a race between spoilage and the time it takes for enough salt to penetrate the meat at a level ample enough to retard spoilage. The salt must travel (diffuse) from the brine to the center of the meat, and the bigger the diameter the longer it takes for the salt to travel to the center of the piece (or in pork leg to the bone). If the process takes too long, there is a greater risk that bacteria will win the race. You can also speed up the process by increasing the amount of salt in the brine. This is how dry-cures for country hams and prosciutto work, but it's still a race, and even the best commercial dry-cure ham makers lose a fair percentage of their products to spoilage. There is also the risk that your ham, even if not spoiled, will be overly salty. The last way to speed up the diffusion of salt from the brine to the center of the meat is to raise the temperature (diffusion is a function of temperature), but if you were to do that then the growth of bacteria would always outpace the passive diffusion. That's why all curing of meat is carried out under refrigeration temperatures. As long as you follow the tips and advice in the recipes and keep everything clean and fresh, you should end up with great-tasting cured meats.

No recipe that I provide for curing will be exact. There are simply too many variables and my brining times may be too long or too short to suit your own tastes. If the results are too salty for you, you may want to decrease the brining time the next time around. Or, if not salty enough, then you want to increase the brining time. I wouldn't mess with the saltiness of the brine recipe itself, though. You can only lower the salt concentration so far. The meat must remain in the brine long enough for adequate levels of salt and sodium nitrite (if you're using it) to penetrate the center of the meat (this is most critical if you're smoking). Otherwise the meat may spoil during the exposure to warm smoke. If you have any doubt whatsoever about your meat, if by feeling it and smelling it you suspect it's gone bad, you *must* throw it out. In each recipe, I give a range for curing times. Start with the longest time for your first attempt and if the result is too salty, decrease the curing time in 12-hour increments until you reach the minimal time, which you should not go below. Another way (and *only* if you use sodium nitrite) to find out if the cure has adequately penetrated the center of the meat is to cut the piece in half crosswise. If it's not uniformly pink all the way through and has a gray circle in the center, then it needs to cure longer. While the meat is safe to eat, you may want to cure it longer so that it is uniformly pink. Put it back in the brine for at least 12 hours more.

Keeping a Journal I recommend that you keep a journal so that you can remember what you've done and learn from your mistakes. Here's a sample of the journal I keep:

Sample Brining Journal

Date	Cut	Weight and Diameter	Cure	Time in Cure	Results and Comments
9/20/03	Boneless Loin	4 lbs 2½ × 3½"	Basic	48 Hrs	Too Salty!

Smoking This term is defined as meat that is exposed to smoke that is absorbed, diffusing from the surface to the interior. Smoking reduces moisture in meat, concentrating flavors and firming up texture. The resultant smoked meat tastes terrific. In addition, smoke has a preserving effect and, if done long enough and combined with adequate salt and air-drying, can completely preserve meats (like country ham) so that they no longer spoil at room temperature.

Generally there are two types of smoking processes based on the temperature of the smoke. **Hot-smoking** is done at high enough temperatures (200° to 250° F) to actually cook the meat as it smokes. Barbecuing (see Real Barbecued Pork on page 174) is an example of hot-smoking. **Cold-smoking** is done at temperatures too low to cook the food. The term "cold" is a bit misleading since the smoke is not actually cold but is at a lower temperature range (80° to 120° F) when compared to "hot" smoke. Cold-smoking doesn't cook the food but it does dry it out. Cold-smoking can take anywhere from a few hours for small items to a couple of days for large items like whole hams. Country hams can take weeks. Meat that is cold-smoked is almost always cured first, and sodium nitrite must be used in the cure. Usually meat that is to be cold-smoked is removed from the cure, patted dry, and allowed to dry for a few hours hanging at room temperature. A fan can help facilitate this process. Meat with a dry surface absorbs smoke more evenly and more quickly than meat with a moist surface and it will have a lovely mahogany exterior after smoking.

For the purposes of this book, all my cold-smoked recipes are done in a covered kettle-type barbecue, using hardwood sawdust. Many other types of manufactured and homemade smokers do the job well. If you use one of these smokers, please familiarize yourself with the instruction manual.

For my recipes I find that I can get an adequate cloud of smoke using hardwood sawdust, which imparts a wonderful smoky flavor after 6 to 8 hours. Smoking times will be less if your smoke is dense and longer if your cloud of smoke is thin or less intense. Final results will depend on your taste. As with curing, I highly recommend that you keep a journal so that you can refer to what you did previously and be able to make appropriate adjustments (see Sample Smoking Journal). One variable you may enjoy playing with is the type of sawdust or wood chips you use for smoking—each has its own unique flavor. Hardwood sawdust can be purchased from barbecue specialty stores, hardware stores, and mail-order outlets (see Sources on page 318). Some types of wood available are hickory, apple, cherry, alder, and oak. Never use softwood sawdust—fir or pine—or yard clippings. Use only sawdust or chips sold for the specific purpose of smoking food.

Sample Smoking Journal

Date	Cut	Dimensions	Cure & Time	Type of Wood	Air Temp	Smoking Temp	Final Temp of Meat	Smoking Time	Comments
9/22/03	Boneless Loin	2½ × 3½"	Basic 48 Hrs	Hickory	80° F	120° F	115° F	6 Hrs	Needs a little more smoke— too salty

Hygiene and Safety for Preparing Fresh Sausage, Pâté, and Cured Meats That Are Not Aged

1 Start with impeccably fresh meat and fresh ingredients, meaning no old or processed garlic and only fresh herbs and onions.

2 Meat must be kept refrigerated at all times; meat, especially after it's ground, should not exceed 45° F. If making several sausage varieties at one time, grind each mixture separately, add the spices, and refrigerate. Then move on to the next mixture until all of them are ground. Pull one mixture at a time out of the refrigerator right before stuffing into casings or filling pâté molds and return it to the fridge before starting on the next batch. Always work with the meat during the coolest hours of the day (unless your kitchen is air-conditioned). Your kitchen should not exceed 72° F and 65° F is even more ideal.

3 Plan ahead and have all your ingredients measured and any cooked ingredients, like onions or cooked pork skin, chilled to refrigerator temperatures. You can do this a day ahead.

4 Before you begin, wash all your equipment in hot, soapy water and cool it in the freezer before use. Wash all surfaces, especially cutting boards, with a diluted bleach solution and sterilize knives with bleach as well. Periodically wash down the work surface.

5 Wash your hands well and often.

6 Never let meat sit around in the grinders, choppers, stuffers, or anywhere. Clean your equipment, even if you're only taking a 15-minute break. When you're done for the day, wash up immediately in hot, soapy water with a little bit of bleach added.

7 Never taste raw meat for seasoning. Make a small patty of the mixture and cook it until done in a pan before tasting.

8 Once you make sausages, they should be refrigerated and eaten within 3 days; otherwise freeze them for up to 3 months. If you know you're not going to use the sausage in the next 3 days, freeze them as soon as they're made.

9 For pâtés, let them cool down at room temperature for 2 hours before refrigerating them loosely wrapped.

10 For cured meats and smoked meats, refrigerate them for up to 10 days after they're cured, or after they're smoked, or after they are cured and cooked. Otherwise freeze them right away. When smoking on a grill, make sure you clean the surface well with a wire brush and soap and water before smoking.

11 Water used for curing and sausage-making must be safe for drinking; if you're not sure of its pedigree, boil it first.

Finally, chill everything, clean everything, and *when in doubt, throw it out.*

13
Sausages

Master Recipe: How to Make Sausage

Making sausage is so easy and the results so satisfying that I think you'll want to become a frequent sausage maker in your own kitchen. You can use the meat in bulk form in any of your favorite recipes that call for sausage, or simply form the meat into patties to be fried or grilled. The only equipment required is a food processor, meat grinder (hand-cranked or electric), or just a sharp knife. If you're feeling lazy, purchase freshly ground pork from you butcher, but it's always best to grind your own meat so that you know exactly how fresh it really is and exactly how much fat it contains. Best of all, even after just one attempt, your homemade sausage will taste better than most any kind you can buy.

Should you want to put the sausage you make into casings, you'll need to purchase a sausage attachment for your meat grinder. Or, if you're really into it, you might want a special sausage stuffer (see Sources on page 318). You can get by, however, using a pastry bag fitted with a large, plain tip for stuffing small batches of sausage.

Before you begin, read over the general information on preserving that begins this section and especially the points on Hygiene and Safety (pages 253 to 254). If you will be smoking your sausage, then read about Curing and Smoking (pages 249 to 251) as well.

The world of sausages is huge, with just about every country on the earth offering up its own flavors (Eskimo reindeer sausage?). This is not surprising when you consider that sausage-making grew out of the tradition of using up the bits and pieces left over after pigs were butchered. However, pork of course was not the only meat used to make sausage. Any meat, poultry, seafood, or animal protein will do. Once the meat is ground, the universe for flavoring is infinite and includes all kinds of available spices, herbs, and various vegetables, such as leafy greens, artichokes, and sweet peppers; or fruit, such as apples, blueberries, cranberries, or dried cherries. With such a vast array of ingredients to choose from, I realize that I've just scratched the surface with the 8 recipes I've offered in this book, so vary the spices or substitute other ingredients that strike your fancy (add dried cranberries, for instance, or blueberries in the Brown Sugar and Sage Breakfast Patties on page 259). Two ingredients you may not want to modify are the salt and the fat. Both are at the minimal level to give you juicy and tasty sausage, and, if anything, you may end up adding more salt.

To Make Sausage Using a Meat Grinder. You can use a hand-cranked or electric meat grinder to make sausage (the grinder attachment to the KitchenAid mixer works very well), but you'll need the type of grinder that has interchangeable plates with several sizes of holes. Cut the meat and fat into ¾-inch-wide strips, spread them out on a plate (separating the meat and fat), and put the plate in the freezer for 10 minutes to firm up the meat and fat and make it easier to grind. Using a ⅜-inch plate, grind the lean meat into a large bowl and put the bowl in the refrigerator. Change to a ⅛- or ¼-inch plate and grind the fat. Combine the meat, fat, and remaining ingredients and mix everything together with your hands, squeezing, kneading, and folding to blend the mixture well. Do not overmix, however, to the point where the fat begins to melt—you just want the ingredients well distributed. Make a small patty with the mixture and cook it in a small pan over medium heat. Refrigerate the rest. Taste patty and adjust the salt, pepper, spices, and sugar as necessary.

To Make Sausage Using a Food Processor. Cut the meat and fat into ¾-inch cubes, spread them out on a plate (separating the meat and fat), and put the plate in the freezer for 10 minutes to firm up the meat and fat to make them easier to chop. Put the food processor bowl and metal blade in the freezer as well for the same amount of time. Set up the processor and add just enough meat to cover the blade (depending on the size of the bowl, about 1 pound). Pulse to form approximately ⅜-inch pieces; transfer the meat to a bowl and put the bowl in the refrigerator. Repeat with the rest of the meat, adding it to the bowl to chill. After all the meat is chopped, process the fat into approximately ⅛- to ¼-inch pieces and add it to the meat. Combine the meat, fat, and remaining ingredients and mix everything together with your hands, squeezing, kneading, and folding to blend the mixture well. Do not overmix, however, to the point where the fat begins to melt—you just want the ingredients well distributed. Make a small patty with the mixture and cook it in a small pan over medium heat. Taste and adjust the salt, pepper, spices, and sugar as necessary.

How to Make Sausage Links To stuff sausage meat into casings, you will need either the sausage horn attachment for a meat grinder, or a pastry bag fitted with a plain round tip. You'll also need about 16 feet of medium pork casings for each recipe, available from specialty butchers or by mail-order (see Sources on page 318). Soak the casings, which come packed in salt, in warm water in a large bowl for 30 minutes to 1 hour. Then put one end of a casing over the end of a faucet and wash the inside with warm water. Change the water in the bowl and soak the casing again.

If you're using a meat grinder, remove the plate and blade and fit it with the sausage horn. Pull the entire length of soaked casing over the tip of the horn, gathering it up and leaving a little bit dangling. Tie a knot in the dangling end. Fill the bowl of the grinder with the chilled sausage meat and crank the meat through the grinder to begin filling the casing. Continue to feed the meat through the grinder into the casing until all the meat is used. Have a skewer, pin, or needle at hand to prick any air bubbles that form as the casing fills. The casing should be full, but not too tightly packed, or it will burst when you make the links. Remove the casing from the horn.

If you're using a pastry bag, pull the entire length of the soaked casing over the end of the tip, gathering it up and leaving a little bit dangling. Tie a knot in the dangling end of the casing and fill the pastry bag with the chilled sausage meat. Squeeze the bag with one hand to push the meat into the casing while you use your other hand to hold the casing on the metal tip. Fill the casing with all the sausage meat as described above. When it's filled, remove the casing from the tip. Prick any air bubbles that form as the casing fills.

To form sausage links, begin at the knotted end and pinch the casing between your fingers about 6 inches from the end; you may vary the length if you wish. Move down the casing another 6 inches and pinch again, about 12 inches from the knot. Twist the second 6-inch section with your fingers to make the first two links (twisting the link will twist both ends and seal both links). Proceed down the casing, twisting every other pinch to make links. When you reach the end, tie another knot.

To separate the chain into individual links, use a sharp knife to cut through the twisted casings. Refrigerate the sausages immediately and use within 2 to 3 days; or wrap the sausages well in plastic wrap or foil and freeze for up to 3 months.

Brown Sugar and Sage Breakfast Patties

This is the classic, slightly sweet breakfast sausage. You may substitute pure maple syrup for the brown sugar or, if you can find it, Steen's Pure Cane Syrup or golden treacle syrup. I usually make the sausage mixture a day ahead so the flavors can mellow and meld. This sausage is good to use in Thanksgiving stuffing, or use the mixture to stuff pork chops (Stuffed Molasses-Brined Chops on page 123).

Read How to Make Sausage—Master Recipe (page 256) and Hygiene and Safety for Preparing Fresh Sausage, Pâté, and Cured Meats (pages 253 to 254). MAKES ABOUT 1½ POUNDS, SERVING 6 TO 8

---

1 Place half the cubed Boston butt and half the pork fat in a food processor bowl fitted with the steel blade. Process the batch with short pulses until the mixture is roughly chopped, with pieces about the size of large peas. Scrape the chopped mixture into a large bowl and repeat with the remaining pork and fat. 2 Add all of the remaining ingredients to the pork mixture. Wash your hands well, using soap and warm water, then mix the sausage mixture by hand, kneading and squeezing the meat until everything is well blended. Make a small patty and cook it in a small skillet until done. Taste and adjust the salt, pepper, and sugar as needed. At this point, you can wrap the sausage mixture in plastic wrap and refrigerate it for 2 or 3 days until you are ready to cook it. 3 When ready to cook the sausage, shape it into 12 to 16 equal-sized oval patties, each about ½ inch thick. 4 Heat a large, heavy frying pan over medium-high heat and add the patties, without overcrowding. (You will need to cook the patties in batches.) Cook for about 5 to 6 minutes or until nicely browned. Flip and cook for 5 minutes more. When done, the centers of the patties should be faintly pink or gray. Transfer the patties to paper towels to drain. Cook the remaining patties in the same manner and drain. Arrange them on a serving platter and serve at once.

1 pound Boston butt, cut into 1-inch cubes

½ pound pork back fat, cut into ½-inch cubes

1½ teaspoons kosher salt

1 to 2 teaspoons dark brown sugar, 1 to 2 teaspoons real maple sugar, or 1 to 2 teaspoons Steen's Pure Cane Syrup

1 teaspoon finely chopped fresh sage or 1 teaspoon ground sage

¼ teaspoon freshly grated nutmeg

½ teaspoon ground coriander seed

1 teaspoon freshly ground black pepper

¼ cup cold water

½ teaspoon Tabasco sauce, or more (optional)

Italian-Style Sausage with Rosemary and Grappa

 Village butcher shops in Italy can be very convivial places and often the butcher will greet regulars and friendly looking newcomers with a slice of housemade salami, a glass of wine, or even a glass of *grappa* (a distillate made from grape must). I've been fortunate enough to participate in this ritual many times. Because of my shared interest in sausage-making, I've been invited to observe the making of the *salsicce* (fresh sausage). I noticed that not only does the butcher imbibe some of the welcoming wine or grappa, but that some of the beverage also makes its way into the sausage. While the alcohol taste is not overpowering, the wine and *grappa* provide a great background flavor to enhance the sweetness of the pork in the sausage. Here's my version of a great Italian sausage. MAKES ABOUT 3½ POUNDS

2½ pounds Boston butt, cut into ¾-inch-wide strips

6 ounces pork back fat, cut into ¾-inch-wide strips

4 ounces pancetta, cut into ¾-inch-wide strips (see Chef's Notes)

2 teaspoons kosher salt

2 teaspoons freshly ground black pepper

1 tablespoon crushed fennel seeds

1 teaspoon fennel pollen or 1 teaspoon ground fennel seed

2 teaspoons finely chopped fresh rosemary

2 teaspoons minced garlic

¼ cup dry white wine

2 tablespoons *grappa* or other grape *eau de vie*

Grind the meat, the fat, and the pancetta and mix with the remaining ingredients as described in How to Make Sausage—Master Recipe (page 256). Make a small patty and cook it in a small skillet. Taste for flavor and make adjustments for salt, pepper, and other ingredients. Stuff the ground mixture into pork casings and tie into 6-inch links as described in How to Make Sausage Links (page 257).

CHEF'S NOTES: Italian butchers will often hang fresh sausage in the shop for a day or two to allow the flavors to mellow and develop a slight aged flavor. I don't consider this a safe practice for the home cook, but I do like the aged flavor, which I achieve by adding some pancetta (cured pork belly) to the ground pork. You may substitute fresh fat or salt pork if you don't want to use pancetta. This sausage mixture (no casings) makes great Italian cheese–stuffed sandwiches. For 4 sandwiches, combine 1 cup diced tomatoes, 3 tablespoons chopped basil, and 1 cup shredded mozzarella or fontina in a bowl. Make

8 patties with 1½ pounds of the sausage and mound equal amounts of the tomato-cheese mixture on 4 of them. Top with the remaining 4 patties and press the edges together to seal. Shape into rough ovals, then grill or broil the patties until done, about 4 to 5 minutes per side. Place each patty in an Italian or French roll and serve with roasted bell peppers and sautéed onions on the side. 🐖 Directions above are for making sausages using a meat grinder. See page 257 for method using a food processor.

Toulouse Sausage

🐖 Of all the French sausages, this is the most basic, really nothing more than fresh pork seasoned with salt, pepper, and a bit of curing salt. The sausages are then allowed to age a couple of days to let their flavors mature and develop. This approach is fine if you have available some of the truly wonderful pork that is sold in France. Few of us in this country, however, have access to this full-flavored meat, so I have developed my recipe using the leaner pork sold in our supermarkets. To get a more aged flavor, I've added a bit of pancetta and I've increased the flavor a bit with the addition of white wine, fresh thyme, and *Fines Épices* (page 279). To my taste, the resulting sausage is subtle and quite tasty. Make sure to grind the meat through a coarse plate (I use the one with ⅜-inch holes), but switch to the ⅛-inch plate for the fat and pancetta. MAKES ABOUT 3½ POUNDS

Using a meat grinder fitted with a ⅜-inch plate, grind the pork shoulder into a large bowl and refrigerate. Change the plate to ⅛ inch and grind the fat and pancetta. Combine with the ground pork. Add the remaining ingredients and mix as described in How to Make Sausage—Master Recipe (page 256). Make a small patty and cook in a small skillet. Taste for salt and pepper. Stuff the ground mixture into pork casings and tie into 6-inch links as described in How to Make Sausage Links (page 257). Let the sausages mellow, uncovered, in the refrigerator for 1 to 2 days before using.

2⅓ pounds Boston butt, cut into ¾-inch-wide strips

7 ounces pork back fat, cut into ¾-inch-wide strips

3 ounces pancetta, cut into ¾-inch-wide strips

2½ teaspoons kosher salt

¼ teaspoon Insta-cure No. 1 (optional, see Chef's Notes)

1 teaspoon coarsely ground black pepper

¼ teaspoon *Fines Épices* (page 279)

½ cup dry white wine

2 teaspoons chopped fresh thyme

CHEF'S NOTES: Insta-cure No. 1 is a mixture of 1 part sodium nitrite to 15 parts salt and is in the recipe solely to give these sausages their traditional pink color. Leave it out if the color is not important to you. 🐷 These sausages freeze well, so freeze enough to make some of your favorite sausage dishes when the weather turns cold. 🐷 See page 257 for making sausage with a food processor.

Boulevard's Pork and Mushroom Sausage

🐷 This sausage is the result of some experimentation on the part of the fine chefs who work at my wife Nancy's restaurant, Boulevard. Each chef has added to and tweaked the recipe that Nancy originated. Jacob Kenedy, a gifted young chef from London, came up with this current rendition, which he inherited from John Desmond, another talented chef from Cork, Ireland. This process of evolution and refinement of recipes, which reflects contributions of individual chefs, is to my way of thinking what keeps a great restaurant innovative and vital even after 11 years in business.

At Boulevard, the sausages are made with fresh porcini mushrooms in season and frozen ones out of season. These magnificent mushrooms are expensive and hard to come by for most of us so when I make these sausages I use the common brown mushrooms called cremini. You could also use portobello mushrooms, which are actually mature overgrown cremini. The important step in this recipe, no matter which kind of mushroom you use, is to roast the mushrooms first in a hot oven to intensify their flavor. While you can substitute dried porcini mushrooms for fresh, I find that they contribute a muddy flavor to the finished sausages. MAKES ABOUT 4 POUNDS

1 Put 8 of the garlic cloves and 1½ tablespoons of the oil in a small microwaveable container, cover, and microwave on high for 2 minutes. Set aside to cool. 2 Preheat the oven to 400° F. 3 Slice the remaining 4 garlic cloves and toss them in a bowl with the whole mushrooms, the onions, the remaining 2½ tablespoons oil, a sprinkling of salt, and freshly ground black pepper. Scrape the mushroom mixture and all the oil into a roasting pan and roast in the preheated oven for 5 minutes. Stir and roast for 5 minutes more or until the mushrooms are soft and fragrant. Set aside to cool. 4 Using a meat grinder fitted with a

⅜-inch plate, grind the pork and roasted mushroom mixture into a bowl and refrigerate. Change to the ⅛-inch plate and grind the fat and reserved cooked garlic and its oil. Combine the ground mixtures in a large bowl and add the remaining ingredients with 1 tablespoon kosher salt and 1 teaspoon pepper. Mix as described in How to Make Sausage—Master Recipe (page 256). Make a small patty and cook in a small skillet. Adjust the salt, pepper, and herbs to suit your taste. Stuff the ground mixture into pork casings and tie into 6-inch links as described in How to Make Sausage Links (page 257).

CHEF'S NOTES: The mushroom-sausage mixture makes a tasty filling for appetizer turnovers (page 76) and is great to use in a bread stuffing for chicken, turkey, or stuffed pork loin (see Apple and Cornbread–Stuffed Pork Loin with Roasted Apple Gravy on page 158). ꝏ See page 257 for making sausage with a food processor.

12 garlic cloves

4 tablespoons olive oil

1 pound cremini, portobello, or fresh porcini mushrooms

1 cup chopped onions

Kosher salt

Freshly ground black pepper

2½ pounds Boston butt, cut into ¾-inch-wide strips

½ pound pork back fat, cut into ¾-inch-wide strips

2 teaspoons chopped fresh sage

1 teaspoon chopped fresh basil

2 tablespoons chopped Italian flat-leaf parsley

1 tablespoon kosher salt

1 teaspoon freshly ground black pepper

Nancy's Artichoke and Piquillo Pepper Sausage

My wife and I developed this recipe after a visit to a farmer and his wife in the Basilicata region of Italy. We were invited for lunch, but ended up staying for three days. The farm produced not only sun-dried tomatoes, but also some of the best artichokes I've ever eaten, which were canned in olive oil. When we arrived home with our suitcases packed with these little gems, we quickly set about experimenting with them in numerous recipes. This sausage recipe was one of our hits. MAKES ABOUT 4 POUNDS

6 garlic cloves

2½ pounds Boston butt, cut into ¾-inch-wide strips

6 ounces pork back fat, cut into ¾-inch-wide strips

6 ounces pancetta, cut into ¾-inch-wide strips

½ cup piquillo peppers or Spanish pimentos, drained and cut into ⅜-inch pieces

2 cups artichoke hearts, frozen or jarred, cut into ⅜-inch dice (see Chef's Notes)

¼ cup dry white wine

2 teaspoons fennel seeds

1 teaspoon crushed red pepper flakes

2½ teaspoons kosher salt

1 tablespoon freshly ground black pepper

1 teaspoon sugar

1 Put the garlic and 1 tablespoon of water in a small microwaveable container, cover, and microwave on high for 2 minutes. Drain the garlic and set aside.

2 Using a meat grinder fitted with a ⅜-inch plate, grind the pork shoulder into a bowl and refrigerate. Change to the ⅛-inch plate and grind the fat, reserved garlic, and pancetta. Combine the ground mixtures in a large bowl and add the remaining ingredients. Mix as described in How to Make Sausage—Master Recipe (page 256). Make a small patty and cook it in a small skillet. Taste for salt and pepper and adjust. Stuff the ground mixture into pork casings and tie into 6-inch links as described in How to Make Sausage Links (page 257).

CHEF'S NOTES: You can also use artichoke hearts packed in oil or in brine. If using the brine-packed, decrease the salt in the recipe by ½ teaspoon.

For a different flavor, large fresh artichokes can be used. First pare them down to the heart, scrape out the choke, then cook the hearts in boiling salted water for 20 minutes or until tender. Drain and cool thoroughly before dicing and adding to the recipe.

See page 257 for making sausage with a food processor.

Chorizo de Los Angeles

My first contact with Mexican-style chorizo was as a lad growing up in Los Angeles. During my summer vacations my mother found me too much to have underfoot, so she often sent me off for the day with my father who worked at my grandfather's nursery near the Hispanic barrio of East Los Angeles. The highlight of my day and a break from the monotonous job of wrapping an endless number of plants with newspaper was the arrival of the catering truck or "roach coach," as the workers called it. I would always choose one of the many types of hot burritos that the vendor sold from his warming box, and my favorite was the one with refried beans and lots of spicy crumbled chorizo, which was delicious. Over the years I've experimented with many different chorizo recipes, and one of my favorites is this version, made with whole dried chilies, pork, and lots of fresh cilantro. Normally chorizo is used in bulk and doesn't need to be put into casings, making it a little easier on the home cook. Not only is chorizo used in burritos, it is used as a filling for tacos and enchiladas and as an accompaniment to eggs.

MAKES ABOUT 3 POUNDS

2 dried ancho chilies, steamed and seeded, or 3 tablespoons pure ancho or New Mexico chili powder (see Chef's Note)

2½ pounds pork shoulder, cut into ¾-inch-wide strips

½ pound pork back fat, cut into ¾-inch-wide strips

1 tablespoon kosher salt

1 teaspoon freshly ground black pepper

2 teaspoons ground cumin seed

1 teaspoon dried Mexican oregano

⅛ teaspoon ground cinnamon

⅛ teaspoon ground allspice

1 tablespoon minced garlic

¼ cup red wine vinegar

1 jalapeño, serrano, or other fresh hot chili, stemmed, seeded, and finely chopped

1 cup chopped cilantro

1 Tear the dried chilies into pieces and put in a glass measuring cup with 1 cup boiling water. Soak for at least 15 minutes or up to several hours. Put the softened chilies with ¼ cup of the soaking liquid in a blender and process to form a puree. Cool the mixture in the refrigerator. 2 Grind the meat and the fat and mix with the remaining ingredients including the chili puree (if using pure chili powder, add ¼ cup water to the mixture) as described in How to Make Sausage—Master Recipe (page 257). Mix in the cilantro. Make a small patty and cook in a small skillet. Taste for flavor and make adjustments for salt, pepper, and other ingredients. Wrap in plastic wrap.

CHEF'S NOTES: Pure ancho or New Mexico chili powder refers to the specific variety of dried chili that is ground to a powder. This should not be confused with "chili powder" that you find in the grocery store, which is a blend of ground dried chilies, cumin, and other spices. Besides ancho and New Mexico dried chilies, both of which are mild, you can also use dried Anaheim chilies (also called California chilies) or Hungarian or Spanish paprika. See page 257 for making sausage in a food processor.

Smoked French Country Sausage

Some of the greatest French sausages are mildly spiced country-style sausages that are smoked. One of the best is Morteau, from the mountains of eastern France, but many regions have their own variations. Often the sausages are eaten as is with potatoes or cabbage, or they're served in classic dishes such as Choucroute Garni (page 242), and they're very good used in bean or vegetable soups. Since these are cold-smoked (page 252), you must use Insta-cure No. 1 (see Chef's Notes). MAKES ABOUT 3 POUNDS

1 Using a meat grinder fitted with a ⅜-inch plate, grind the lean meat into a bowl and refrigerate. Change to the ⅛-inch plate and grind the fat, bacon, or pancetta, and optional skin. Combine the ground mixtures in a large bowl. Add the remaining ingredients and mix as described in the How to Make Sausage—Master Recipe (page 256). 2 Make a small patty and cook it in a small skillet. Taste for salt. Keep in mind that smoked sausage should be a bit saltier than fresh sausage. Stuff the ground mixture into pork casings and tie into 8-inch links as described in How to Make Sausage Links (page 257). Hang the sausages in the kitchen for 4 to 6 hours or until they are dry to the touch. Then cold-smoke them for 6 to 8 hours as described on page 252. The sausages can be refrigerated after smoking or hung overnight in the kitchen to allow the flavors to develop. Then refrigerate for up to 1 week.

CHEF'S NOTES: Insta-cure No. 1, a mixture of 1 part sodium nitrite to 15 parts salt, is in the recipe to prevent the growth of botulism and so must be used. See page 257 for making sausage with a food processor.

2½ pounds lean pork shoulder, cut into ¾-inch-wide strips

½ pound pork back fat, cut into ¾-inch-wide strips

¼ pound lean smoky bacon or pancetta, cut into ¾-inch-wide strips

¼ pound cooked pork skin (optional, page 79), cut into ¾-inch-wide strips

2 teaspoons chopped fresh sage

½ teaspoon chopped fresh thyme

½ teaspoon chopped fresh oregano

2 tablespoons sweet Hungarian paprika

¼ teaspoon *Fines Épices* (page 279)

2 teaspoons freshly ground black pepper

4 teaspoons kosher salt

2 teaspoons sugar

½ teaspoon Insta-cure No. 1

2 teaspoons minced garlic

½ cup dry white wine

John Desmond's Blood "Puddy" 🐷

John Desmond, who hails from County Cork, Ireland, is one of the best cooks I know. Fortunately, he works at my wife's restaurant, Boulevard, where he oversees sauces, special projects, and a little bit of everything else. He is also the resident *charcutier*.

Cork is justifiably famous for its blood "puddy," as John calls it, or blood pudding, and Clonakilty is a Cork town whose blood pudding is identified on the menus of better restaurants throughout Ireland. Usually Irish blood pudding is a mixture of blood, oatmeal, spices, and onions, stuffed into a wide casing (2 to 3 inches in diameter). Thick rounds are sliced off and fried in a bit of butter until just barely crisp. It's eaten with eggs for breakfast or with fried apples for lunch. Instead of just using blood and oatmeal, John adds ground pork to his blood pudding, which gives it better texture and body, as well as added flavor. And because John has cooked all over the world (Australia, France, New Zealand, Ireland, and California), he's been exposed to many more spices than are customarily used in Irish cooking. He incorporates these flavors into his blood pudding, and, to my taste, he makes it better than any I've ever tasted, in Ireland, France, or Italy. Also, John bakes his pudding in a loaf pan rather than stuffing it into casings. To serve, these firm puddings are unmolded, cut into individual servings, and briefly pan-fried.

Usually at Boulevard, the blood pudding is featured on the appetizer side of the menu, paired with fried scallops, lobster, or other seafood. These dishes have become so popular that John has to make up batches of 40 to 50 pounds, and that's a lot of blood "puddy." This recipe is much smaller. MAKES 2 LOAVES, SERVING ABOUT 24

---

2 tablespoons lard, bacon drippings, or olive oil

2 cups coarsely chopped onions

6 garlic cloves

¼ cup port, sherry, or Madeira

½ teaspoon fennel seeds

1 teaspoon coriander seeds

2 teaspoons mustard seeds

1 teaspoon cumin seeds

1 bay leaf, crumbled

1 Heat the fat or olive oil in a medium skillet over medium heat. Add the onions and garlic, cover, and cook, stirring from time to time, for 5 minutes. Stir in the port, cover, and cook for 20 minutes more or until the onions are quite soft. Transfer the onions and any liquid to a bowl and cool in the refrigerator while you prepare the rest of the ingredients.

2 Heat a small skillet over medium heat and add the fennel seeds, coriander seeds, mustard seeds, cumin seeds, bay leaf, and red pepper flakes. Shaking the pan continuously, toast the spices until aromatic, 2 to 3 minutes. Let cool for a few minutes, then grind

in a spice grinder; set aside. 3 Combine the pork, fat, and reserved onions in a bowl. Using a meat grinder fitted with the ¼-inch plate, grind the mixture into a large bowl. If you have the bowl that comes with a standing mixer, choose it as you'll be using the mixer to combine the pudding ingredients. Otherwise you'll mix the old-fashioned way by hand. Add the blood, reserved ground toasted spices, cooked rice, barley, oats, parsley, sage, thyme, marjoram, allspice, *fines épices,* pepper, paprika, salt, and eggs. Fit the bowl on the mixer and stir on medium speed until the mixture is well combined, 2 to 3 minutes, or mix by hand for about 5 minutes. Pour equal amounts of the mixture into 2 loaf pans (9½ by 5½ inches each, with a 7-cup capacity). Seal each pan tightly with foil. 4 Preheat the oven to 325° F. Put on some water to boil. 5 Put the pans in a large roasting pan or baking dish. Put the pan in the oven on the middle rack and add enough boiling water to come two thirds of the way up the loaf pans. Bake the puddings for 1½ hours or until they reach an internal temperature of 160° F on an instant-read thermometer. Remove from the oven. Take pan out of the water and let cool for 2 hours, then wrap and refrigerate overnight. 6 To serve, unmold the blood puddings and cut into ½-inch-thick slices. Heat a small bit of butter or oil over medium heat in a nonstick skillet, then add a few slices of the blood pudding, enough to fit comfortably in the pan. Cook until lightly browned, about 3 to 5 minutes. Turn and cook the other side until browned. Serve with fried or poached eggs or pan-fried apples. 7 Wrapped well, blood pudding will keep for a week in the refrigerator or up to 3 months in the freezer.

1 teaspoon crushed red pepper flakes

1½ pounds Boston butt, cut into cubes

½ pound pork back fat, cut into cubes

3 cups blood (pork or beef, see Chef's Notes)

¾ cup cooked rice

¾ cup cooked pearl barley

½ cup cooked steel-cut rolled oats

½ cup chopped parsley

1 teaspoon chopped fresh sage

1 teaspoon chopped fresh thyme

1 teaspoon chopped fresh marjoram or oregano

½ teaspoon ground allspice

1 teaspoon *Fines Épices* (page 279)

2 teaspoons freshly ground black pepper

1 tablespoon Spanish paprika

2 tablespoons kosher salt, or more to taste

2 eggs, lightly beaten

Butter, for frying

CHEF'S NOTES: If you can't find blood from a Chinese butcher or other ethnic source, it can be ordered frozen from the Niman Ranch website (see Sources on page 318).

Serve slices of fried blood pudding instead of the pork confit in Warm Pork Confit and Frisée Salad (page 82). Add a slice of fried blood pudding as a hearty garnish to Italian Pork and Greens Soup with Skillet Cornbread (page 88).

14
Pâtés and Terrines

Pâtés are the rich relatives of the meat loaf clan, and though they are eaten cold and sometimes arrive at the table dressed to the nines in their formal jackets of glazed pastry or glistening aspic, they are barely more difficult to make than Mom's meat loaf. What distinguishes them is the quality and variety of their ingredients, which may include some or all of the following: ground pork, poultry, liver often marinated in wine or brandy; diced fresh pork fat; sliced or cubed tongue, ham, or game; cream, eggs, spices; pistachios, or, for the *ne plus ultra* touch, truffles. Endless combinations are possible to tempt you. The texture may be smooth if all the meat is finely ground or pureed, or rough if the meat is coarsely chopped and some of the ingredients are diced to present a beautiful mosaic when the loaf is sliced.

Technically, if you're a student of classic French *charcuterie, pâté* is a blend of forcemeats (ground or chopped meats) cloaked in pastry. *Terrines* are more rustic; they're simply a mixture of ground meats packed into a mold or loaf pan (called a *terrine*), which is sometimes lined with strips of fat or bacon. Today *pâté* refers to both the pastry-cloaked version as well as the terrine. Most pâté in America no longer sports a cloak of pastry.

In my experience I find that lining a terrine or loaf pan with fat is not necessary. Simply press the meat directly into the pan. In fact, the coarsely textured Pâté de Campagne (page 278) can even be baked free-form by shaping the meat mixture directly on a baking sheet as you would for a meat loaf. Many recipes instruct you to weight a pâté down after it's been cooked, which compacts the loaf so it stays together better after it's sliced. Usually I find this step unnecessary as well because the skin and other ingredients in my recipes provide enough natural gelatin to hold the slices together firmly.

It's important to cook most pâtés or terrines in a water bath, or *bain-marie,* especially the finely textured smooth pâtés, so that they cook slowly and evenly. Pâtés are cooked to an internal temperature of 160° F so that all the ingredients can slowly tenderize and release their gelatin.

Once baked, a pâté should be removed from its water bath, but left in the pan to cool for 2 hours before refrigerating. After a day or so in the fridge, you can unmold it, wrap it well in plastic wrap, and keep refrigerated for 7 to 10 days. You can serve the pâté the day after it is made, but it will taste better after 2 or 3 days, giving the flavors time to mellow and mature. Never freeze a pâté, as when thawed it loses texture and becomes wet and grainy.

Pâtés contain lots of fat, particularly liver pâtés. The fat is necessary for good flavor, but also for texture. Do not decrease the amount of fat called for in the recipes that follow or your pâté will be dry and grainy. Do have fun, however, altering the grind and the texture of the ingredients to suit your taste, or change the combination of spices. It's perfectly okay to make substitutions like poultry liver for pork liver, or use some ground veal for pork, or to exchange smoked turkey for ham or smoked tongue for smoked sausage, and so on, and on . . .

Rustic Pork Liver Terrine

🐷 I've made this terrine for years, beginning back in the '70s when I was the chef at Poulet, a small charcuterie in Berkeley. It was our biggest-selling pâté and is still one of my enduring recipes—I've changed it very little over the years. It has a coarse texture and is seasoned simply with classic spices and a little brandy and Madeira. I like to serve it with some hearty country bread and cornichons or pickled onions as a starter to a casual dinner with friends. Any extra pâté is great to have around for lunch with a salad. MAKES 2 TERRINES, EACH SERVING ABOUT 10

2 pounds pork liver

2 cups milk

1 tablespoon sugar

2 tablespoons lard, bacon drippings, or olive oil

3 cups coarsely chopped onions

1½ pounds pork back fat, cut into 1-inch cubes

3 large eggs

¼ pound boiled pork skin, cut into 1-inch pieces (see Chef's Notes)

1 cup heavy cream

2 tablespoons brandy

2 tablespoons Madeira or port

1 garlic clove

5 teaspoons kosher salt

1 tablespoon freshly ground black pepper

2 teaspoons sugar

¼ teaspoon allspice

1 Cut away any large blood vessels and connective tissue from the pork liver and cut it into 2-inch pieces. Put the milk in a large bowl or storage container and stir in the sugar. Add the liver and stir to combine. Cover and refrigerate for 2 hours or up to 24 hours. 2 When ready to make the terrine, drain the liver into a colander and wash well under cold running water until all the milky coating is removed. 3 Heat the fat or oil in a large skillet over medium-low heat. Add the onions, cover, and cook, stirring occasionally, until quite soft, about 20 minutes. Transfer the onions to a bowl and refrigerate, covered, for at least 30 minutes or overnight. 4 Using a meat grinder fitted with a ⅜-inch plate, grind 1 pound of the pork liver into a large bowl. (Use the bowl that comes with a standing electric mixer, if you have one, as you'll be using the mixer to combine the ingredients.) Change to a ⅛- or ¼-inch plate. 5 In another bowl, stir together the remaining liver, fat, chilled cooked onions, and pork skin. Grind the mixture into the bowl with the liver. Add all the remaining ingredients except the bay leaves. Fit the bowl on the mixer and stir on medium speed until the mixture is well combined, 2 to 3 minutes. 6 Preheat the oven to 300° F. Put on some water to boil.

7 Pour the ground mixture into 2 loaf pans (9½ by 5½ inches each, with a 7-cup capacity). Lay 2 bay leaves on top of each loaf for garnish. Put the pans in a large roasting pan or baking dish. Put the pan in the oven on the middle rack and add enough boiling water to come two thirds of the way up the loaf pans. Bake, uncovered, for 2 to 2½ hours or until they reach an internal temperature of 160° F on an instant-read thermometer. Remove the pan from the oven, remove the loaf pans to a rack, and let cool for 2 hours. Cover with plastic wrap and refrigerate overnight. **8** To serve the pâtés, unmold (see Chef's Note) and cut into slices ⅜ to ½ inch thick. Serve with bowls of cornichons and pickled onions alongside some rustic peasant bread.

⅛ teaspoon ground nutmeg

¼ teaspoon ground ginger

¼ teaspoon ground coriander

1 tablespoon chopped fresh thyme

½ teaspoon Insta-cure No. 1 (optional)

4 bay leaves

CHEF'S NOTES: Boiled pork skin provides gelatin to the pâté so that the slices don't fall apart. It also contributes an earthy taste. To prepare the skin, simmer it in water to cover for at least 2 hours or until very soft. Drain and store in a covered container in the refrigerator for 3 or 4 days or in the freezer for up to 3 months. If you can't find fresh pork skin, use the rind from slab bacon. Or substitute 3 packets plain dissolved gelatin. 🐖 Soaking the liver overnight in milk helps to subdue its strong porky flavor. 🐖 Insta-cure No. 1 gives the terrine a pinkish color. If you don't mind serving a terrine with a gray tinge, then by all means leave it out. 🐖 Wrapped tightly in plastic, the terrines will keep refrigerated for 2 weeks, so consider using the one of the loaves for sandwiches or snacks. 🐖 If you don't have a meat grinder, use a food processor. Coarsely chop the pork liver and finely chop the fat.
🐖 To unmold a terrine, place pan in a roasting pan with 2 to 3 inches of hot water. After a minute or two the gelatins will melt. Flip and dump the terrine onto a sheet pan and the terrine loaf will slip out.

Franco's Polpettone Napoletano   *Polpettone*

is Italian for giant meatball. In Italy this dish is made not as a ball, but shaped as a rolled cylinder that is stuffed with eggs, cheese, and cold cuts, wrapped in cheesecloth, and poached in a fresh tomato sauce. Franco Dunn, chef/owner of Santi restaurant in Geyserville, California, likes to bake his version of *polpettone*, as you would any meat loaf—*polpettone* is really just a glorified meat loaf. Then he serves the tomato sauce on the side. You can make the *polpettone* with all ground pork or blended with ground turkey or beef. This recipe is intentionally quite large so it makes lots of leftovers; it makes the best meat loaf sandwiches in the world, particularly on Italian bread with a little of Lisa's No-Fuss Tomato Sauce (see Chef's Notes). SERVES 12 TO 16

---

2 tablespoons olive oil

2 cups chopped onions

6 garlic cloves, chopped

1 cup fresh bread crumbs

½ cup milk

1 cup (6 ounces) finely chopped pancetta

1½ pounds ground pork

1¼ pounds ground turkey or beef (or use all ground pork)

2 eggs

1 cup freshly grated Parmesan cheese

2½ teaspoons kosher salt

2 teaspoons freshly ground black pepper

1 tablespoon chopped fresh oregano

½ cup chopped Italian flat-leaf parsley

1 Heat the olive oil in a medium skillet over medium heat, add the onions, and cook until softened and beginning to color, about 7 minutes. Add the garlic and cook 2 minutes. Set aside to cool to room temperature.
2 In a small bowl, soak the bread crumbs in the milk for 15 minutes. Drain and discard the milk. Squeeze the bread crumbs to remove the excess liquid. Put in a large bowl and set aside. 3 Put the pancetta in the bowl with the bread crumbs. Add the ground pork, ground turkey or beef, eggs, Parmesan cheese, salt, pepper, oregano, and parsley. Using the "squeeze, knead, and fold" technique for sausage (page 257), combine the mixture well.
4 Preheat the oven to 350° F. 5 Lay a large rectangle of parchment paper or foil (about 18 by 20 inches) on a rimmed baking sheet with the long edge facing you. Spread and pat the meat mixture out into an evenly thick 10- by 13-inch rectangle, again with the long edge facing your body. Put a layer of mortadella and then a layer of salami on top of the meat, leaving at least a 1-inch border on all sides. 6 Slice ⅛ inch off the ends of all the hard-cooked eggs and lay them end to end down the middle of the rectangle. Line the cooked carrots and strips of cheese alongside both sides of the eggs. 7 Using the parchment

or foil, lift the long side of the meat rectangle and gently fold and roll it over the eggs and onto the other side, making sure that the two long sides meet evenly. With your hands, pinch the open side to seal well so that the cheese doesn't leak out when cooked. Plump up the loaf and seal the two ends. Unroll parchment or foil and spread back over pan. Cut off any parchment or foil that overhangs the baking sheet. 8 Put the loaf in the oven and bake until the internal temperature reaches 150° F on an instant-read thermometer, 1¼ to 1½ hours. When taking the reading, make sure you take it from several places in the loaf as you don't want to stick the thermometer directly into the eggs. 9 Remove the loaf from the oven and allow to cool for 30 minutes before slicing and serving. Cut into ½- to ¾-inch slices and serve warm or at room temperature with or without the tomato sauce.

¼ pound sliced mortadella

¼ pound sliced Italian salami

7 eggs, hard-cooked

1 carrot, peeled, quartered lengthwise, cut once crosswise, blanched in boiling water until just tender, and drained

4 ounces fontina or provolone cheese, cut into strips about 3 inches long and ½ inch wide

Lisa's No-Fuss Tomato Sauce (see Chef's Notes)

CHEF'S NOTES: This is a versatile dish. You can use deli meats such as prosciutto or smoked ham or coppa. Leave out the hard-cooked eggs and just put more cheese down the center and layer with more sliced meats. In addition to the carrot, try zucchini or black pitted olives, and embed black olives in the meat as well. Use your imagination. 🐖 Lisa's No-Fuss Tomato Sauce: Sauté ¼ cup each of finely chopped carrots, celery, and shallots in 1 tablespoon olive oil. Add 2 cups good-quality Italian canned tomatoes, drained, and simmer for 30 minutes. Add ½ teaspoon chopped fresh rosemary and cook 5 minutes more. Puree in a blender or food processor, adding water to thin if necessary, and season to taste with salt and pepper. Makes about 2 cups.

Pâté de Campagne

I've always loved pâtés and terrines, particularly those that are rough-textured and robustly flavored, akin to classic American meat loaf. This recipe is very similar to Rustic Pork Liver Terrine (page 274), but contains diced smoky ham, bacon, or pancetta, and is chunkier. It's a great pâté for picnics or rustic meals. MAKES 2 TERRINES, EACH SERVING ABOUT 10

1 pound pork liver

1 cup milk (see Chef's Notes)

1 teaspoon sugar

2 tablespoons lard, bacon fat, or olive oil

1 cup finely chopped onions

¼ pound slab bacon or pancetta, diced

2 pounds boneless Boston butt, cut into 1-inch cubes

¼ pound boiled pork skin, cut into 1-inch pieces (see Chef's Notes)

¾ pound pork back fat, cut into 1-inch pieces

½ pound smoked ham, cut into ½-inch cubes

½ cup Madeira or dry sherry

2 tablespoons brandy

1 tablespoon kosher salt

1 teaspoon coarsely ground black pepper

1 tablespoon chopped fresh thyme

2 large eggs, lightly beaten

½ teaspoon *Fines Épices* (opposite)

2 bay leaves or sprigs thyme

1 Cut away any large blood vessels or connective tissue from the pork liver and cut it into ½-inch pieces. Put the milk in a large bowl or storage container and stir in the sugar. Add the liver and stir to combine. Cover and refrigerate for 2 hours or up to 24 hours. 2 When ready to make the pâté, drain the liver into a colander and wash well under cold running water until all the milky coating is removed. 3 Heat the fat or olive oil in a medium skillet over medium-low heat. Add the onions, cover, and cook, stirring occasionally, until quite soft and beginning to color, about 25 minutes. Transfer the onions to a bowl and refrigerate, covered, for at least 30 minutes or overnight. 4 Using a meat grinder fitted with a ⅜-inch plate, grind the bacon or pancetta and pork butt into a bowl. (Use the bowl that comes with a standing electric mixer, if you have one, as you'll be using the mixer to combine the ingredients.) Change to a ⅛- or ¼-inch plate. 5 In another bowl, stir together the pork skin and back fat. Grind the mixture into the bowl with the coarsely ground bacon and Boston butt. Add the reserved soaked liver, cubed ham, Madeira, brandy, salt, pepper, thyme, eggs, and *Fines Épices*. Fit the bowl on the mixer and stir on medium

speed until well combined, 2 to 3 minutes.   6 Preheat the oven to 300° F. Put on some water to boil.   7 Pour the pâté mixture into 2 loaf pans (9½ by 5½ inches each, with a 7-cup capacity). Lay 2 bay leaves or thyme sprigs on top of each pâté for garnish. Put the pans, uncovered, in a large roasting pan or baking dish. Put the pan in the oven on the middle rack and add enough boiling water to come two thirds of the way up the loaf pans. Bake for 2 to 2½ hours or until the pâtés reach an internal temperature of 160° F on an instant-read thermometer. Remove the pan from the oven, remove the loaf pans to a rack, and let cool for 2 hours. Cover with plastic wrap and refrigerate overnight.   8 To serve the pâtés, unmold (page 275) and cut into slices ⅜ to ½ inch thick. Serve with bowls of cornichons and pickled onions alongside some rustic peasant bread.

CHEF'S NOTES: Boiled pork skin provides gelatin to the pâté so that the slices don't fall apart. It also contributes an earthy taste. To prepare the skin, simmer it in water to cover for at least 2 hours or until very soft. Drain and store in a covered container in the refrigerator for 3 or 4 days or in the freezer for up to 3 months. If you can't find fresh pork skin, use bacon rind. Or substitute 3 packets plain dissolved gelatin.   Soaking the liver overnight in milk helps to subdue its strong porky flavor.

Fines Épices

Every *charcuterie* master has his own unique spice blend that he/she uses in pâtés, sausages, and other porky morsels. Some chefs prefer the traditional blend quatre-épices (four spices, such as black pepper, clove, nutmeg, and cinnamon), while others prefer a more elaborate blend of aromatic spices and herbs called *fines épices* (often sold here as Spice Parisienne). I favor the latter for pâtés and some of my sausages. Once you make a batch, it will keep for 2 to 3 months in a sealed jar. If you wish to change my basic recipe with your own touches (fennel, mace, and cardamom are all good, too), please feel free. MAKES ABOUT ½ CUP

6 bay leaves

1 tablespoon ground cloves

1 tablespoon ground coriander

2 tablespoons dried thyme

1 tablespoon ground nutmeg

1 teaspoon ground cinnamon

1 tablespoon dry sage

2 teaspoons ground ginger

Crumble the bay leaves and toast them in a small skillet over medium heat until they become brittle and begin to smoke, about 2 minutes. Grind the leaves to a powder in a spice grinder. Put the toasted bay leaves in a lidded glass jar and add the remaining ingredients. Seal the jar and shake well to blend the spices. Store in a dark cupboard for up to 2 to 3 months.

Phony Baloney

As the old adage goes, there are two things one should never see being made: sausage and the law. Well, for me, making sausage turned out to be the beginning of a wonderful romance.

My first date with Nancy Oakes (who is now my wife) took place in my kitchen, where we got together to make a very special "sausage" for a group of serious wine aficionados. Annually during the Christmas holidays, this San Francisco wine-tasting group conducts a large tasting of champagne. It's a very fancy event, and chefs from the area are invited to bring a special pâté for the guests to sample with the champagnes and sparkling wines. I had participated in the event for several years and had decided that these guys were way too serious about wine and pâté. I had decided that this year I was going to tease them a bit. Nancy agreed they needed a little "loosening of their stuffed shirts." Our plan was to make the most elegant, over-the-top pâté we could come up with, then stuff it into a baloney casing, cook it, and call it "Phony Baloney."

I picked Nancy up at the BART station near my house and unpacked the heavy duffle bag she had lugged over, full of ingredients to make our "Phony Baloney." Besides pork tenderloin and blanched sweetbreads, it appeared that Nancy had robbed the piggy bank. She also had a pound of fresh black truffles and one entire duck *foie gras*. This was going to be one phony baloney indeed.

While Nancy cleaned the foie gras and diced the truffles, I wrote a working recipe. Three hours later, the mixture was done. The next day I brought it to my sausage plant, where the mixture was stuffed into a couple of huge bologna casings and then slowly cooked. I had our graphic designer make us a label that said "Phony Baloney, Made in the USA, by Nancy Oakes and Bruce Aidells." The finishing touch to our *petit farce* was that at the tasting we presented our Phony Baloney on a cheap checked tablecloth with a loaf of supermarket white bread and a jar of Miracle Whip. Ours was by far the most popular pâté served that evening, but I realized the president of the group didn't see the humor when he asked in all seriousness why we would serve the pâté with Miracle Whip. Neither Nancy nor I have been invited back. We did, however, get along so fabulously during our "baloney"-making session, that we spent the rest of the evening at a local restaurant and went on to have many more dates. Six months later we were married.

Of course, that's really the last time we cooked together without an argument. Both of us are so used to being the "head chef," with very different styles, that we're unable to compromise. But the baloney brought out our best behavior. Now what was that adage about sausage-making again? MAKES 2 LOAVES, SERVING 32

ABOUT THE RECIPE Even though we called it "baloney," it really is a pâté and like all pâtés, can be made in a loaf pan. While there are several expensive ingredients, you can make substitutions according to your budget and still come out with a great-tasting and elegant pâté: You can leave out the sweetbreads or use diced cooked chicken, turkey, or rabbit. Instead of the truffles, you can used dried porcini or morel mushrooms. Instead of *foie gras,* use diced chicken, duck, or pork liver. Smoked ham can fill in for the tongue. Most of the ingredients for this pâté are diced, which means that when the pâté is sliced it has a beautiful mosaic-like appearance. Your guests will be impressed. Serve our Phony Baloney as a first course to an elegant dinner or special buffet and tell your guests the story if they have good senses of humor.

Marinated Meats

¼ pound sweetbreads, blanched, peeled, and diced, or ¼ pound cooked skinned turkey or chicken (about ½ cup diced)

1¼ pounds pork tenderloin, cut into ¾-inch cubes

2 ounces fresh or canned black truffles, cut into ¼-inch dice, or 1 ounce dried porcini, soaked and cut into ¼-inch dice, or 1 ounce dried morels, soaked and cut into ¼-inch dice

¼ cup chopped shallots

2 tablespoons cognac or brandy

2 teaspoons kosher salt

1 teaspoon chopped fresh thyme

½ teaspoon freshly ground black pepper

Pinch of allspice or ⅛ teaspoon *Fines Épices* (page 279)

Diced Meats

6 ounces smoked tongue, cut into ½-inch dice, or 6 ounces smoked ham, cut into ½-inch dice

6 ounces pork back fat, cut into ½-inch dice

½ pound fresh *foie gras,* cut into ¾-inch dice, or chicken, duck, or pork liver, cut into ¾-inch dice

Ground Meats

1½ pounds boneless Boston butt, cut into ½-inch strips

½ pound pork back fat, cut into ½-inch strips

2 teaspoons kosher salt

2 teaspoons freshly ground black pepper

2 teaspoons chopped fresh thyme

¼ teaspoon ground allspice or ¼ teaspoon *Fines Épices* (page 279)

2 tablespoons cognac or brandy

2 large eggs

3 packets plain gelatin

3 ounces (½ cup) shelled pistachios

1 To prepare the marinated meats: Toss together in a medium bowl the diced sweetbreads or poultry, pork tenderloin, truffles or mushrooms, shallots, cognac, salt, thyme, pepper, and allspice. Make sure the meats are well coated. Marinate, covered, at room temperature for 1 or 2 hours. 2 For the diced meats: Combine the tongue, fat, and *foie gras* or other liver in a medium bowl. Cover and refrigerate until ready to use. 3 To prepare the ground meats: In a meat grinder fitted with the ¼-inch plate, grind the strips of pork alternating with the strips of fat, until all the meat and fat are ground. If you don't have a meat grinder, you can cut the meat and fat into 1-inch pieces and process them in a food processor in 2 or 3 batches until chopped to ¼-inch pieces. 4 To assemble: Put the ground mixture in the bowl of a standing electric mixer. Add the salt, pepper, thyme, allspice, cognac, eggs, and gelatin. Stir on medium speed until well combined, about 1 minute. Reduce the speed to the lowest setting and add the marinated meats and any juices, all of the diced meats, and the pistachios. Stir for 2 to 3 minutes until the ingredients are well distributed and well combined. 5 In a small skillet, cook a small patty of the mixture and taste for salt, pepper, and spices. Adjust the uncooked mixture as necessary. 6 Preheat the oven to 300° F. Put on some water to boil. 7 Scrape equal amounts of the mixture into 2 loaf pans (9½ by 5½ inches each). Cover the pans tightly with aluminum foil and place them in a large roasting pan. Put the pan in the oven and pour in enough boiling water to come two thirds up the sides of the loaf pans. Bake for 2 to 2½ hours or until the internal temperature reaches 160° F on an instant-read thermometer. Remove the pâtés from the water pan. Put a foil-wrapped brick or other heavy object on top of each pan that fits in the pan to weight the pâtés. Set aside to cool completely. When cool, put the pâtés, still weighted, in the refrigerator for at least 24 hours before serving. 8 To serve, unmold (page 275), slice the "phony baloney" into ½-inch slices. Serve with cornichons as a first course.

Herbed Pork Rillettes

Rillettes technically are not pâté but they are what the English call "potted" meat. Fatty chunks of pork are braised slowly until the moisture evaporates. Then the meat is shredded, mixed with the fat, and packed into a mold. Rillettes are best after they have been refrigerated for 2 to 3 days. Like pâté, however, the mixture is brought to room temperature to be spread over toast for serving. SERVES 6 TO 8

1 Cut the pork and fat or belly meat into ½-inch pieces. Put the meat and fat in a large saucepan and add water to cover. Add the thyme, rosemary, bay leaves, sage leaves, shallots, garlic, coriander seeds, and salt. Bring the liquid to a boil over high heat, then reduce the heat to maintain a simmer and cook for 3 to 4 hours, until the meat is extremely tender, the water is evaporated, and only melted fat remains. Stir occasionally to prevent the meat from sticking to the bottom of the pan. 2 Remove and discard the bay and sage leaves and let the mixture cool for 20 minutes. Using a fork or potato masher, mash and break up the mixture. Add the pepper and stir to combine. Taste for salt. Pack the mixture into a 1-quart terrine or soufflé mold. Cover with plastic wrap and refrigerate the rillettes for at least 12 hours or preferably 2 to 3 days before serving. The rillettes will keep, well wrapped, in the refrigerator for 2 weeks.

1 pound boneless Boston butt

1 pound pork fat from the Boston butt or belly

1 teaspoon chopped fresh thyme

½ teaspoon chopped fresh rosemary

2 bay leaves

2 fresh sage leaves

2 shallots, chopped

3 whole garlic cloves

6 coriander seeds

2 teaspoons kosher salt

1 teaspoon freshly ground black pepper

Jambon Persillé (Molded Ham in a Parsley Aspic)

Jambon persillé is the traditional dish to serve for Easter lunch in Burgundy. Ham is first poached in stock and white wine, cut into chunks or shredded, and packed into a mold. Stock with lots of chopped fresh parsley is added and the whole is chilled to set. This cold loaf is too good to be reserved just for special occasions and has become standard fare in charcuteries throughout France, where each charcuterie master has his or her own variation and special touch. I, too, could not resist the urge to tinker with this dish, replacing the traditional chopped tarragon and/or tarragon vinegar with chopped French cornichons, those lovely little pickles flavored with tarragon and usually served as an accompaniment to pâté.

One thing I would not change is the type of ham used. Plain old American supermarket smoked ham won't do, and our excellent country-style smoked hams would be too salty and overpowering. This is best made with a very mild unsmoked ham (see York-Style Ham on page 290), or you can use a pork shoulder cured as in Petit Salé of Pork (page 292). Neither of these home-cured meats is difficult for a home chef to make and are well worth the effort, both to enjoy on their own or to use in this wonderful jellied ham and parsley loaf. SERVES 8

1 To make the stock: Combine the white wine and all of the remaining stock ingredients in a large casserole or soup pot. Bring to a boil over high heat and add the meat. Make sure the meat is covered completely by liquid; add water or stock if necessary. Return the liquid to a boil, reduce the heat to maintain a simmer, and cook, uncovered, until the ham is fork-tender (taste a bit, too), 2½ to 3 hours. 2 Line a large strainer or sieve with cheesecloth or a clean kitchen towel that has been moistened with water and wrung out. Remove the meat from the stock and set aside. Strain the stock through the cheesecloth into another large saucepan. Over high heat reduce the stock by half. (You will need 2 cups to finish the dish.) Pour the reduced stock into a bowl or storage container and cover. Wrap the poached ham in plastic wrap and refrigerate it and the stock overnight. 3 To assemble the *jambon persillé:* Remove the 2 cups stock from the refrigerator and scrape away and discard any congealed fat or foam on the surface. Rewarm the stock over low heat until it's no longer gelled. 4 In a small bowl, stir the gelatin with ¼ cup cool tap water and let stand for 1 minute to soften. Stir into the warm stock and continue to stir until dissolved completely, about 2 minutes. Remove from the heat and let cool at room temperature for 20 minutes. Stir in the shallot, parsley, celery leaves, and cornichons, making sure the liquid has not started to gel. If so,

gently rewarm to liquefy. Add the vinegar to taste.

5 Remove and discard any gristle or large pieces of fat from the meat and cut the meat into 1- to 2-inch pieces. You should have 3 to 4 cups. 6 In a 1½- to 2-quart loaf pan, terrine, or bowl, spoon ½ cup of the stock/parsley mixture. Add a layer of ham and cover it with some of the warm stock mixture. Continue to layer ham pieces and cover them with stock until the ham and stock are all used, making sure that the ham pieces are completely covered by the stock. Cover with plastic wrap pressed directly against the surface of the stock. Refrigerate overnight or up to 5 days. 7 To serve, invert the *jambon persillé* onto a platter and cut into ½-inch slices, or into wedges if molded in a bowl.

CHEF'S NOTES: Some recipes instruct you to clarify the stock for *jambon persillé* to produce a clear aspic, but I don't think a cloudy stock detracts from the appearance of the dish. If, however, you'd like to go that extra step, it's easily accomplished: After you strain the stock, chill it in the refrigerator until very cold. Whisk 1 cup of the cold stock with 2 egg whites in a medium bowl and bring the remaining stock to a boil in a large saucepan. Slowly whisk the hot stock into the egg white mixture, then add it back to the saucepan and bring to a simmer, stirring with the whisk until the egg whites have coagulated on the surface. Let simmer for 15 minutes. Push the egg whites aside and gently ladle the stock through a cheesecloth-lined sieve into a bowl. Discard the egg whites. Proceed to reduce the stock as directed in the recipe. To unmold, immerse the loaf pan or bowl in a larger pan of hot water for 30 seconds to soften the aspic slightly. Invert the ham onto a platter.

Ham Stock

2 cups dry white wine

2 to 4 cups Dark Pork Stock (page 87) or the stock used to make Pickled Pig's Feet Terrine (page 286)

1 sprig fresh thyme

2 sprigs fresh tarragon

2 bay leaves

Handful of parsley sprigs

1 medium onion, sliced

2 garlic cloves, unpeeled

1 carrot, thickly sliced

1 celery stalk, thickly sliced

3 pounds home-cured York-Style Ham (page 292) or Petit Salé of pork shoulder

3 packets gelatin

2 tablespoons finely chopped shallot

1 cup finely chopped Italian flat-leaf parsley

¼ cup chopped celery leaves

2 tablespoons chopped cornichons

2 tablespoons white wine vinegar, or more to taste

Pickled Pig's Feet Terrine

Folks who love eating pig's feet must really love the texture of soft skin and soft cartilage because there's not much meat on a trotter. To add a little more meat to this dish, I added pork neck bones, which give the terrine a meatier texture and taste, which I prefer. (See Chef's Notes on eating trotters on the bone or using pig's tails for the feet.) SERVES 6 TO 8

2 pig's feet (trotters; about 1 pound each)

3 pounds meaty pork neck bones

1 cup dry white wine

Kosher salt

¼ teaspoon crushed red pepper flakes

½ large onion, thinly sliced

3 garlic cloves

1 lemon, sliced

2 bay leaves

10 whole black peppercorns

6 juniper berries

2 sprigs fresh thyme

1 teaspoon pickling spice

1 teaspoon coriander seeds

1½ cups Dark Pork Stock (page 87), homemade chicken stock, or canned low-sodium chicken broth

4 teaspoons white vinegar

Freshly ground black pepper

¼ cup dill pickles or cornichons, cut into ¼-inch dice

1 Put the pig's feet and neck bones in a large casserole or saucepan with water to cover. Add the wine, 1 teaspoon salt, the pepper flakes, onion, garlic, lemon, bay leaves, peppercorns, juniper berries, thyme, pickling spice, coriander, and stock. Bring to a boil over high heat. Reduce the heat to maintain a simmer and cook, uncovered, until the feet are falling apart and the cartilage is quite soft, 4 to 5 hours. Add more water as needed to keep the meats covered. Remove the meats from the liquid and transfer to a bowl. Strain the stock through a fine sieve in to a bowl, discarding the solids, then return the stock to the pot. Over high heat reduce the stock by one third. 2 When cool enough to handle, remove the meat from the neck bones and the meat, skin, and soft cartilage from the trotters. Discard the bones and any hard cartilage. Coarsely chop the meat and skin, and return both to the bowl. Pour the reduced stock over the meat and skin and stir in the vinegar, 1 teaspoon each of salt and pepper, the pickles, parsley, thyme, and coriander. Adjust the salt, pepper, and vinegar. Pour the mixture into an oiled 5-cup loaf pan or terrine and refrigerate until firm. 3 To serve, slice and serve cold, with a splash of vinegar, and garnished with chopped cornichons and red onion.

CHEF'S NOTES: Instead of using them in a terrine, serve the trotters whole, right out of the pot. Or cool and let the bone suckers go for it. 🐖 For pickled pig's tails, prepare them as you would feet, but eat the tails warm from the pot. Tails will take less time to cook, 1½ to 2 hours. Serve with Tabasco or a splash of cider vinegar. 🐖 Serve the terrine sliced in place of the Warm Pork Confit and Frisée Salad (page 82). 🐖 Save any leftover stock to use in Jambon Persillé (page 284) or in pâtés to add extra flavor and gelatin.

½ cup chopped Italian flat-leaf parsley

1 teaspoon chopped fresh thyme

Pinch ground coriander

Garnish

White wine vinegar

Chopped cornichons

Finely diced red onion

15
Bacon, Other Cured Cuts, and Salami

York-Style Ham 🐖 Read the strategy for Preserving Pork at Home on page 249.

York-style ham is mildly cured (that means not too salty). After brining it can be cooked in a court-bouillon, or you can remove the ham from the brine and smoke your ham following the instructions on page 297 for Smoked Pork Butt Bacon and page 300 for Smoked Pork Loin. Once smoked, the meat can be baked and glazed it as you would any store-bought ham, but don't overcook it. You'll want to remove it from the oven at 145° to 150° F. Because your homemade ham is much smaller than a whole store-bought ham, you should start checking the internal temperature as early as 45 minutes after it starts roasting.

Since the ham cured in this recipe is not too salty, it will not keep for long. Once fully cured and removed from the brine, plan to use it in 2 to 3 days. Your homemade ham is good in Choucroute Garni (page 242), Jambon Persillé (page 284), Ham in Tangy Chablis and Mushroom Sauce (page 196), or as part of a boiled dinner (Pot-au-Feu on page 213). Or just cook in court-bouillon as directed below and slice it up for some of the best ham sandwiches you've ever eaten. Or use your homemade ham, smoked or unsmoked, in any of the Baked Glazed Ham recipes (page 190). MAKES 8 TO 10 POUNDS

Mild Ham Cure

1 pound (3 cups) kosher salt

½ pound (1 cup) light brown sugar

3 tablespoons Insta-cure No. 1 (Required if you're going to smoke your ham; optional if you're not) (see Chef's Notes)

1 gallon ice water

8 to 10 pounds Fresh Ham Inside or Fresh Ham Outside (see Chef's Notes); boneless blade-end loin roasts, or Boston butt

1 To cure the ham: Put the salt, brown sugar, and optional Insta-cure No. 1 in a 3-gallon or larger plastic tub, stainless-steel bowl, or crock or glass container. Add the ice water and stir until the salt is completely dissolved. Submerge the meat in the brine and weight it down with a plate so it stays submerged in the liquid. Refrigerate for 3 days. 2 Remove the meat, stir the brine, and return the meat to the brine. Weight down with plate. Refrigerate 3 more days. 3 Remove the meat from the brine. Now cook the meat in court-bouillon, or smoke it (pages 249 to 253), or use it in a recipe.

Court-Bouillon for Cooking Homemade York-Style Ham

Combine all the ingredients in a large pot or casserole, bring to a boil over high heat, and reduce the heat to maintain a simmer. Add the ham. Continue to cook at a simmer or just below a simmer until the meat is tender and has an internal temperature of 145 to 150° F, about 2 hours. Remove the ham and strain the court-bouillon, saving it for bean or vegetable soups or Jambon Persillé (page 284).

CHEF'S NOTES: For smoking ham follow instructions for Smoking in Makin' Bacon (page 297). 🐖 Insta-cure No. 1 is a mixture of 1 part sodium nitrite and 15 parts salt. It is used to give the meat a reddish color and to discourage the growth of bacteria, especially botulism. If you're not smoking the ham and don't care whether it's red or not, then leave it out. If smoking the ham, you must use it since the temperatures for smoking are ideal for bacterial growth. 🐖 Fresh Ham Inside, also called pork leg top roast, is a boneless roast from the top round portion of the leg and weighs 4 to 6 pounds. Fresh Ham Outside, also called pork leg bottom roast, is a boneless roast from the bottom round portion of the leg and weighs 4 to 6 pounds.

2 (12 ounce each) bottles lager or 3 cups dry white wine

2 quarts water

3 bay leaves

4 sprigs fresh thyme

16 whole black peppercorns

6 juniper berries

2 unpeeled onions, studded with 4 cloves each

2 carrots

4 garlic cloves

2 celery stalks

¼ cup cider vinegar

Petit Salé of Pork

🐷 In the olden days, no French butcher worth his salt (pun intended), would open up shop without at least a crock or two filled with various porky chunks curing away in an aromatic brine. Patrons would purchase their preferred cut, a belly, some shoulder, a blade chop or two, and use these pickled meats to make a Pot-au-Feu (page 215), the renowned French "boiled dinner." They may also have braised the meat in court-bouillon and the local vin blanc to make jambon persillé (ham loaf with parsley in aspic). For me, the best cuts for brining this way are the picnic shoulder or Boston butt, but the belly and ribs are good, too.

Making a brine is dead easy, nothing more than stirring together a solution of water, salt, sugar, and spices. The brine not only provides the meat with flavor and makes it juicy, it also helps tenderize it a bit, and the resulting pork is packed with subtle ham flavor. Use this Petit Salé of pork in the recipes for Pot-au-Feu (page 213), Jambon Persillé (page 284), and Choucroute Garni (page 242). MAKES ENOUGH BRINE FOR 8 POUNDS OF MEAT

---

8 cups water

½ pound kosher salt (1½ cups)

¼ pound brown sugar (½ cup)

1½ tablespoons Insta-cure No.1 (optional, page 14)

6 bay leaves

12 juniper berries

10 sprigs fresh thyme

1 tablespoon coriander seeds

1 tablespoon whole black peppercorns

1 tablespoon pickling spice

8 garlic cloves, crushed

4 to 6 pounds picnic shoulder meat, Boston butt, cut in half, spareribs, or fresh pork belly

1 In a large pot, bring the water to a boil over high heat and stir in the salt and brown sugar until dissolved. Add the remaining ingredients except the meat and remove the pot from the heat. (This step will extract more flavor from the spices than just using cold water.) Cool the liquid in the refrigerator until the brine is no more than 45° F.

2 Submerge the meat in the brine and weight it with a plate so that remains submerged. Cover and refrigerate for 2 to 4 days, depending on how large the chunk of meat is that you're curing. A whole Boston butt, cut in half, will take about 3 days, while a 3- to 4-pound chunk of picnic should take 2 to 3 days; spareribs will take 2 days, and fresh pork belly 3 days. All curing times are estimates. Keep a brining journal (page 252), as I do, and adjust aging times to suit your taste. Once the meat is cured, rinse and use in Pot-au-Feu recipe (page 213).

Pancetta (Italian-Style Cured Air-Dried Pork Belly)

Before you make Pancetta, you must read Making Salami and Air-Dried Meats (page 301).

Pancetta is very easy to make, especially this flat version that is not rolled and stuffed into a casing like the store-bought kind. The key to success is to have a space like a cellar or basement that can maintain temperatures between 40° and 55° F for at least 6 continuous weeks during the year. The spice rub that I use on the pancetta is one that suits my taste, but you can experiment. If you prefer less aromatic spice, then cut the allspice, cinnamon, and nutmeg in half. Some pancetta makers use cloves, but I only like cloves in mulled wine and spice cake. Besides fresh rosemary, you could use fresh thyme, savory, or sage, and even fresh bay leaves if you can find them. I found rosemary my personal favorite—but this is a very flexible recipe. White mold flourishes in my basement, and my pancetta was splotched with it. I found the taste pleasant and, therefore, did not wash it off. If you find mold—we're talking harmless mold here—unpleasant, then wash it off with a stiff brush and make sure you dry your pancetta thoroughly before you wrap it for storage.

2½ quarts water

2½ cups (¾ pound) kosher salt

½ pound (1 cup) light brown sugar

2 ounces (¼ cup) white sugar

3 tablespoons Insta-cure No. 1 (page 14)

1 skinned pork belly (about 8 pounds), cut into 3 equal pieces

3 cups ice cubes

Spice Rub

3 tablespoons fresh coarsely ground black pepper

¼ teaspoon ground cinnamon

½ teaspoon ground allspice

½ teaspoon ground nutmeg

3 tablespoons chopped fresh rosemary

10 bay leaves, crushed

1 Pour the water into a large plastic tub or pot. Add the salt and stir until dissolved. Add the brown and white sugars and the Insta-cure No. 1, stirring until dissolved. 2 Put pork belly in a nonreactive container and pour in the cure until the pork is completely submerged. If necessary, weight the pork with a plate. Cover and store in the refrigerator for 10 days. 3 Remove the pork from the cure, discard the cure, and pat the belly dry. 4 To make the spice rub: Combine the spices for the rub in a bowl. 5 Use one third of the spice rub to coat each piece of belly on all sides. Hang the belly in a cool basement, cellar, or garage where the temperature does not exceed 55° F (see Making Salami and Air-

Dried Meats, page 301). After about a month, the pancetta should be firm when squeezed, which means it is ready to eat. If not, continue to dry it until firm when squeezed. 6 Cut off a thin slice and cook it to see if it tastes good. Pancetta may take from 4 to 8 weeks to age if your room is more humid or colder than mine. White mold that may develop on the pancetta is harmless and actually helps to give it a good flavor. Store pancetta in the refrigerator, loosely wrapped in paper, not plastic wrap, for up to 3 weeks.

CHEF'S NOTES: When properly cured and aged, the pancetta should have a deep, salty flavor redolent with herbs and spices. The texture may be chewy when raw but should be fine when thinly sliced and cooked. 🐖 While the pancetta may be usable after a month, you may continue to age it another 4 to 6 weeks depending on the temperature and humidity (see discussion on Making Salami and Air-Dried Meats, page 301).

Lardo (Cured and Air-Dried Back Fat) 🐖

Before you make *lardo*, you must read Making Salami and Air-Dried Meats (page 301).

Lardo, a slightly salty, creamy, and herbaceous fat, is really something special. Colonnata, in Tuscany, where the Carrara marble quarries are located, is *lardo* central. The thick slabs of back fat are layered and cured in large, rectangular marble vats called *conca di marmo*. In these vats the fat slabs are layered with salt, pepper, rosemary, bay, sage, and maybe other aromatics. Eventually water is leached from the fat to immerse it in its own brine. The *lardo* ages in this brine at least 6 months before it is eaten. While *lardo* can be used in pastas and risottos, it was traditionally served on country bread with fresh tomatoes and sliced onions as a high-calorie snack for the marble workers. In Italy, I've mostly eaten *lardo* thinly sliced over warm toasted country bread or draped over freshly baked flat bread. My method for making *lardo* uses a liquid brine. Then the salted back fat is removed, flavored with herbs, and allowed to age and air-dry in a cool basement. With this method, delicious *lardo* can be produced in 2 to 3 months in a home kitchen.

When properly cured, thin slices of *lardo* should be moderately salty, soft and slightly creamy, and have a mellow herbaceous taste from the herb and black pepper coating. If the flavor still seems underdeveloped, hang the *lardo* for another week or so.

Don't confuse *lardo* with "fat back" or salt pork, which is salted and becomes quite hard and salty-tasting. Fat back and "salt pork" are used mostly in Southern cooking to flavor various beans and vegetables and are never eaten raw in thin slices.

1 To cure the back fat: Dissolve the salt, sugar, and Insta-cure No. 1 in 2 quarts tap water and cool in the refrigerator for 30 minutes. 2 Cut the pork back fat into rectangles to fit snugly in an approximately 8-inch square clean, noncorrosive container. Put in one layer of fat and sprinkle generously with some of the pepper, garlic, and rosemary. Place 6 bay leaves on top. Put another layer of fat in the container and repeat the order of seasoning, continuing layering fat and seasonings ending with a layer of seasoning. Pour in brine to cover. Use a plate as a weight to keep the fat submerged in the liquid. Cover the container and label it with the date. Refrigerate for 3 weeks. 3 Drain the back fat and discard brine and old seasonings and shake off the extra moisture. 4 Make the herb coating: In a bowl, combine the pepper, sage, rosemary, and bay leaves and sprinkle all of it generously over the fat. Hang the fat on meat hooks suspended from a pole in a cool basement (below 55° F) for 4 to 8 weeks. Cut a thin slice and taste. If it is soft, creamy, and tastes good, then it's ready to serve. (See headnote.) To store, wrap the lardo loosely in paper and refrigerate for 3 to 4 weeks.

CHEF'S NOTE: Insta-cure No. 1 is a mixture of sodium nitrite and salt and **must** be used in this recipe to retard the growth of spoilage bacteria, especially botulism.

Cure

1 pound (3 cups) kosher salt

2 quarts water

5 pounds pork back fat (the thicker the better—mine was 2 to 3 inches but most will only be 1 inch thick)

¼ pound (½ cup) sugar

1½ tablespoons Insta-cure No. 1 (see Chef's Note)

¼ cup coarsely ground black pepper

¼ cup chopped garlic

½ cup chopped fresh rosemary

20 bay leaves

Herb Coating

¼ cup freshly ground black pepper

2 tablespoons chopped fresh sage

¼ cup chopped fresh rosemary

10 bay leaves, crushed

Lonza (Cured and Air-Dried Pork Loin)

Before you make *lonza,* you must read Making Salami and Air-Dried Meats (page 301).

While making prosciutto at home is beyond what most of us home cooks can handle in terms of time or curing conditions, *lonza* is much more doable and is a good stand-in in many recipes for prosciutto. It's quicker to make, yet when thinly sliced yields the same slightly sweet, and silky meat that the best imported prosciutto provides. I like to serve *lonza* thinly sliced with fresh figs and drizzled with an excellent olive oil. The recipe below provides enough cure for 3 (3-pounds each) pieces of center-cut boneless pork loin. MAKES ABOUT 6 POUNDS

4 quarts water

1 pound kosher (3 cups) salt

10 ounces (1¼ cup) light brown sugar or white sugar

¼ cup Insta-cure No. 1 (page 14)

3 (3-pounds each) pieces center-cut pork loins with ¼-inch fat layer (make sure there is fat on the loins; it helps to keep the meat from becoming too dry during the aging)

3 tablespoons coarsely ground black pepper

1 Pour the water into a large plastic tub. Add the salt, sugar, and Insta-cure and let dissolve. 2 Put the pork loin pieces in a large rectangular storage container so that they lie flat. Pour in the cure until the loins are completely submerged. Weight down the loins with a small plate. Cover and store in the refrigerator. 3 After 5 days, remove the loins, stir the cure, then return the loins to the liquid. After a total of 12 days, remove the loins and discard the brine. Pat the loin pieces dry and sprinkle each with a tablespoon of black pepper. Hang the loins in a cool basement where the temperature never exceeds 55° F, for 2 months and up to 3 months. To tell if the loins are properly dried, cut one in half crosswise and cut a thin slice. It should have the texture of good prosciutto, not too dry, but no longer as soft as uncooked meat. 4 Once the *lonza* are air-dried, wrap it in paper and store in the refrigerator for up to 1 month. Or you can continue to hang it as long as the temperature never exceeds 55° F.

CHEF'S NOTES: You can make air-dried pork shoulder (coppa) by following the same procedures to make *lonza.* Cut a boneless Boston butt (5 to 7 pounds) into 2 equal pieces, 2 to 3 inches thick and 3 to 4 inches wide by the length of the butt. Tie it in several places so it holds its shape. Cure for 15 days and air-dry in a 55° F or cooler basement or room for at least 2 or up to 4 months. During the drying and aging time, a white mold may appear on the surface of the meat. It provides good taste but you may scrub it off with warm water and a stiff brush, if you wish.

Makin' Bacon

Before you make bacon, read strategy for Preserving Pork at Home, page 249.

When I was a lad, my sleeping habits were famous within the family. These habits became legendary when I slept completely through a fairly sizable earthquake that rolled its way through Southern California early one morning. But my mother knew one sure-fire way to raise me from my bed. All she had to do was fry up a little bacon and I would be grabbing at the pan within minutes.

The sweet, smoky, pork-laden aroma of bacon frying is pretty much irresistible for most folks. I can say that I have seen committed vegetarians as well as devout fat-fetishers grab for a slice when a platter is passed under their noses.

Years ago the bacon that I ate was simpler and more delicious than what is sold today in most supermarkets, made by curing pork in nothing more than salt, sugar, and curing salt (sodium nitrite), then smoking it slowly over sweet hickory or fruit wood. It came as a chunk with the rind on, and my mother cut it into thick slices that browned and crisped.

The bacon sold in supermarkets today is overfussed with and tampered with by the addition of flavorings and other commercial tricks to give it taste it doesn't need nor want. I yearn to return to those simpler times of straightforward bacon.

How I Make Bacon

Making bacon couldn't be easier: The process consists of soaking a chunk of pork belly or other cut for a few days in a solution of salt, sugar, curing salts, and water; then it's patted dry and cold-smoked right in a backyard kettle barbecue for several hours. When it's done, all that is necessary is to slice it thinly and fry it with some eggs or pancakes.

---

1 Make a brine by dissolving salt, sugar, and Insta-cure No. 1 in water and chill to 45° F or less as described in the individual recipes. 2 If using a whole pork belly, cut it into 3 equal pieces. If using boneless Boston butt, butterfly and cut it into 2 equal pieces. Put the meat into a plastic storage container and submerge it in the brine. Refrigerate for 2 to 3 days (see individual recipes) then remove from the brine. Pat dry. 3 Now the meat is ready to be cold-smoked. The goal of cold-smoking is to keep wood (usually in the form of hardwood sawdust) smoldering to produce smoke, but not to produce enough heat for cooking. Several hardwood sawdusts suitable for smoking are available. These include aromatic hardwoods

such as hickory, apple, alder, cherry, oak and mesquite (see Sources). Backyard wood clippings, shop sawdust, or other wood chips not specified for the purpose are not suitable for smoking because they may contain chemicals and toxins that may be harmful. The method I use for cold-smoking bacon is also ideal for smoking sausages such as Smoked French Country Sausage (page 266), or York-Style Ham (page 290). 4 To cold-smoke, I remove the top grill from my kettle-type barbecue and place a large pie pan or small disposable aluminum roasting pan on the lower grate. I then pour 6 cups of sawdust into the pan. Next I put 4 charcoal briquettes (never use the self-igniting variety) into a chimney starter and ignite with newspapers. When the coals are fully lit and completely covered with gray ash and glowing embers, I'm ready to start smoking. Using tongs, I place the briquettes on top of the sawdust so they're well spaced. When the sawdust begins to smolder I open the bottom vents of the barbecue, replace the top grill and lay the meat to be smoked on the grill in a single layer with some space around each piece. Then I replace the lid and open the top vent all the way. I insert an instant-read thermometer into a vent hole to monitor air temperature inside the grill, which I want to be between 80° F and 120° F. 5 What I'm looking for is smoke gently rising out of the vents. If it comes bellowing out I know that it will take less time to get a nice smoky taste, and if the smoke rises in gentle wisps I need to smoke the meat longer or add another glowing briquette or two to the sawdust. After about 1½ hours, I stir the sawdust to get it to burn evenly. As it burns down, I add 2 or 3 more cups of fresh sawdust to the pan. For a nice smoky flavor I smoke the meat for 6 to 8 hours. I always keep a journal and decide once the bacon is done and tasted if it's too smoky or if it's not smoky enough (see Sample Smoking Journal, page 253.) Next time out I adjust the smoking time and intensity to suit my taste. 6 When the bacon is done I take it out, cool it, wrap it tightly in plastic before storing it in the fridge. Smoked bacon will last a week to 10 days in the refrigerator. It can also be frozen, well-wrapped, for up to 2 months.

CHEF'S NOTE: Bacon made with Boston butt can be chewy when it's sliced and fried. To make it more tender I recommend slow-roasting the meat after it's smoked. To do this, roast whole chunks in a 225° F oven until the internal temperature reaches 155° F, about 1½ to 2 hours. Once it is roasted, cool it and store it as above.

Molasses-Cured Pork Shoulder Bacon

MAKES ABOUT 4 TO 6 POUNDS, ABOUT 16 TO 24 SERVINGS

1 To cure the pork: Lay the pork butt, fat-side up, and cut it in half horizontally, parallel to the table, to make 2 pieces each 1½ to 2 inches thick. Set aside. 2 In a 1- to 2-gallon plastic storage tub or large stainless-steel bowl, combine the water, salt, brown sugar, and Insta-cure. Using a large spoon, stir until the solids are dissolved completely. Stir in the molasses, then add the ice cubes to cool the liquid down. Submerge the 2 pieces of pork in the cure and weight them down with a plate to keep the meat submerged. Cover the tub with a lid or plastic wrap and refrigerate for 2 days. 3 To smoke the pork: Remove the meat from the brine and discard the liquid. Pat the meat with paper towels to remove excess moisture. If you wish to make some pepper bacon, generously sprinkle 2 tablespoons of the pepper over each piece so that all surfaces of the pork are seasoned. (You may want to do smoke one piece as pepper-bacon and leave the other piece plain.) 4 Set up your kettle-type barbecue for cold-smoking (page 252) and lay the shoulder pieces on the grill so that they do not touch. Cold-smoke for 6 to 8 hours. Remove, wrap with plastic wrap, and chill for later enjoyment or slice to use immediately. 5 To cook the bacon: Slice it thinly. Fry it in a heavy nonstick frying pan over medium heat until one side begins to brown, 2 to 3 minutes. Turn the slices and continue frying another 2 to 3 minutes or until both sides are nicely browned. Pork shoulder bacon does not get as crisp as belly bacon but has a great taste and meaty texture. 6 If the sliced bacon is too chewy for your liking, then roast the whole piece slowly. (Slow-roasting will make the meat more tender.) To do this, preheat oven to 225° F and roast the bacon until it reaches an internal temperature when tested with an instant-read thermometer of 155° F, 2 to 2½ hours. Cool, wrap in plastic wrap, and refrigerate until you are ready to slice and fry.

1 boneless Boston butt, about 4 to 6 pounds

6 cups tap water

1 cup kosher salt

⅔ cup dark brown sugar

2½ tablespoons Insta-cure No. 1 (see Chef's Notes)

½ cup dark unsulfured molasses

3 cups ice cubes

2 to 4 tablespoons coarsely ground black pepper (optional)

CHEF'S NOTES: Insta-cure No. 1 (see Sources on page 318) is a mixture of 1 part sodium nitrite to 15 parts table salt. The small quantities of sodium nitrite needed for curing cannot be measured in the kitchen, necessitating a curing mixture to deliver the active ingredient.

It must be used in this recipe to prevent the growth of spoilage bacteria during the smoking period. 🐷 The method and preparation for making traditional belly bacon is the same as for shoulder bacon. Because bellies are fattier, the curing time is longer. Cut a 6- to 8-pound fresh pork belly crosswise into 2 pieces and cure for 3 days instead of 2. Cold-smoke as directed for shoulder bacon. Pepper-coated belly bacon is very tasty.

Maple-Cured Canadian Bacon (Smoked Boneless Pork Loin) 🐷 I prefer to use pork

from the rib end of the loin because it has a little more fat and a better flavor. The loin should be 2 to 3 inches in diameter. MAKES 4 POUNDS, ABOUT 16 SERVINGS

6 cups water

1 cup kosher salt

⅔ cup dark brown sugar

2½ tablespoons Insta-cure No.1 (see Chef's Notes)

2 teaspoons pure vanilla extract

½ cup maple syrup

3 cups ice cubes

2 (2-pound) boneless pork loins, preferably from the rib end

1 To cure the pork: In a 1- to 2-gallon plastic storage tub or large stainless-steel bowl, combine the water, salt, brown sugar, Insta-cure No. 1, and vanilla. Using a large spoon, stir until the solids are dissolved completely. Stir in the maple syrup, then add the ice cubes to cool the liquid down. Submerge the 2 pieces of pork loin in the cure and weight them down with a plate to keep the meat submerged. Cover the tub with a lid or plastic wrap and refrigerate for 2 days.

2 To smoke the loins: Remove the meat from the brine and discard the liquid. Pat the meat with paper towels to remove excess moisture. 3 Set up your kettle-type barbecue for cold-smoking (page 252) and lay the loin pieces on the grill so that they do not touch. Cold-smoke for 6 to 8 hours. Remove, wrap with plastic wrap, and chill for later enjoyment or slice to use immediately. 4 To cook the bacon: Slice it ⅛ to ¼ inch thick. Fry in a heavy nonstick frying pan over medium heat until one side begins to brown, 2 to 3 minutes. Turn the slices and continue frying another 2 to 3 minutes or until both sides are nicely browned. Canadian bacon will not crisp like belly bacon but should be firm and juicy.

CHEF'S NOTES: You may also roast a piece of your smoked pork loin whole: Bake in a preheated 350° F oven until the meat reaches an internal temperature of 140° to 145° F. Slice it and eat it hot out of the oven with sautéed apples and roast sweet potatoes. Also see Glazed Smoked Pork Loin (Canadian Bacon) (page 64). 🐖 Insta-cure No. 1 contains 1 part sodium nitrite and 15 parts salt and is necessary for cold-smoking to prevent the growth of harmful bacteria.

Making Salami and Air-Dried Meats

Salami is a mixture of seasoned chopped or ground meat packed in a casing and allowed to mature and air-dry until enough water is evaporated to make it firm and sliceable. Most salami is served raw but some, such as pepperoni, are smoked and even cooked. Some salami, such as kosher salami, which is made with beef, are cooked right after stuffing into the casings and are not air-dried at all.

I'm not going to beat around the bush—making salami and air-dried meats in a home kitchen or restaurant can be a risky business. Spoilage by bacterial contamination is a real issue, especially with salami because the meat is ground and then fermented. Grinding meat exposes each little particle to the ambient bacteria present in the environment, while fermentation provides ideal temperatures and humidity for bacterial growth. The key to successful salami making is to encourage the right bacteria (lactobacillus) to flourish while discouraging harmful ones and to ultimately reduce the water in the meat and replace it with salt so that no detrimental bacteria can survive.

The critical elements in making salami are temperature and humidity. The most important consideration in any recipe on how to make salami and air-dried meat is the aging room. You can no more make salami without the right room than you could prepare a pork roast without an oven. In fact, the environment is even more important than the aging and maturing process is to cheese making. Usually the ideal temperature and amount of humidity are present in a basement or cellar, but only if you live in an area with the proper climate. You must have a space that does not exceed 55° F or drop below 40° F for any extended period of time (meaning a day or two) and where that temperature can be maintained for a minimum of 4 months—the time it takes for a salami to cure and meat to air-dry. For those of us on the

Pacific Coast that usually means from between October to mid-March, unless the basement or cellar is so well insulated and deep in the ground that it can maintain 55° F even on hot days or stay above 40° F when the temperatures are freezing. For the Midwest and East, the ideal time for salami making is fall to early winter, September to January, unless your basement is well insulated so that it does not freeze during the coldest times. So what do you do if you don't have such a place for drying and aging your salami? Well, you could move. Or, more realistically, you could build an insulated room or walk-in box that artificially maintains the temperature range and humidity needed for salami aging and drying. Simply put, if you live in the desert, for instance, or the South, particularly around New Orleans, where the ground is too wet to dig basements, or in Minnesota or North Dakota, where your basement is not adequately insulated or so cold that it's below freezing, then you do not have the right conditions for making salami and you'll need to build a temperature- and humidity-controlled room.

FERMENTATION As I mentioned earlier, salami is a fermented sausage that derives its characteristically tangy flavor from the friendly bacteria, lactobacillus, which converts sugars to acids. Lactobacillus is also used in cheese and other fermented foods. In modern commercial salami manufacturing, specialized cultures of lactobacillus are added to salami in precise amounts along with dextrose, a sugar that the lactobacillus metabolizes and converts to acids. This process is carefully monitored with pH meters, instruments that measure acidity. The goal is to increase the acidity in the salami so that the pH is reduced to 5.0. This is accomplished in special rooms with controlled temperatures of 68° F to 85° F and 80 to 85 percent humidity. The fermentation is usually complete in 48 hours after which the sausages are placed in another cool room at 70 percent humidity to age slowly and dry.

All this attention to detail reduces the risk that the wrong spoilage bacteria will grow, forcing the salami maker to throw out the batch.

Unfortunately, most of us home cooks are not likely to use frozen starter cultures, pH meters, and temperature and humidity-controlled rooms for making salami. While I do agree that these details can vastly improve your chances for success, I'm not convinced that they are a feasible step for us home cooks or restaurant chefs. If, however, you plan to make salami and air-dried meats on a regular basis and have an adequate cellar or basement for aging them and you are prepared to spend a little time and money, then you may wish to go to the next step of setting up a fermentation room, using starter cultures, and monitoring pH levels. Paul

Bertolli, chef/owner of Olivetto Restaurant in Oakland, California, makes salami and cured meats comparable to the best I've ever eaten in Italy. In his book, *Cooking by Hand* (Clarkson Potter, 2003), he discusses how a committed home cook or restaurant chef who wishes to make salami and cured meats at home can do so with the aid of a fermentation room, starter cultures, pH meters, and aging rooms, without the huge expenditure of setting up a commercial-type operation. Paul also describes in detail how to use these instruments and provides excellent recipes for various salami, prosciutto, and even mortadella.

Successful salami and air-dried meat-making goes back many centuries in Italian peasant life. The recipes and methods were handed down from generation to generation and resulted in unique time-honored products. These methods obviously preceded the use of starter cultures, pH meters, and fermentation rooms and are still practiced today throughout Italy in small butcher shops, restaurants, and on family farms. Since these methods are not scientifically controlled, they're more prone to environmental fluctuations and errors, but time-honored methods repeated over and over enabled the primitive salami maker to determine if a batch was successful or not. I have adapted these peasant-derived methods for the recipes in this book, and I have done my best to point out a few critical steps and signs to which you should pay particular attention in order to have success at making salami. However, I'm not going to be there to guide you through the process and although I've made enough salami to predict some of the problems you might experience, I, too, am still a home salami maker, and I can't predict all that can go wrong. (Although the truth is that very few of my batches have gone bad or failed.) You may have a problem that I've not encountered. If you suspect that something is not right about the salami or air-dried meat you've made, then please throw it out.

That said, the information I've provided here for making salami and air-dried meat *is* done in good faith but is accurate only with respect to my own experiences. Because conditions and methods that you may use are out of my control, I can't make any guarantees as to your own success. You must rely on all of your senses, especially those of smell, feel, sight, and taste, to determine if what you produce is safe to eat. My publisher and I cannot be held responsible for damages that may result from the use or reliance upon any of the information I've provided in this book.

For all recipes where there are a lot of variables, I recommend that you keep a journal describing in detail what you've done and what the results were, so that you can make changes the next time you make it.

Sample Salami and Air-Dried Meat Journal

Date	Recipe	Beginning Weight	Casing Diameter	Temperature of Aging Area During 1st Week	Days to Cure	Final Weight	Comment
9/20	Basic Salami	20 ounces	3 inches	53° F	67	14 ounces	Salt good— should be tangier
10/1	Pancetta	16 ounces	2 inches	54° F	49	13 ounces	Good salt

How I Make Salami

1 Before I start, I make sure I've read over the basic information on Strategy for Preserving Pork at Home (page 249), especially the points on Hygiene and Safety (pages 253 to 254), as well as all the info on How to Make Sausage (page 256). 2 The first thing I do is prepare the meat by separating all the lean from the fat. I cut the lean into strips and the fat into strips or chunks and weigh each portion: Ideally I'm looking for about 80 percent of the total weight as lean and about 20 percent as fat. That means for 10 pounds total, there should be 8 pounds meat and 2 pounds fat. Once weighed the meat and fat go into the refrigerator for an hour or so or into the freezer for about 20 minutes so that they chill down to between 35° to 40° F. 3 While the meat and fat are chilling, I measure out all the other ingredients and combine all the spices with the salt and sugar. I also combine the Insta-cure No. 1 with the wine and water so that it is mostly dissolved. Then I proceed with grinding the meat and fat and store-bought salami, add the Insta-cure No. 1, liquid, spices, salt, and sugar, and mix it well by kneading and squeezing the meat. I continue to knead and squeeze the mixture until it's well combined and sticky, but not so much that the fat has begun to melt from the warmth of my hands. 4 I do not use a starter culture, but I do use some ground-up commercial salami to seed the batch with lactobacillus organisms. I use Molinari brand salami, which I find works well, but you can use whatever brand is available in your area. You will want to buy the salami covered with white mold, which you will also use to brush on to your salami so it too becomes coated with white mold), not pasteurized salami, i.e., presliced or vacuum packed. (Pasteurization kills the bacteria you want.) 5 I stuff the meat mixture into casings and tie each end. 6 Then I remove any air bubbles under the casings with a sharp, clean needle. Puncturing any air pockets is crucial since trapped air could lead to spoilage. 7 I remove and soak the white moldy casings from store-bought (meaning not pasteurized) salami in warm

water, which provides the seeding white mold culture. 8 Once my salamis are stuffed in their casings they can be dipped into a small bowl of the soaked casings water, or the water can be brushed all over the salamis after they're hung. This process adequately seeds the salamis with spores of white mold that eventually coat the surface. 9 I tie a string around the end of each salami and attach a tag that records the date, flavoring, and the weight. I note this info and more in a journal (page 304). Then I hang the salamis on a horizontal pole in my cellar where the temperature never exceeds

55° F. This is a lower temperature than is recommended for fermentation using starter cultures, which means that this fermentation will take longer than 48 hours. I usually allow a week. It's very important that during this first week the salami does not dry too quickly, otherwise you can have a condition develop called "case hardening" in which the exterior becomes dry and hard and prevents air from reaching the interior of the salami so that it can dry. Salamis that have "case hardening" will remain squeezable even after a month or two because the interior does not dry out completely; it remains loose and susceptible to spoilage. If you cut into a case-hardened salami, the interior will be full of air spaces and the meat loose; this salami *must* be thrown out. To avoid the risk of case hardening, I always increase the humidity around the salami by draping 33-gallon plastic trash bags over the pole the salamis hang from, which creates a humid micro environment around them. I also put in a stick crosswise under the bags so the plastic does not actually touch the salami. I usually leave the plastic covering up until little spots of white mold begin to appear on the surface of the salamis. This white mold is just what I'm looking for. Not only does it create a barrier to slow down evaporation to just the right amount, it also contributes great flavor and a pleasant aroma to the finished salamis. The whole point of the drying and aging time is for moisture to move from the interior of the salami to the exterior so that it can evaporate from the exterior at the same or at a slightly greater rate. If other molds appear on the salami that are blue-green or brown or that have an "off" smell, then the salami needs to be washed in a diluted vinegar solution and step number 7 (seeding the surface with white mold) needs to be repeated. 10 The length of time it takes for the salamis to be ready depends first on the diameter of the sausage, then on the temperature and humidity of the space where they hang. In an artificially maintained drying room of 50° to 55° F, salami made in 1½-inch wide hog casings may be ready in 20 to 30 days, while salami made in 3-inch wide casing, called beef middles, will take 50 to 70 days. These times, however, are approximate. Basically the salamis are done when they are completely firm to the touch and have lost about 30 percent of their original weight due to evaporation. Monitor salamis made in 1½-inch wide (35 to 40 millimeters) hog casings by gently squeezing them, beginning after 2 weeks. When they are firm or solid, they are probably done. To really be sure, sacrifice one by cutting into it; the slices should be tightly textured and firm. If they're not done, I let the rest of the batch hang a week or so longer. (Individual tastes vary, as does preferences for "hardness," so the final decision as to whether or not they're done can only be suggested.) For the 3-inch diameter salamis, I begin checking them after 4 weeks and the guidelines are the same. 11 When the salamis are done, I wrap them in paper and store them in the refrigerator for up to 1 month. I always weigh the salamis and record the results in my journal so that I can compare the final weight to the beginning weight to see how much evaporation has occurred and to determine how dry I like them.

Basic Italian Salami (Genoa Style) with Variations

Before you make this or any salami recipe that follows, you must read Making Salami and Air-Dried Meats (page 301).

This is a basic Italian salami recipe and produces very good results. The variations (pages 308 to 309) start with 5 pounds of the basic mixture and then distinctive spices are added, otherwise all the procedures and curing and aging times are the same. *The amount of salt, sugar, and Insta-cure No. 1 called for in the recipes should not be decreased*—they're the minimal amounts needed for safety as well as taste. MAKES 6 TO 8 POUNDS SALAMI (WHEN DRIED)

1 Cut the Boston butt into 1-inch wide strips and cut the fat into strips or chunks. Chill in the freezer for 10 to 20 minutes. Meanwhile, measure out all the remaining ingredients. Grind the meat and fat through a meat grinder fitted with a ¼-inch plate into a large bowl. Cut the store-bought salami into chunks; grind it through the same plate into the bowl. In a medium container, combine the Insta-cure, wine, and water and stir to dissolve. Pour over the meat mixture. Add the remaining ingredients. 2 Using your (clean!) hands, knead and squeeze the meat mixture until all the spices are well blended and the mixture becomes

sticky; do not overmix to the point the fat begins to melt. If you're making any of the variations, divide the mixture into each variation and chill until you're ready to proceed with the recipe. **3** Stuff, hang, and monitor the salami according to the instructions in How I Make Salami (page 304). **4** After 1 week, check the salami. Spots of white mold should be apparent and the salami should be slightly moist. Now you can remove the trash bags. Continue to hang the salami for another 3 weeks. By that time, it should be covered with white mold and be somewhat firm when squeezed. If the salamis are dry on the outside but soft when firmly squeezed, they may be "case-hardened" and must be thrown away. Continue to monitor the salami every week. To become completely firm when squeezed may take from 7 to 10 weeks, depending on the humidity and temperature of your basement or cellar. (Warmer, less-humid basements will take less time than colder more humid ones). You can also check to see if the salamis have sufficiently dried by weighing them and comparing the current weight to the original weight recorded on the tag. The salami should have lost about 30 percent of its moisture. Another way to tell if the salami is done is to cut one in half and taste a slice; it should be firm and tight, never loose, or full of air pockets. If you detect any "off" odors your salami needs to be *thrown away*.

10 pounds Boston butt, lean and fat separated

3 ounces store-bought salami, casings removed and reserved (about ⅓ cup)

1 tablespoon Insta-cure No. 1 (see page 14)

½ cup dry red or white wine

½ cup water

¾ cup kosher salt (4 ounces)

¼ cup whole black peppercorns

1 tablespoon freshly ground black pepper

1 teaspoon minced garlic

2 tablespoons sugar

3-inch (65 mm) beef middles casings (see Chef's Note)

CHEF'S NOTE: There are two types of beef casings: beef middles and beef rounds. The rounds, which are used for bologna or kielbasa, range in diameter from 2 to 3 inches. Beef middles are often sold sewed and are used to make large semi-dry sausages and salamis. An individual sewed middle will range in diameter from 2 to 4 inches and will hold 2 to 3 pounds of meat. Casings are usually sold in bundles called "hanks." Depending on the type and size, a hank will take care of 50 to 150 pounds of meat. That's a lot of salami, but because they're packed in salt they can last several years in the refrigerator. Butchers who make their own sausage will often sell you smaller amounts, or you can order them from butcher supply houses or by mail-order. (See Sources on page 318.)

Italian Salami Variations

All the following variations start with the basic salami mixture and then specific ingredients are added. Stuff, hang, and age the salamis according to the directions in How I Make Salami (page 304).

Finochiana

This fennel seed-flavored variation is popular in Tuscany and often is eaten when still somewhat soft, but it can also be aged until completely firm.

MAKES 3 TO 4 POUNDS SALAMI (WHEN DRIED)

Combine all of the ingredients. Stuff into 3-inch diameter (65 mm) beef middles. Proceed as directed for Basic Italian Salami.

5 pounds Basic Italian Salami mixture (before drying)

2 teaspoons whole fennel seeds

2 teaspoons ground fennel seed or fennel pollen

Calabrese (Pepperoni)

In Italy, pepperoni does not exist as a type of salami. In Italian, *pepperoni* means chili pepper. But spicy Calabrese is very similar to what we Americans know as pepperoni although it is air-dried and pepperoni in America is usually smoked. If you wish to smoke the Calabrese instead of air-drying it, follow the smoking instructions in How I Make Bacon on page 297.

MAKES 3 TO 4 POUNDS SALAMI (WHEN DRIED)

Combine all of the ingredients. Stuff into 3-inch diameter (65 mm) beef middles. Proceed as directed for the Basic Italian Salami.

5 pounds Basic Italian Salami mixture (before drying)

1½ teaspoons fennel seeds

½ teaspoon ground fennel seed

2 teaspoons crushed red pepper flakes

2 tablespoons New Mexican chili powder

2 tablespoons paprika

½ cup Chianti or other dry red wine

Basilicata 🐖

Even spicier than the Calabrese, this variation comes from the neighboring state of Basilicata. You can also turn this version into pepperoni by smoking it (see How I Make Bacon on page 297). MAKES 3 TO 4 POUNDS SALAMI (WHEN DRIED)

Combine all of the ingredients. Stuff into 1½- to 2-inch diameter whole hog casings. Because the casings are narrower, these salamis should be dried and aged in 3 to 5 weeks, instead of 7 to 10 weeks, or until they've lost 30 percent of their weight in moisture.

5 pounds Basic Italian Salami mixture (before drying)

1 tablespoon sugar

3 tablespoons New Mexico chili powder

3 tablespoons paprika

1 teaspoon minced garlic

1 tablespoon whole anise seed

½ teaspoon ground allspice

1 tablespoon crushed red pepper flakes

1 teaspoon ground coriander seed

Soppresatta 🐖

Soppresatta is made with pork that has a coarser grind than Basic Italian Salami and the fat is cubed by hand, which gives this salami a very satisfying texture and eye appeal. The method for making, drying, and aging this salami is the same as for Basic Italian Salami so follow the instructions for that recipe. MAKES 3 TO 3½ POUNDS SALAMI (WHEN DRIED)

Grind 2 pounds of the pork butt in a meat grinder fitted with the ⅜-inch plate into a bowl. Grind the remaining 2 pounds pork using the ½-inch plate into the same bowl. Add the remaining ingredients. Proceed as directed for Basic Italian Salami and stuff into 2- to 4-inch diameter beef middles casing.

CHEF'S NOTE: You will need 4 pounds lean meat to make Soppresatta, so I suggest you buy a 4½-pound pork butt and trim away any external and visible fat. Discard or use it in another dish.

4½ pounds boneless Boston butt, trimmed of fat (see Chef's Note)

¼ pound pork back fat, diced into ¼-inch pieces

1½ teaspoons Insta-cure No. 1 (page 14)

6 tablespoons kosher salt

½ cup Chianti or other dry red wine

¼ cup water

2 tablespoons whole black peppercorns

1 teaspoon finely minced garlic

1 tablespoon sugar

2 teaspoons freshly ground black pepper

¼ cup finely ground store-bought salami

Pork Confit (Slow-Cooked Pork Perserved in Fat)

This recipe is a much less salty version of the Southwestern French classic. I've adapted a recipe that is used by my wife, Nancy, at her restaurant in San Francisco, Boulevard. In these days of modern refrigeration, it's no longer necessary to preserve meat with salt and fat. We do, however, love the flavor of meats cured with salt and then cooked slowly in fat. The good news is that we need much less salt to cure the meat because we're not actually preserving it for a year, and packed in the fat in which it was cooked, the pork will still keep for 2 months in the refrigerator, ready to dig out and crisp up for an impromptu dinner. In the times before refrigeration, when pigs were butchered and the meat preserved, confit was made from bits and pieces left over from the hog kill. I use Boston butt, which is both inexpensive and has ample fat, to give good results. MAKES ABOUT 3 POUNDS

Dry Rub

2 teaspoons *herbes de Provence*

1 teaspoon chopped fresh thyme

1 tablespoon kosher salt

2 teaspoons freshly ground black pepper

¼ teaspoon ground allspice

6 bay leaves, crushed

½ teaspoon ground coriander

2 fresh sage leaves, chopped

4 pounds boneless Boston butt, cut into 3-inch chunks (don't trim too much fat from the meat)

2 onions, sliced

8 garlic cloves

6 sprigs fresh thyme

1 sprig fresh rosemary

Enough melted lard and/or olive oil to cover meat (about 1 quart)

1 To make the rub: In a small bowl, combine the *herbes de Provence,* thyme, salt, pepper, allspice, bay leaves, coriander, and sage leaves. 2 Rub the herb mixture generously over the pork cubes. Put the pork into a zip-lock plastic bag or covered bowl and refrigerate overnight. 3 Preheat the oven to 225° F. 4 Put the onions, garlic, thyme, and rosemary sprig on the bottom of a large casserole. Pat the pork dry with paper towels and lay it on top of the onions and herbs. Pour in the melted lard and/or olive oil to cover the pork. Bake, turning the meat in the fat occasionally, for 4 to 5 hours or until quite tender. (The meat should be completely covered with fat at all times; add more if necessary.) 5 Using a slotted spoon, remove the pork from the fat and pack it snugly into a storage container. Strain the fat and juices into a glass measuring cup, discarding the onions, thyme, garlic, and rosemary, and let

the juices settle to the bottom, about 15 minutes. Pour the fat (leaving the juices in the measuring cup) over the pork so it's completely covered by an inch of fat. Seal the container. Refrigerate for at least 2 weeks before serving and up to 2 months, making sure the pork is always completely immersed in fat. 6 Pour the juices remaining in the measuring cup into another container and save for another use (see Chef's Note). 7 To serve the pork, remove the chunks of meat from the fat and heat them in a nonstick skillet over medium-high heat until lightly crisped. Serve as part of salad or with white beans or lentils.

CHEF'S NOTE: The meat juices from the pork confit can be refrigerated or frozen and used in vinaigrettes or other dishes to lend an intense porky flavor.

Lard—A Lot Healthier Than You Think

About 75 years or so ago, pigs were raised not only for their meat, but also for the fat they produced, familiarly known as lard. Lard was the primary source of cooking fat for many Americans, especially those with Eastern European, Latino, or Asian ethnic roots. In the early part of the twentieth century, manufactured vegetable shortenings (or fake fats) such as Crisco were invented and these products began to dominate the market. Lard continued to be used until the 1950s and early 1960s but research that saturated fats, i.e., animal fat, were bad for us and our hearts, in particular, made people turn away from lard. Well, the tide has turned. Fake fats like vegetable shortening and margarine, it turns out, are very bad for us. Because they're partially or wholly hydrogenated, they're packed with nasty trans-fatty acids. In a word, trans-fats are toxic and can contribute to heart disease by raising LDL and lowering HDL. Trans-fats inhibit insulin bonding to cells, which exacerbates insulin resistance and diabetes, and generally raise free radicals in the body—not a good thing for our health. Trans-fats are now considered enough of a health risk that they will soon be listed on labels, and, to my way of thinking, they should be avoided altogether.

The saturated fats with which lard and other animal fats are loaded are actually helpful in counteracting some of the negative effects of trans-fats. When I recommend lard, I'm not talking about those packaged bricks of "lard" sold in supermarkets, which are partially hydrogenated and highly processed and don't taste anything like real lard. Either you must make your own lard (page 313), or purchase it from a mail-order source (see Sources on page 318) or from an ethnic supplier where it is made fresh.

Here are some of the health benefits of lard: The saturated fat in lard contains about one third of stearic acid, which may have a beneficial effect on cholesterol, and it helps to relax blood vessels. Lard, which is 40 percent unsaturated, belongs in the high oleic group, which has a similar lipid profile to olive oil (meaning it has lots of beneficial monounsaturated fatty acids). Also, lard has antimicrobial properties, so things fried in lard don't spoil as quickly. That's one of the reasons it is still used to fry some commercial brands of potato chips. Lard is a good choice for frying because it doesn't break down as easily as vegetable oil, causing the production of nasty trans-fats.

Health issues aside, I think you will be sold on lard the first time you make a piecrust with it. Oh, okay, some all-butter pie crusts are good, but they don't cut a cuff to piecrusts made with lard. A piecrust made with lard is a wonder—delicious and delicate in flavor, but flaky, and a bit crisper, meaning that the bottom browns better and is less prone to getting soggy than a crust made with just butter. I do love the taste of butter, so I like to add some to my lard dough, but you can make an all-lard piecrust, which would still taste terrific. All-lard crusts work particularly well with savory pies such as the Tourtière (page 236). To make an all-lard crust, simply replace the butter in the recipe with lard, but you may need to add a tablespoon or so of water because lard contains less water than butter.

If you're a baker and you've never used lard, I think you'll be surprised at how light your biscuits will be—not to mention how well lard works in cornbread, gingerbread, cookies (lard is what makes Chinese almond cookies so tasty), and steamed pudding.

Lard is also great for frying. The next time you make fried chicken, fried fish, or any coated pan-fried or deep-fried foods, use lard instead of vegetable oil or (God forbid!) vegetable shortening. Food fried in lard absorbs much less frying fat than food fried in vegetable oil and that's because saturated fats are not absorbed into fried food as easily as vegetable oils are, assuming the food is fried at the proper temperature, about 350° to 365° F. Another reason to use lard for frying is that it does not chemically break down at 365° F, yet it produces wonderfully crisp food.

Potatoes cooked in lard are plain irresistible, no matter whether they are deep fried, oven-roasted, or pan-fried. Shredded potatoes pressed into cakes and fried in lard with a tad of butter for flavor make the best and crispiest hash browns you've ever tasted.

If you're cooking some of the traditional dishes in this book that call for lard as a choice such as Pork Confit (page 310), Choucroute Garni (page 242), Pörkölt (page 226), or many of the Asian dishes, lard is the fat of choice. If you don't have homemade lard, my next choice would be bacon fat.

If you're now convinced about lard but don't know a friendly pig farmer or live in an area with a large Chinese or Mexican community, it's going to be difficult for you to find the pork back fat or kidney fat you need to make lard. However, you can mail-order back fat (see Sources on page 318), or you can trim off the fat from the loins, Boston butts, pork chops, etc., that you buy and stockpile it in your freezer. When you've amassed 5 pounds of fat or more, then follow the recipe for making lard (below). It's a very simple process.

Rendering Lard 🐖 MAKES ABOUT 3 QUARTS

1 Preheat the oven to 300° F. 2 Put the cubed fat in a large pot or Dutch oven, making sure that it's no more than half full. Slip into the oven and bake until the fat begins to melt. Stir the mixture and continue to stir every 45 minutes until the bits of fat (cracklings) brown and float to the top. It may take up to 4 hours to render the lard. Strain the lard into a clean container and ladle it into canning jars. When the jars have cooled, cover them and refrigerate. Lard will keep in the refrigerator for 6 months. 3 The cracklings are incredibly irresistible and I dare you not to eat them. Use them in Hot Water Cornbread with Cracklins (page 89), biscuits, or as a garnish on salads.

6 pounds pork back fat, cut into ½-inch cubes

CHEF'S NOTE: If you have a meat grinder and a strong arm, you can grind the back fat instead of dicing it, which will speed up the melting and rendering process.

Specialty Pork

EXCEPT FOR CUTS SUCH AS fresh belly, pork cheeks, and fresh shank, which are not usually sold at supermarkets (unless they're in ethnic neighborhoods), all the pork we used in our recipe tests for this book came from large chain grocery stores. Basically, the meat was unbranded commodity pork, pretty much what is sold everywhere. Some of the national chains now sell only pumped ("enhanced") pork, so we avoided buying it. During the course of writing this book I did have many opportunities to sample pork that was not the usual commodity pork—from pigs kept in confinement—but was from pigs that were raised outdoors and allowed to roam freely (pasture pork). Some of the meat I sampled came from animals whose diet was free of any growth stimulants or antibiotics and some of it came from pigs raised entirely on organic diets. Some pork came from specific pure breeds of pigs, and some came from small family hog farms, where only a few pampered animals are raised. In most cases, the pork from these special animals was superior to any purchased at our local supermarket.

Many factors affect how an animal develops and, hence, the quality of its meat. Some of the obvious ones are its breed (genetics), age, the health of the animal, its feed, its housing environment (comfortable or stress-free), the conditions and slaughtering methods. And we haven't even mentioned how the meat is processed.

You may have your own reasons for searching out pork that is different from what can be purchased at the typical grocery store. Your motivation may be philosophical, political, health-driven, or just serendipitous—to find better taste or unusual cuts. For every preference there is pork to suit your needs if you're willing to search it out. Here is a selection of places to start.

Suppliers of Hard-to-Find Cuts

Niman Ranch (nimanranch.com) not only produces pork that is better tasting than most supermarket pork, but they offer hard-to-find cuts such as fresh pork belly, pork shank, fresh leg-of-pork, and pork blood for blood sausage. In addition, Niman only contracts with small family farms that produce pork without antibiotics and growth stimulants. Unlike large industrial pork producers, Niman's pigs are raised outdoors and not in cement pens. The result is some very tasty pork that has more marbling and juicier texture. Niman pork is costlier than supermarket pork, but it's definitely a case of getting what you pay for. Niman Ranch pork is also sold in some upscale and natural food stores, so be on the lookout.

Enzo's Meat Market in Oakland, California, is a high-quality meat market that sells excellent pork from Canada. Besides the traditional cuts, you can purchase hard-to-find ones such as pork belly, leg, and shank. They do mail-order. Telephone: (510) 547-5839, or email mmurphy173@aol.com.

Preferred Meats in San Francisco (preferredmeats.com) sells all-natural antibiotic- and hormone-free pork from Beelers in Iowa, as well as the superb-tasting Berkshire pork from Eden Farms in Iowa. Hard-to-find cuts such as belly, leg, and shank can be ordered as can excellent applewood-smoked bacon and hams from Nieske's in Wisconsin.

Special Breeds

By far, the best-tasting pork I've encountered comes from an old breed called Berkshire. The breed originated in England 400 years ago and was very popular in the United States up until fifty years ago. It not only tastes great, with strong porky flavor, it's also quite tender and juicy. In Japan the pork from Berkshire pigs, which is a black-coated breed, is revered and is known as *kurobuta* (which means black pig). Today, many small farms are raising 100 percent Berkshire pigs, about 95 percent of which are sold to Japan. But as consumers become aware of how delicious pork from Berkshire pigs is, the market for this meat is expanding.

The following vendors sell Berkshire pork. All offer hard-to-find cuts as well as traditional ones. Some raise their animals without antibiotics or growth stimulants and are so noted. Some ranchers who raise Berkshire pigs have formed an association where you can learn more about this superb meat. You can go to their website at americanberkshire.com. Also, berkshiremeats.com in

Minnesota sells all cuts of Berkshire pork raised on small family farms. They also sell ham, sausage, and other smoked meats made with Berkshire pork. Telephone: (507) 256-7214.

Henry's Butcher Block (henrysbutcherblock.com) sells all cuts of hormone- and antibiotic-free Berkshire pork at their shop near Austin, Texas.

Snake River Farms (snakeriverfarms.com), a consortium of small family farms that raise all-natural and organic pigs in Idaho, sells Berkshire pork (all cuts) under the Japanese name Kurobuta.

All-Natural and Organic Pork

The term "all-natural" when it comes to pork means that the animals were raised without antibiotics, hormones, or other growth stimulants. In contrast, the term "certified organic" means that the animals were raised as "all-natural," but were fed only certified organic feed and allowed to graze on organically fertilized and chemical-free pastures.

Now that the USDA has established criteria for certified organic meat, several farms have begun to supply it:

Du Breton of Quebec Canada (dubreton.com) sells organic pork as well as all-natural pork, humanely raised on small family farms. The pork is excellent and all cuts are available. The pork is sold in many stores in the United States, so contact the company to find out where it's sold in your area.

Organic Valley (organicvalley.com) in Wisconsin also sells organic pork but through retail outlets. Contact the company to see where it's sold.

Diamond Organics (diamondorganics.com) sells all-organic pork raised on straw from small family farms and offers hard-to-find cuts such as fresh leg-of-pork. They also sell organic pork from Sara Joe, which makes nitrite-free bacon, hams, and sausage.

Sara Joe (sarajoe.com) also sells its organic pork through an online store called the meatshop-tacoma.com. You should be able to find fresh leg-of-pork, shank, and belly at both websites.

Heritage Breeds and Small Family Farms

Heritage breeds are old breeds no longer raised because their genetic traits make them less than ideal for modern industrial farms. Most often their meat is particularly wonderful to eat. Some of the best of the old breeds are Berkshire, Gloucester Old Spot, Large Blacks, Tamworths, and Herefords, and all have exceptionally great flavor. Flying Pigs Farm (www.flyingpigsfarm.com) in upstate New York offers all cuts from some of these heritage breeds. In addition, the New England Live Stock Alliance (www.nehbc.org) has information on heritage breeds, as does the American Livestock Breeds Conservatory (www.albc-usa.org). The New England Livestock Alliance (www.nelivestockalliance.org) has information on heritage animals and on pigs raised in pastures. Sap Bush Hollow Farm raises excellent pork in pastures in upstate New York (sapbush@midtel.net. Telephone: [518] 234-2105)

Fancy Meats from Vermont is a meat company that sells pork from small family farms. Telephone: (802) 875-3159. The pork can be purchased from Frank's Butcher Shop in the Chelsea Market in New York City. Telephone: (212) 242-1234.

Vermont's Quality Meats also offers pork from small farms. Telephone: (802) 394-2558.

Prairie Grove Farms in Illinois specializes in high-quality pork raised in nonindustrial conditions (www.prairiegrovefarms.com). They're wholesale only, but sell their meat to high-end stores and natural groceries across the country. Contact them for outlets in your area.

Many small family farms and growers of pasture-raised pork sell their meat at farmers' markets or directly to the public. I have listed many of these farms in Sources (page 318) and they are worth checking out. Many of these can be found at www.eatwild.com, www.meadowraisedmeats.com, or www.eatwellguide.org.

Sources

ASIAN INGREDIENTS

Kam Man Market
(212) 571-0330
www.kammanfood.com

Oriental Pantry
(800) 828-0368
www.orientalpantry.com

Uwajimaya Market
(206) 624-6248
www.uwajimaya.com

Tokyo Fish Market
(510) 524-7243

BACON AND OLD-FASHIONED BRINE-CURED HAMS AND SAUSAGES

Aidells Sausage Company
(800) 546-5795
www.aidells.com

Grateful Palate
(888) 472-5283
www.gratefulpalate.com

Jones Dairy Farm
(800) 635-6637
www.jonesdairyfarm.com

Nueske's
(800) 392-2266
www.nueske.com

Summerfield Farm
(800) 898-3276
www.summerfieldfarm.com

COUNTRY HAMS

Burger Smokehouse
(800) 624-5426

Early's Honey Stand
(800) 523-2015

Finchville Farms
(800) 678-1521

Gratton Farms
Father's Country Ham
(502) 525-3437

Gwaltney's
(800) 292-2773

Johnston County Country Hams
(800) 543-4267

Scott Hams
(502) 338-3402

Smithfield Collection
(800) 628-2242

Stadler's Country Ham
(800) 262-1795

Tripp Country Hams
(901) 772-2130

Wallace Edwards & Sons
(800) 222-4267

HARDWOOD SAWDUST AND SMOKERS

Cabela's
(800) 237-4444
www.cabelas.com

Luhr Jensen
(800) 535-1711
www.smoke-house.com

The Sausage Maker
(888) 490-8525
www.sausagemaker.com

NATURAL LARD (UNHYDROGENATED)

John F. Martin and Sons
(717) 336-2804

MEXICAN/ SOUTHWESTERN INGREDIENTS/ BANANA LEAVES

The Chile Shop
(505) 983-6080
www.thechileshop.com

El Nopalito #1
(760) 436-5775

The Kitchen Food Shop
(888) 468-4433
www.kitchenmarket.com

Melissa's Specialty Foods
(800) 588-0151
www.melissas.com

Texas Spice Company
(800) 880-8007

SAUSAGE-MAKING SUPPLIES AND EQUIPMENT, INSTA-CURE #1

Cabela's
(800) 237-4444
www.cabelas.com

Carlson Butcher Supply
(800) 662-6212

The Sausage Maker
(888) 490-8525
www.sausagemaker.com

SPECIALTY PRODUCTS, HERBS, SPICES, AND PRESERVED LEMONS

Adriana's Caravan
(800) 316-0820
www.adrianascaravan.com

Dean & DeLuca
(800) 221-7714
www.deandeluca.com

Frieda's
(800) 241-1771
www.friedas.com

G.B. Ratto's International Grocers
(800) 325-3483

Kalustyan's
(800) 352-3451
www.kalustyans.com

Penzey's, Ltd.
(800) 741-7787
www.penzeys.com

The Spanish Table
(510) 548-1383
www.spanishtable.com

Zingermans
(888) 636-8162
www.zingermans.com

Index

adobo:
   Filipino pork, 224
   Spanish, grilled thin pork
      chops in, 109
air-dried and cured:
   back fat, 294–95
   pork belly, Italian-style,
      293–94
   pork loin, 296
   see also cure(d), curing; salami
air-dried meats, 301–13
albóndigas soup with chili
      broth and cilantro salsa,
      92–93
Alex's *pierna* (banana leaf-
      wrapped pork), 204–5
ancho chilies:
   in *albóndigas* soup with
      chili broth and cilantro
      salsa, 92–93
   in chorizo de Los Angeles,
      265–66
anchovy:

fillets, in pork stew à la
      Provençale, 221
   in sauce gribiche, 71
andouille:
   crostini with shrimp, red
      bell pepper and, 66–67
   in smoked sausage and
      hominy filling for pork-
      filled turnovers, 76–77
apple:
   cider marinade, 137
   and cornbread–stuffed pork
      loin with roasted apple
      gravy, 158–59
   and ham breakfast pie,
      Pam's, 61
apricot sauce, grilled North
      African marinated pork
      kebabs on couscous with,
      138–39
arroz con puerco y chorizo,
      Spanish (pork and chorizo
      paella), 238–39

artichoke and piquillo pepper
      sausage, Nancy's, 264
   in pork-filled turnovers,
      76–77
Asian dipping sauce, spicy,
      pearl balls with, 74–75
aspic, parsley, molded ham in
      (*jambon persillé*),
      284–85
avocado, in El Profé *pozole
      blanco*, 90–91

back fat, pork, *see* pork, back
      fat
bacon:
   in Hungarian goulash,
      226–27
   makin', 297–98
   molasses-cured pork
      shoulder, 299–300
   in smoked French country
      sausage, 266–67
   in *tourtière*, 236–38

pork cutlets, 126–27
Jeff's lard piecrust, 238
jerk-marinated ribs, 148
John Desmond's blood
"puddy," 268–70
Johnson and May Koo's
Burmese shredded pork
ear salad, 84
juniper berries, in choucroute
garni, 242–43

kale stuffing for Spanish pork
tenderloin roulade, 168–69
kebabs, 136–42
grilled pork, 137
Jacob's pork skewers with
pancetta-wrapped figs,
139
pork, grilled North African
marinated, on couscous
with apricot sauce,
138–39
tamarind-marinated pork
belly skewers, 142
kirsch, in braised stuffed pork
loin wrapped in cabbage
leaves, 208–9
Kirsten's fried pork chops with
country gravy, 62–63
kiwis, in Alex's *pierna*, 204–5

lager:
in casserole-roasted pork on
a bed of cabbage and
sauerkraut, 202–3
in court-bouillon for York-
style ham, 290–91

lard, 311–13
piecrust, Jeff's, 238
in pork confit, 310–11
lardo (cured and air-dried
back fat), 294–95
lasagna, Nancy's meatball,
234–35
leeks, in pot-au-feu, 213–14
leg-of-pork roast (fresh ham)
with cumin and fresh herb
crust, 170
lemon:
-soy marinade for Lisa's
chopped grilled vegetable
salad with grilled pork
medallions, 80–81
-tarragon brine, 107
lime juice:
in citrus-marinated red
onions, 204–5
in grill-roasted pork shoulder Cuban style, 172–73
lime-oregano rub, 106
Lisa's chopped grilled vegetable salad with grilled
pork medallions, 80–81
Lisa's no-fuss tomato sauce,
277
liver, pork, rustic terrine,
274–75
lobster, in Thai seafood and
pork dumplings, 72–73
loin, *see* pork loin
lonza (cured and air-dried
pork loin), 296
Los Angeles, chorizo de,
265–66

Madeira:
in pâté de campagne, 278–79
in rustic pork liver terrine,
274–75
maple:
brine for stovetop-smoked
pork tenderloin, 164–65
-cured Canadian bacon,
300–301
marinades:
apple cider, 137
Cam Van's tamarind, 142
coffee-molasses, spareribs
with, 147
Cuban, 172–73
lemon-soy, 80–81
North African, 138–39
see also flavor brines; rubs;
sauces
marinated:
pork belly skewers,
tamarind-, 142–43
pork chops, grilled yogurt-,
108
pork kebabs on couscous
with apricot sauce, grilled
North African, 138–39
red onions, citrus-, 204–5
ribs, jerk-, 148
marmalade:
in basic fruit glaze, 193
in fruit-flavored sauce, 194
master recipes:
baked glazed ham, 190
braised chops, 116
grilled, brined, fresh herb–
coated pork chops, 105

North African grilled,
marinated pork kebabs on
couscous with apricot
sauce, 138–39
nuoc mam, in tamarind-
marinated pork belly
skewers, 142

old-fashioned pan gravy, 113
olives, black Niçoise, in pork
stew à la Provençale, 221
olives, green:
in pork stew à la
Provençale, 221
in Spanish *arroz con puerco
y chorizo*, 238–39
-stuffed pork tenderloin,
165
onions:
braised green, 126–27
citrus-marinated red, 204–5
orange:
brine, 107
-soy brine, 162–63
-thyme rub, 107
orange juice:
in braised pork cheeks with
pappardelle and
radicchio, 228–29
in citrus-marinated red
onions, 204–5
in grill-roasted pork
shoulder Cuban style,
172–73
oregano-lime rub, 106
organic pork, 316
oven-roasted ribs, 145–46

paella, pork and chorizo
(Spanish *arroz con puerco
y chorizo*), 238–39
pancetta, 293–94
in baked rigatoni with pork
rib ragù, 230–31
in braised pork cheeks with
pappardelle and radicchio,
228–29
in Italian-style sausage with
rosemary and grappa,
260–61
in my best Bolognese,
232–33
in Nancy's artichoke and
piquillo pepper sausage,
264
in tigelle, 78
in Toulouse sausage, 261–62
-wrapped figs, Jacob's pork
skewers with, 139
pan gravy, old-fashioned, 113
panko-crusted pork cutlets
(*tonkatsu*) with tangy
Japanese dipping sauce,
126–27
pan sauce:
fig, 115
for longer braising, beer
and mustard, 119–20
mushroom, roasted double
pork tenderloin stuffed
with prosciutto and herbs
with, 166–67
prune, 115
sautéed pork chops with,
110

sweet red pepper, 114
pappardelle, braised pork
cheeks with radicchio
and, 228–29
Parmesan cheese:
in baked rigatoni with pork
rib ragù, 230–31
in Franco's *polpettone
Napoletano*, 276–77
in involtini, 131–32
in pork cutlets Milanese,
128–29
Parmigiano-Reggiano, in
tigelle, 78
parsley aspic, molded ham in
a, 284–85
parsnips, in pot-au-feu,
213–14
pasta:
baked rigatoni with pork rib
ragù, 230–31
braised pork cheeks with
pappardelle and
radicchio, 228–29
Nancy's meatball lasagna,
234–36
pâtés and terrines, 271–87
de campagne, 278–79
definition of, 272–73
pickled pig's feet, 286–87
rustic pork liver, 274–75
patties:
brown sugar and sage
breakfast, 259
in tomato sauce, warm pita
stuffed with Turkish meat,
68–69

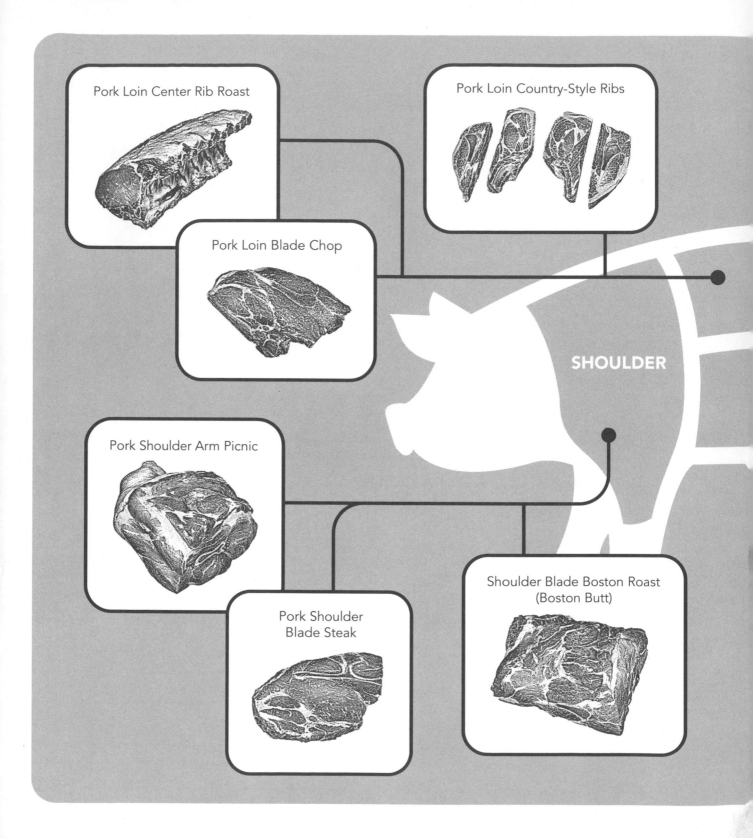

Pork Loin Center Rib Roast

Pork Loin Country-Style Ribs

Pork Loin Blade Chop

SHOULDER

Pork Shoulder Arm Picnic

Pork Shoulder Blade Steak

Shoulder Blade Boston Roast (Boston Butt)